POLICY-MAKING
IN THE
FEDERAL EXECUTIVE
BRANCH

POLICY-MAKING IN THE FEDERAL EXECUTIVE BRANCH

edited by
Randall B. Ripley
Grace A. Franklin

THE FREE PRESS
A Division of Macmillan Publishing Co., Inc.
NEW YORK

Collier Macmillan Publishers
LONDON

The Free Press
A Division of Macmillan Publishing Co., Inc.
866 Third Avenue, New York, N.Y. 10022

Collier Macmillan Canada, Ltd.

Library of Congress Catalog Card Number: 74–33093

Printed in the United States of America

printing number
1 2 3 4 5 6 7 8 9 10

Library of Congress Cataloging in Publication Data
Main entry under title:

Policy-making in the Federal executive branch.

   Bibliography: p.
   Includes index.
    1. United States—Executive departments—Addresses,
essays, lectures. 2. Budget—United States—Addresses,
essays, lectures. 3. Policy sciences—Addresses,
essays, lectures. I. Ripley, Randall B. II. Franklin,
Grace A.
JK421.P59   353   74-33093
ISBN 0-02-926490-1

Contents

Preface

Virtually all of the existing literature on policy-making in the federal executive branch of government is of two kinds: substantive case studies or studies explaining budget figures. The case studies focus on individual decisions in a given policy area and explain that decision using a variety of variables. The analysis may range from systematically empirical to impressionistic, and the longitudinal focus may range from the first perception of need for governmental attention in the policy area to the stage of legislation passage ("legitimation"). Some case studies go even further to examine (or speculate about) the impact of a policy decision both on the policy actors and on groups in society; some strive for generalizability by focusing on more than one policy area, or on several decisions over time within the same area.

The second kind of policy study focuses on policy in a less substantive way—it conceives of policy in budgetary terms (amounts of appropriations or expenditures) and seeks to explain change in dollars, usually using previous amount of dollars as the principal, or only, determinant variable.

Both of these approaches to policy study have shortcomings. The case study is rich (sometimes too rich) in detail that describes a variety of participants and the environmental and political influences impinging on their behavior. Usually the case approach lacks comparability to other policy areas and other case studies. The budgetary approach allows comparisons between policy areas since policy is measured in relatively comparable dollars (although some would argue that this constitutes a sterile and colorless conception of policy), but the dearth of explanatory variables employed in this approach results in an analysis that is quite devoid of situational politics. Usually neither approach is part of an integrated theoretical framework, and thus, contributions to knowledge are erratic and unsystematic.

We base the policy research reported in this book on a comprehensive theoretical framework developed explicitly to facilitate systematic, scientific study of policy and policy-making. The framework combines the advantages of comparability between policy areas and adequate attention to non-budgetary explanatory variables, and its use represents what we feel is a new broader way of looking at policy-making at the federal level.

The framework used here, and the tests of it reported in this volume are the product of an ongoing research project on policy-making sponsored by the Mershon Center at the Ohio State University. This book represents an interim report on the status of that research project. The chapters by the six authors (all of whom have been associated with the Mershon project for several years) stand on their own as independent empirical studies, but taken together, they constitute an integrated book because of their commonly employed framework, language, and methodologies. Only parts of three of the chapters have appeared in print elsewhere (Ripley et al., 1973a, 1973b, and 1974).

The central purpose of the research project from which this volume stems is to say something important and interesting about many aspects of policy-making in the Executive branch of the national government of the United States. The phase of the project represented by the papers here has focused on a variety of specific policy actions by the Executive branch (and, in effect, by Congress too), especially in the budgetary sphere, as dependent variables. What we call agency maturity has been explored rather fully in explaining variations in these actions, and a number of aspects of the external social, economic, and political environment have also been explored as independent variables. In subsequent phases of the project we expect to explore the explanatory power of aspects of agency structure other than maturity, and we also expect to delve more deeply into the societal, economic, and especially, political environment surrounding agency behavior. We also aspire to examine a variety of agency actions in addition to spending—an examination begun in Chapter 5. And, above all, we hope ultimately to have a considerable amount to say about the impact of agency actions on intended beneficiaries and on society in general.

The conceptual framework underlying the empirical work reported here has undergone a number of transformations during the life of the project. These transformations have always been for the purpose of facilitating empirical research. Changes have not been made for the sake of elegance alone, but in response to newly perceived demands of empirical endeavor. An article of faith with all of the authors is that social science is at its best when it mixes deductive theory with empirical tests that then may lead to further restatement of the theory.

The generous intellectual and financial support provided by the Mershon Center has made both this book and the larger research enterprise possible. We are particularly grateful to Richard C. Snyder, Director of the Mershon Center, and Charles F. Hermann, Associate Director, for their intellectual encouragement, insights, and understanding. To Rose Goodyear and Debi Harper go a special thank you for their cheerful patience and diligence in typing the manuscript.

We have incurred many other personal debts from individuals both at Ohio State and elsewhere who gave freely of their time and intellect to comment on drafts of the papers printed here. For this aid (although not always comfort!) we wish to acknowledge Philip M. Burgess, Aage R. Clausen, C. Richard Hofstetter, John H. Kessel, Warren Kostroski, Harold D. Lasswell, Thomas Milburn, Arthur H. Miller, Saad Nagi, Ira Sharkansky, Richard H. Sinnreich, and Donald S. Van Meter. No doubt a number of these individuals may still have reservations about portions of what follows, but there is also no doubt that what follows is better than it would have been had they not paid it the compliment of their serious critical attention.

Officials of the agencies studied in the various chapters were most helpful and generous in providing us with data not available in public documents. We found a uniform degree of interest and cooperation in the federal Executive branch that was gratifying as well as essential.

Finally, we wish to thank the Instruction and Research Computer Center at the Ohio State University, without whose resources these analyses could not have been performed. The Polimetrics Laboratory of the Ohio State Department of Political Science also provided helpful assistance in file building and program usage.

RANDALL B. RIPLEY
GRACE A. FRANKLIN

About the Editors

RANDALL B. RIPLEY, professor and chairman in the Political Science Department at Ohio State University, has written a number of books and articles on public policy and governmental institutions in the United States.

GRACE A. FRANKLIN, research associate at the Mershon Center of Ohio State University, has been engaged in research on national public policy-making for the past five years and is coauthor of a monograph and an article stemming from that research. She earned her M.A. in political science at Ohio State.

About the Contributors

WILLIAM M. HOLMES, assistant professor in the Sociology Department at Case–Western Reserve University, earned his Ph.D. at Ohio State. He has been engaged in research on national public policy-making for the past four years and is coauthor of a monograph and an article based on that research.

LANCE T. LELOUP, assistant professor in the Political Science Department at the University of Missouri at St. Louis, earned his Ph.D. at Ohio State. He has been engaged in research on both national and state policy-making.

WILLIAM B. MORELAND, associate director of the Force and Policy Program at the Mershon Center of Ohio State University, earned his Ph.D. in political science at Ohio State. He is author or coauthor of three articles and a monograph on various aspects of American politics and policy-making.

STEVEN A. SHULL, assistant professor in the Political Science Department at the University of New Orleans, earned his Ph.D. at Ohio State. He has been involved in research on national and state policy-making.

POLICY-MAKING
IN THE
FEDERAL EXECUTIVE
BRANCH

1

Policy-Making: A Conceptual Scheme

Randall B. Ripley

In this chapter a conceptual framework ("the bureaucratic policy arena") is introduced for investigating policy both scientifically and comprehensively. The framework represents a synthesis of several major "schools" of policy-related literature: the comparative study of American states, the substantive typologies of public policy, the discussion and description of stages of policy-making, and the systems approach. Although the framework was developed explicitly for the analysis of policy-making by agencies within the federal government, it is adaptable to any other bureaucratic setting.

The bureaucratic policy arena is comprised of four components: the environment external to the agency, the internal environment of the agency, the policy actions of the agency, and the policy results of agencies' policy actions. The external environment encompasses events, conditions, and trends that are not generally within the agencies' control—public opinion, social conditions, economic conditions, and political conditions within society and government. The internal environment encompasses characteristics inherent to the agency that are, at least in theory, subject to some degree of agency manipulation—characteristics of agency structure, personnel, and decision-making processes. Policy actions are simply the activities in which an agency engages as it implements its policies (usually in the service of its clients or beneficiaries). These activities include such diverse things as writing checks, building facilities, maintaining local service offices, and otherwise spending money. Policy results are the changes that occur in society as a result of agencies' policy actions.

Nine pairs of general hypotheses are presented. Three pairs of the hypotheses link concepts of the internal environment—agency maturity, structural rigidity, and traditional/nontraditional nature of the agency—to change in policy actions. Three pairs of hypotheses relate concepts of the external environment—political party identification of the society and government, visibility of agencies' coalitions, and changes in social and economic conditions—to change in policy actions. Two pairs of hypotheses explore the relationship between two concepts involving the external environment—change in social and economic conditions and the agencies' public opinion context—to the agencies' ability to achieve desired policy results. The final pair of hypotheses links change in agencies' policy actions to ability to achieve desired policy results.

FROM TIME TO TIME every social scientist pauses to ponder the directions in which his or her discipline is moving. One result of such musings is that policy-oriented studies in political science have become fashionable in recent years. The focus on policy stems from two desires: first, to achieve "relevance" to society by studying not just the organizations, institutions, and personnel that comprise government, but also the outputs of the government, the policies that daily affect the lives of citizens in multitudinous ways; and second, to achieve "relevance" to government actors by advising them on aspects of their policies—planning, implementation, probable impact, and evaluation. Within the body of policy-oriented writing that has emerged, it is possible to distinguish good work from bad work on a case-by-case basis and also to delineate different areas of focus (for example, social indicators, or impact evaluation, or comparative state policy), but, in many ways, it is not yet possible to distinguish the development of a cumulative scientific enterprise focused on public policy or policy-making in a broader sense.

In this volume we present a conceptual framework (or model) for investigating policy both scientifically and comprehensively. The framework represents a synthesis of several elements of policy-related literature and was developed explicitly for the study of policy-making by executive agencies at the federal government level, but, in principle, the framework is adaptable to other bureaucratic policy-making settings, including American state and local governments, foreign governments, and nongovernmental bureaucracies.

Policy-Oriented Literature

Elements from three principal areas of public policy literature have been incorporated into the framework. First, the comparative study of policy in the American states is important. Dawson and Robinson (1963), Dye (1965, 1966), Hofferbert (1966), Sharkansky (1967), and others treat the American state system as a semi-experimental model; they examine the differential effects of varying state government structures (competitive party systems, control of legislative apportionment) on the delivery of various state-produced public benefits (expenditures for education, welfare, public roads), while controlling for the economic environment of each state (per capita income, industrialization, urbanization). Their concern derives in part from an older debate extending back to the late 1940s about the differential effects of state political party competition on the distribution of social welfare benefits (Eulau, 1957; Key, 1949; Lockard, 1959; and Schlesinger, 1955). The units of analysis in these studies were either states or political party systems within states. Explanations of variation and conclusions about differences in these studies were dependent upon relatively abstract findings about the behavior of large social or geographic aggregates.

Second, in the last decade some scholars have given their attention to the description and explanation of political behavior at the national level in a concern for rectifying the almost exclusive focus upon "process" to the exclusion of the substance of governmental policy. Froman (1968), Lowi (1964), Salisbury (1968), and Salisbury and Heinz (1970) developed and applied the notion of policy type as both an independent and dependent variable. Lowi's classification of governmental policy (as distributive, redistributive, and regulatory) and Salisbury's similar scheme are major examples of attempts to develop a general, substantively oriented public policy typology. One of the constraints imposed by considering the policy type as an important variable is the necessity of using mixed levels of analysis and units of analysis in deriving conclusions. Furthermore, in the absence of extremely large research expenditures, almost by definition this approach will be limited to little more than the aggregation of the findings of centrally directed case studies.

A third approach derives its impetus from a much older literature that deals with the philosophical implications of "rational" social choice. Harold Lasswell's discussion and description of the stages of policy-making (1956) attempts to clarify rules of evaluating the efficiency of rule-making and rule application. Simon's (1957) "satisficing model" of decision-making questioned the "rational man" approach derived from economic theory. Likewise, Braybrooke and Lindblom (1963) have articulated the reasons for adopting the "disjointed incremental" approach in preference to the synoptic or ratio-deductive schemes in the evaluation of social or governmental policy. Dror (1968) picks up this theme with his discussion of "meta" policy-making (rules for making rules governing policy-making) and attempts to distinguish more rational criteria for judgment of policy as relatively more or less efficient in fulfilling the goals of policy-makers. The individual policy-maker in an organizational context faced with imperfect information is the unit of analysis in all of these works. The authors share a common concern for articulating relatively abstract decision rules that could, to a certain extent, be analytically defined as formal (mathematical) models of behavior. While each author draws heavily upon the "real" world for inductive proof by example, very little contact with the real world is used to establish empirical validity. Application in a data confrontation sense comes closest in principles or rules for administrative decisions, such as those developed in the literature of public administration.

Both the strengths and limitations in these three approaches have informed the development of the present perspective. From the state policy literature we adopted the notion that environment (both socioeconomic and political) should be examined for its impact on policy, but we wished to avoid the necessity of depending exclusively on findings about the behavior of large aggregates. From the literature urging a substantive typology of policy we accepted the potential importance of such a typology and also saw the possibility of developing a dynamic model wherein time-dependent relationships are explicitly considered. But we concluded that the limitations of the specific proposed types needed to be overcome with a different conceptualization. From the literature on decision-making we drew the idea that models of policy-making were feasible conceptually, but we rejected the focus on the individual because of the remote possibility of large-scale generalizable empirical testing using such a focus.

It should also be added that the systems perspective as developed by Easton (1953, 1965a, 1965b), and as filtered through the comparative state policy literature, has played a limited part in developing our general framework. The problems with this approach for our interests are several, however. First, "authoritative allocation of values" is not a discriminating category—either it includes everything a government does in all its branches and operations, or it includes only a very small part of what government does (for example, laws formally passed by a legislature and signed by a chief executive, or pronouncements by a high court). In either event, it allows neither the analyst nor the practitioner to know what is more important and what is less important in the policy realm except through the time honored but often confused use of "feel" or "seat of the pants."

Second, the well-recognized boundary problem intrudes: How can an analyst tell when an action in the external environment becomes a part of the interacting web labeled the political or policy system? Third, the systems perspective does not allow the analyst to distinguish between inputs and feedback; the strict chronological implications of a systems approach imposes categories on the analyst that cannot, in this case, be used in any rigorous way. Despite its shortcomings, the systems perspective does provide some useful notions: the conception of government as an agent separate, at least analytically, from an environment or environments; and, by extension, the conception of the goverment as an organism responding to environmental stimuli.

The Bureaucratic Policy Arena

Bureaucratic policy-making is the response of executive branch agencies to stimuli coming from their internal and external environments. Policies take the form of a wide variety of specific actions and, at least logically, help determine a variety of results in society. Results are also directly influenced by external environmental factors and in turn influence the external environment at later periods of time. This mixture of components —agencies, internal and external environments, actions, and results— comprise the bureaucratic policy arena. Within the policy arena the relationships that are of interest to us are presented in Figure 1–1.

The *external environment* contains those events, activities, conditions, and trends of whatever nature that are external to the agencies. We are particularly interested in public opinion, party strength, and economic

FIGURE I-I: THE BUREAUCRATIC POLICY ARENA

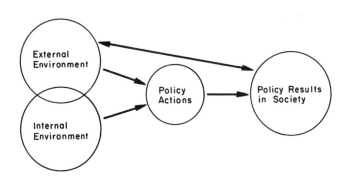

and social conditions as important elements in the external environment. The *internal environment* contains various structural and process features of the agencies themselves. We are particularly interested in characteristics of agency structure, characteristics of agency personnel, and characteristics of decision-making processes within the agencies as important elements in the internal environment. Internal and external environments are shown to intersect because coalitions, which are potentially important in explaining variations in policy actions, may contain actors who are agency members as well as persons who are outside of the agency.

Policy actions are simply the activities in which agencies engage as they implement policy. *Policy results* are what happens in society as a result of policy actions.[1]

This basic set of relationships is conceived to be in constant flux over time. As it is applied in the succeeding chapters, the model is used explicitly in longitudinal terms.

The Research Design

In order to direct our attention to a limited number of meaningful questions, and in order that the empirical answers to those questions would make sense when considered together, we developed a number of specific concepts and then incorporated those concepts into a set of hypotheses. An elaboration of the concepts and the hypotheses follows in the next sections. The present chapter will conclude by specifying briefly those parts of the general research model that will actually be investigated in subsequent chapters.

SPECIFIC RESEARCH CONCEPTS

Nine concepts were developed as the focus for our research. The following discussion offers brief definitions of these concepts, identification of the principal dimension or dimensions of each concept, and illustrative indicators for them.

ECONOMIC AND SOCIAL CONDITIONS

There are two different kinds of economic and social conditions—those that constitute an environment for all agencies (for example, unemployment) and those that are particularly relevant to specific agencies (for example, the changing age distribution of the population considered in relation to the Office of Education). While recognizing the usefulness of the latter type of variable, our attention is presently directed to the former type.

Illustrative indicators of economic conditions include the percent of unemployed civilians in the labor force, the percent of the labor force classified as white collar, per capita income, a standard of living or "real" income index (per capita income divided by the consumer price index), number of new housing starts, and percent disposable income saved. Examples of indicators of social conditions include mobility of the population, percent of the population in urbanized areas, percent of the population with some college education, and the homicide rate. As the present relatively underdeveloped state of economic and (especially) social indicators is rectified, we should have an increasingly sophisticated array of indicators from which to choose.

PARTY STRENGTH

We have focused on two kinds of party strength—in the electorate and in the government. The principal dimension of interest in both of these aspects of party strength is the relative standing of the Republican and Democratic parties—relative gains and losses for the two parties (which can be measured by focusing on only one party since American party politics is almost always a zero sum two-party game). Examples of indicators of party strength in the electorate are percentages of the population identifying themselves with each of the parties, percentages of the two-party vote for the House of Representatives candidates of each of the parties, and percent of the two-party vote for the presidential candidates of each of the parties. Examples of party strength in the government include the control of the presidency (Democratic or Republican), the control of Congress (Democratic or Republican), and the size of the majority party's margin in Congress (in number of seats).

PUBLIC OPINION

For our purposes, public opinion includes mass and elite attitudes toward policy issue areas, actual government programs, government officials in their policy roles, and proposed governmental involvement or noninvolvement in specific issue areas. The principal dimension of interest is whether an agency is set in an opinion context that is more supportive or less supportive of its endeavors. Illustrative indicators include popular rating of the President's handling of his job, various measures of trust in government and governmental institutions, rating of the most serious problems facing the nation, and the affect toward specific policies.

NATURE OF COALITIONS

Coalitions are the clusters of supporters and/or opponents (both governmental and nongovernmental) of specific programs administered by and decisions made by agencies. The principal dimension of interest is the visibility of these coalitions. More visible coalitions are those that are highly active and probably highly partisan. Less visible coalitions are those that are less active and probably less partisan. Illustrative indicators include various measures of activity at congressional hearings, spending of interest groups, measures of presidential interest and support, and measures of partisanship in congressional action on agency related matters.

CHARACTERISTICS OF AGENCY STRUCTURE

Characteristics of agency structure contribute to a dimension called agency maturity or development. This concept encompasses a number of factors that have been suggested in the literature to be important to the way an agency performs its policy actions. We want to investigate five principal aspects of agency maturity—agency age, agency size, hierarchical complexity, functional complexity, and administrative experience. We are principally interested in whether an agency can be called more mature or less mature.

Illustrative indicators for agency age (older agencies are considered more mature) include the number of years since an agency was first established, the number of years between replacements of the agency head, and the number of years since the agency was last formally reorganized.

Illustrative indicators for agency size (larger agencies are considered more mature) include the total number of full-time permanent positions in an agency and the number of specified geographical locations in which federal employees work.

Illustrative indicators for hierarchical complexity (more complex agencies are considered more mature) include organizational shape (Kaufman and Seidman, 1970), span of control (Blau and Scott, 1962), number and percentage of middlegrade employees, and number and percentage of supergrade employees. (Middlegrades are those with a rank of GS13 through GS15 or the equivalent; supergrades are those with a rank of GS16 through GS18 or the equivalent.)

Illustrative indicators for functional complexity (more complex agencies are considered more mature) including the number of distinct occupational titles of nonclerical staff (Blau et al., 1966) and a measure based on division of labor and the relative uniformity of the number of people in each subunit performing separate tasks (Samuel and Mannheim, 1970).

Illustrative indicators for administrative experience (Moreland, 1973) include the span of authority acquired by an agency (agencies with more authority are considered more mature) and annual percent change (turnover) in top echelon agency personnel (agencies with a low turnover are considered more mature).

Indicators for each of the above aspects can be studied singly and in groups. Eventually, indices combining various indicators may be constructed. Subsequent chapters will use indicators for several of these aspects of development. In the final chapter we will summarize what has been discovered empirically about the concept in the reported research, and we will address the question of whether there are one or several kinds of maturity.

CHARACTERISTICS OF AGENCY PERSONNEL

The characteristics of agency personnel structures as a whole contribute to a dimension called structural rigidity. The principal interest here is whether the personnel structure of an agency is more rigid or less rigid. Less rigidity indicates a condition facilitating development, movement, and turnover of personnel. Greater rigidity depresses the development, movement, and turnover of personnel. Illustrative indicators include the mean and median age of employees (agencies with relatively old employees are considered more rigid), the mean and median time in service for employees (agencies with relatively more senior employees are considered more rigid), the ratio of promotions from within an agency to new hiring for jobs for which present employees are eligible for promotion (agencies with a high ratio of in-house promotions are considered more rigid), and years in grade before promotion, by grade to which promotion is made (agencies with a slow rate of promotion are considered more rigid). It should be noted that maturity and structural rigidity may be highly related, with more mature agencies also being more rigid.

CHARACTERISTICS OF AGENCY DECISION-MAKING PROCESSES

Agencies make decisions in different ways. The principal dimension of interest here is whether aspects of those decision processes, when aggregated, can be called more traditional or less traditional. Indicators, based largely on interviews, will be developed for five aspects of traditional/nontraditional agency behavior.

1. Reasons for accepting authority (authority is conceived of as the power of command located in specific individuals holding specific offices) vary from exclusive reliance on a strong tradition of accepting the legitimacy of the formal leaders' actions to heavy reliance on confidence in

and trust of a specific official or set of officials. Agencies in which authority is accepted more for the first, formal reasons are considered more traditional. Agencies in which authority is accepted more for the second, informal reasons are considered less traditional.

2. The degree of hierarchical control of subunit decisions and processes is relatively high in some agencies and relatively low in other agencies. Agencies in which there is a relatively high degree of such control are considered more traditional. Agencies in which there is a relatively low degree of such control are considered less traditional.

3. The mode of managing conflict varies from a relatively high degree of command and relatively low reliance on persuasion at one end of the spectrum to a relatively low degree of command and relatively high reliance on persuasion at the other end. Agencies relying more on command are considered more traditional. Agencies relying more on persuasion are considered less traditional.

4. The patterns of communications within an agency and from an agency to outsiders vary from relatively closed patterns (in which internal horizontal communication is limited, vertical communication is principally downward, and communications with nonagency personnel are highly restricted) to relatively open patterns (in which internal communication is unlimited, vertical communication flows in both directions, and communications with nonagency personnel are unrestricted). Agencies with closed communications patterns are considered more traditional; agencies with open patterns are considered less traditional.

5. The attitude in an agency toward change and innovation varies from being more receptive to being less receptive. Agencies in which the personnel have less receptive attitudes are considered more traditional and agencies in which the personnel have more receptive attitudes are considered less traditional.

POLICY ACTIONS

Policy actions are what agencies do. Traditionally, policy actions have been treated only as dollar measures of activity, for example, appropriations or expenditures. We are proposing a much broader conceptualization of actions that includes nondollar as well as dollar measures of agency activity. This conceptualization consists of three classes of policy actions —rhetorical actions, acquisitive actions, and implementing actions. Rhetorical actions are the easiest form of actions for agency personnel to perform. Quantitative measurement of verbal statements by agency personnel in public documents allows profiles of rhetorical actions to be constructed for the agencies. The acquisition of resources encompasses actions related to the building and maintaining of a resource base from which the agency can implement its programs. Implementing actions are what the agency actually does to put its program in effect. This class of actions differs from acquisitive actions in that it is primarily concerned with expending resources rather than gathering them. Table 1–1 presents examples of indicators for each of these categories.

There are several dimensions of interest within any class of policy actions. First, there is the level of agency involvement in an activity. This dimension focuses on the absolute size of the commitment. Second, there is the direction of change in agency involvement—does a commitment represent an increase or a decrease from previous levels? Third, there is the amount of change in agency involvement in an activity relative to previous levels—is the change relatively greater or smaller? Finally, there is the speed of change in government involvement—is the change relatively slow or relatively rapid?

POLICY RESULTS

Policy results are what happens in society following governmental actions. The principal dimension of interest is the ability of the governmental agencies to achieve desired results—whether they are more able

TABLE 1-1. Indicators for Policy Actions

Type of Action	Illustrative Indicators
1. Rhetorical Actions	Paragraph and page counts of testimony presented by agency personnel at hearings Paragraph and page counts of material from agency reports, administrators' speeches, etc.
2. Acquisitive Actions	Number of authorization statutes and amendments enacted Amount of appropriations New personnel granted Acquisition of physical resources: specialized equipment, land, raw materials
3. Implementing Actions	Disbursal of resources: expeditures, grants, loans, personnel assigned Directives issued Directives enforced ("cases") Information collected and disseminated by agency Contractual relations entered into Establishment of subunits: implementing units, coordinating units, task forces, conferences, etc.

to achieve them or less able to achieve them. Indicators will be developed as the policy results of specific agencies and their major programs are investigated.

HYPOTHESES

Nine pairs of basic hypotheses embracing the concepts discussed above were developed both to illustrate the directions in which our work might move and to serve as stimulants for the first empirical tests. These hypotheses reflect a careful reading of a large and diverse literature in American politics as well as common sense expectations about the hypothesized relationships. Each pair of hypotheses is followed by a brief discussion explaining the reasoning behind the hypothesized relationship and by a citation of supportive literature. It should be noted that although the first six pairs of hypotheses are worded in terms of amount and direction of change, the wording of level of involvement and speed of change could have been inserted in the hypotheses without changing the basic meaning. The appropriate dimensions will be determined by research interests.

H1. The less mature an agency, the greater the changes in its policy actions, usually in the direction of increasing government activity. The more mature an agency, the less the changes in its policy actions.

Maturation can be thought of in two senses. In one sense it is like the physical development of the human organism—that is, an agency must develop the capacity in a physical sense for performing its ordained tasks. At the same time, the number of tasks assigned to it may well grow, thus necessitating further growth in physical capacity. We hypothesize that in this sense younger agencies will have more rapidly changing policy actions, usually in the direction of more government activity. Sometimes the changes may go in the opposite direction because young agencies may also be especially vulnerable to dramatic cuts or shrinkage because they have not entrenched themselves in the policy-making system, may not have had time to develop a substantial supportive clientele, and so on.

In the physical sense a more mature agency is less likely to be subject to the swings of either good or bad fortune. Its tasks will be relatively stable, its place in the governmental scheme will be secure, and its support from beneficiaries and other agencies will all tend to be more stable, and thus stable policy actions are more likely.

At some point, however, it may be that organizational "senility" sets in and that physical capacity for performing tasks begins to shrink—perhaps because the task is no longer highly valued, perhaps because the individuals expected to carry out the task no longer perform efficiently, or perhaps because younger organizations have gradually encroached on the jurisdiction of the agency.

The second sense in which maturation might be applicable to an agency involves the accumulation of experience both in dealing with the subject matter of the agency and especially in dealing with the other actors important to the life and strength of the agency. This kind of maturation may prolong the ability of "middle-aged" agencies to grow programmatically, and it may delay the onset of senility in older agencies, while younger agencies find themselves in a relatively weaker position because they have not yet developed this kind of maturity.

Our general hypothesis is derived using maturation in the first sense. Literature that suggests support for the general hypothesis includes Bailey and Mosher (1968); Downs (1967: Ch. 2); Ripley (1972a, 1969); and Simon (1953).

Maturation in the second sense may well push in opposite directions. In Chapter 3 an empirical exploration of this kind of maturity will be presented. As already indicated, maturity will also receive a fuller discussion in the final chapter.

> **H2. The less the structural rigidity of an agency, the greater the changes in its policy actions, usually in the direction of increasing government activity. The greater the structural rigidity of an agency, the less the changes in its policy actions.**

The qualities of structural rigidity—older employees, more senior employees, more in-house promotions, a slow rate of promotions—are not compatible with growth in policy actions. These characteristics invoke the image of stodgy, unimaginative, routinized leadership where freshness in policy direction is unlikely, aggressiveness in seeking to expand the agency's responsibilities is not practiced, and conservative administration is the norm. Growth in policy actions is enhanced when the agency personnel are willing to be aggressive and to seek new means to implement programs. These conditions are likely to exist only if new blood is encouraged to enter and rise in the agency.

Relevant literature includes Bailey and Mosher (1968); Corson (1963); Downs (1967); Golembiewski (1969); and Palumbo (1969).

> **H3. The more nontraditional an agency is, the greater the changes in its policy actions, usually in the direction of increasing government involvement. The more traditional an agency is, the less the changes in its policy actions.**

The concept of the traditional agency is linked to the concepts of greater physical maturity and structural rigidity in agencies, and its effects on policy actions are similarly depressing. The marks of traditional patterns of decision-making include closed patterns of communications, a high degree of hierarchical control over the decisions of agency subunits, and an unreceptive attitude toward change and innovation. When these characteristics are present, policy actions are likely to be depressed because of the presence of a restrained, conservative intra-agency administrative style. A high degree of control over subunit decisions limits the flexibility and freedom of the subunits to implement their programs and consequently limits the potential range of policy actions. A nonreceptive attitude toward innovation similarly limits the range of actions that agencies can take to those that are "tried and true" or at least nonthreatening. A closed communications pattern limits the interplay between personnel and the opportunity for exchange of ideas that may have payoffs in terms of increasing policy actions.

Supportive literature includes Bailey and Mosher (1968); Corson (1963); Downs (1967); and Palumbo (1969).

> **H4. As the Democratic party gains strength in the electorate and in government, changes in policy actions coming from agencies are greater, usually in the direction of increased government activity. As the Democratic party loses strength in the electorate and in government, changes in policy actions from agencies are less, including some changes in the direction of decreased government activity.**

Since the source of agencies' latitude for action ultimately comes from the interaction of the President and Congress on matters such as statutory authority and appropriations, the fate of agencies is partially dependent on these elected officials. The elected officials generally seek to assure their reelection and the success of their party generally by generating benefits for their supporters, real and potential. Democrats tend to be most strongly supported by individuals in lower socioeconomic strata, who benefit or assume they benefit by increasing government activity in a number of substantive areas. Republicans tend to be most strongly supported by individuals in higher socioeconomic strata, who are less interested in or actively opposed to increasing government activity in a number of areas. Thus, in general, we expect Democratic ascendance and dominance to be associated with increasing policy actions and periods of relative Democratic weakness and Republican strength to be associated with stable or perhaps decreasing policy actions.

It should also be noted, of course, that Republican supporters may well have considerable interest in the activities of some particular agencies if their programs are thought to be sound ideologically. For example, the National Labor Relations Board thought to be stringent in interpreting limits on labor unions might receive strong support from elected Republican officials backed by active interest on the part of corporate managers who are the backbone of Republican support in many districts.

Similarly, Democrats might not be particularly impressed by the utility of governmental activities thought mainly to subsidize the already well-to-do classes in society. For example, if Democrats and their supporters perceive the Communications Satellite Corporation to be in existence mainly to promote the fortunes of large communications companies, they are not likely to be interested in increasing its policy actions. Thus, it may be that there are "Democratic" agencies and "Republican" agencies, depending on the substance of their programs.

The general hypothesis is based on the assumption that growth for agencies will be more supported by Democrats than by Republicans when all agencies are aggregated. However, the more refined possibility of different agencies being related to each party in terms of support will be investigated in some of the subsequent chapters and will again be discussed in the last chapter.

Literature supportive of the general hypothesis includes Berelson et al. (1954); Campbell et al. (1960); Downs (1957); Dye (1966); Key (1966); Lockard (1959); and Rossiter (1960).

> **H5. The greater the visibility of coalitions that support or oppose an agency, the greater the changes in the agency's policy actions. The less the visibility of coalitions that support or oppose an agency, the less the changes in the agency's policy actions.**

High visibility for coalitions is associated with highly politically charged situations—those in which there is a high degree of involvement by top level executive and legislative officials (for example, the President, the Speaker of the House, the Majority Leader of the Senate) and in which there is also a relatively high degree of public awareness of whatever issue or issues are under consideration. In such situations change in policy actions—in either direction—is also particularly likely.

Coalitions also become visible if they are considered important because of a substantial resource base (wealth, good political connections, a large proportion of active members). Such coalitions are more likely to succeed in influencing policy actions in directions favorable to them than less visible, weaker coalitions. Thus, given the presence of such coalitions, change is more likely.

Literature supportive of the general hypothesis includes Connery (1968); Donovan (1967); Feingold (1966); Harris (1966); Kessel (1968); Ripley (1972a, 1969); Sayre and Kaufman (1965); Speigel (1968); and Sundquist (1969).

> **H6. As economic and social conditions change more rapidly, changes in policy actions coming from agencies are greater. As economic and social conditions change more slowly, changes in policy actions coming from agencies are less.**

Policy actions emerge partially because policy-makers are trying to meet perceived needs among their supporters and clientele and to generate benefits for those groups. Unstable conditions, marked by rapid change in economic and social conditions, generate dissatisfaction among groups that perceive themselves to be adversely affected by the changes. To help allay the dissatisfactions among these people, policy actions undergo greater change. When conditions are stable, more groups feel satisfied, and fewer feel negatively affected by the lack of change. The relative satisfaction does not require policymakers to alter policy actions substantially.

Relevant literature includes Berelson et al. (1954); Burns (1956); Campbell et al. (1960); Donovan (1967); Ripley (1972a); Schlesinger (1957); and Sundquist (1968).

H7. As economic and social conditions change more rapidly, agencies are less able to achieve desired policy results. As economic and social conditions change more slowly, agencies are more able to achieve desired policy results.

Unstable conditions, marked by rapid changes in social and economic conditions, inhibit the ability of policy-makers to forecast the impact of their actions accurately. If forecasting is inaccurate or unreliable, desired policy results are more difficult to achieve.

Relevant literature includes Donovan (1967); Hammond (1963); Hitch and McKean (1960); Lindblom (1965); Moynihan (1969); Novick (1965); Ripley (1972a); Schultze (1968); Simon (1957); Speigel (1968); and Wildavsky (1964).

H8. The more supportive the public opinion context in which an agency operates, the more successful it will be in achieving desired policy results. The less supportive the public opinion context in which an agency operates, the less successful it will be in achieving desired policy results.

Hostile public opinion about specific programs and agencies forces policy-makers to spend their time trying to counteract it rather than allowing them to concentrate on forecasting the links between those actions and results and on taking actions consonant with those predictions. It may also lead them to choices within programs aimed at placating public opinion rather than maximizing goal achievement. Even if policy-makers are aware of the consequences of such choices, they may feel forced to make them anyway. And it may be that the necessity of focusing on placating the hostile opinion obscures the consequences of the choice for the policy-makers. Furthermore, if the program depends in part on cooperation from the target population (the presumed beneficiaries), hostile opinion in that population may well slow down or prevent the desired impact for the program. Thus, in at least three senses, hostile public opinion makes goal achievement less likely and supportive public opinion makes it more likely.

Relevant literature includes Aberbach and Walker (1970); Art (1968); Donovan (1967); Hammond (1963); Hitch and McKean (1960); Key (1961); Miller and Stokes (1963); Moynihan (1969); Ripley (1972a); Schultze (1968); Speigel (1968); Stokes (1966); and Wahlke (1967).

> **H9. The slower the changes in the policy actions of an agency, the more likely it is to achieve desired policy results. The more rapid the changes in policy actions of an agency, the less likely it is to achieve desired policy results.**

The slower pace associated with slower change in policy actions provides agency administrators more time to ponder the impact of their actions; thus, their forecasting and policy analysis in general is likely to be more accurate, and policy results are likely to be the desired ones. Also, accurate forecasting is more likely when changes in actions are small or slow because there is less change for which to predict the impact, and deviation from existing conditions (the impacts of which presumably are already known) is less.

Supportive literature includes Connery (1968); Donovan (1967); Feingold (1966); Harris (1966); Ripley (1972a, 1969); Speigel (1968); and Sundquist (1968).

The general research model underlying this volume is presented in Figure 1–2. This model is simply a diagrammatic representation of the nine pairs of hypotheses. The numbers on the arrows in the figure refer to hypothesis numbers. The primary hunch underlying the research effort to be reported in the subsequent chapters is that policy actions, especially when measured by dollars, are not determined simply by previous policy actions. External and internal environmental factors are believed to have an important role in determining the level and kind of change in agency policy actions.

The Present Volume

In the chapters that follow, policy actions, usually measured in dollar terms, are the dependent variables. Independent variables that are explored—in addition to previous policy actions—are economic and social conditions, party strength, the nature of coalitions, and agency maturity. In terms of Figure 1–2, we have chosen to focus on the relationships numbered 1, 4, 5, and 6.

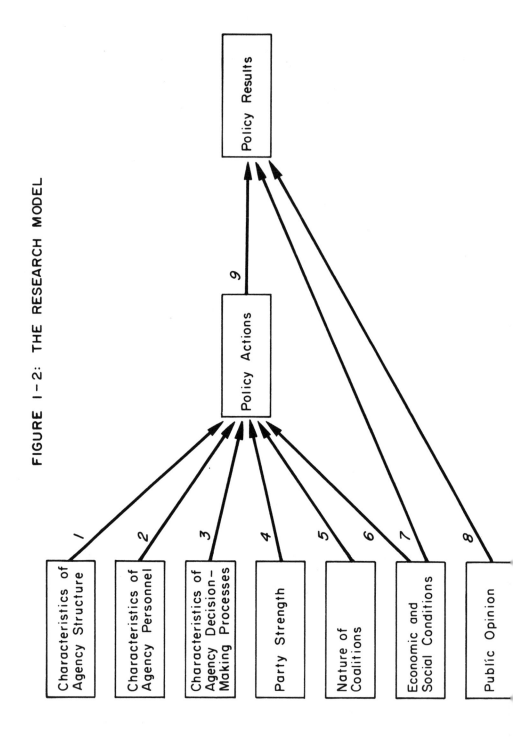

FIGURE I-2: THE RESEARCH MODEL

18

We selected these clusters of independent variables on grounds that were both pragmatic and theoretically attractive. First, given the ambitious and comprehensive nature of the conceptual scheme, it seemed prudent to test only a portion of it rather than trying to tackle all portions simultaneously, in order to assess its empirical promise.

Second, we explored the kinds of data we would need for use in developing indicators for all of the seven independent variable clusters included in Figure 1–2. Because of the longitudinal nature of the model, we were insistent that data for a concept be available for a long period of time. Our survey of data showed that exploration of three concepts—public opinion, agency personnel characteristics, and agency decision-making characteristics—would have to be delayed. In general, public opinion data that related to specific agencies and programs were far too scanty over a long-time period to give us much hope of rigorous testing. After checking with a number of agencies, we concluded that data on characteristics of agency personnel would be extremely difficult to collect in comparable form for a large number of agencies for the requisite time period. Data on characteristics of agency decision-making processes necessarily would have to come largely from interviews. Such interviewing would have been feasible for differentiating between contemporary agencies, but we saw no practical way to extend that kind of data back in time far enough to undertake the kind of testing in which we were interested.

Our initial explorations into data on agency structure, party strength, coalitions, and economic and social conditions, however, convinced us that although problems were present they were surmountable, and we could use these variables with considerable rigor. Naturally, decisions about which specific indicators to use for these variables (because there are numerous logical candidates in each case) still had to be made. Those decisions are discussed, as appropriate, in each of the empirical chapters (Chapters 2–7).

The data problems surrounding the public opinion, personnel, and decision-making concepts are not insurmountable (the primary obstacle is one of time and difficult accessibility), and our decision not to focus on them does not mean that we have abandoned them. The decision was grounded in pragmatism—we wanted to test a substantial part of the model in a relatively short period of time (a few years). To do so it seemed sensible to explore concepts for which data could be gathered with less rather than more time, expense, and effort. The empirical exploration of the currently untested concepts must await a longer data collection period.

Third, in terms of the social science literature that relates various environmental and structural variables to policy actions, we discovered that although such literature in general is thin, it is more developed in dealing with characteristics of agency structure, party strength, coalitions, and economic and social conditions than in dealing with the other variable clusters. Thus, we found a welcome congruence between our opportunities for building on extant work, and our judgment about relative feasibility of sufficient high-quality data for each of the independent variable clusters.

In deciding where to place our efforts in terms of dependent variables we settled first on the policy action cluster rather than the policy result cluster. Within that cluster we chose to examine primarily budgetary policy actions.

The first decision—to explore actions rather than results—was made for two basic reasons: the relatively greater availability of longitudinal data for policy actions and the relatively more developed treatment of actions in the social science literature. The second decision—to work largely with budgetary data of various descriptions in dealing with policy actions —was guided by the existence of a large body of literature that operationalized policy in dollar terms and asserted that budgetary policy actions could be explained solely in terms of previous budgetary policy actions. Such a single-explanatory variable approach offered an explicit challenge to the framework we had developed and provided a natural starting point for selecting analysis topics.

Note

1. Readers of earlier versions of this conceptual framework (Ripley et al., 1973a, 1973b) will notice that the concept of policy statements (statements of intent by agency personnel about agency goals and intentions) has been deleted from the present version. Originally, we intended to study three aspects of policy statements: (1) the relationship between variations in policy statements and variations in the external environment; (2) the fit between policy statements and subsequent policy actions; and (3) the goal content of policy statements as related to assessment of policy results. However, a survey of policy statements in a number of fields has indicated that the first two objectives are not feasible empirically no matter how interesting theoretically. The third objective is still viable, but its study does not depend on a formal addition to the conceptual model.

   The results of the examination of policy statements showed that rhetoric about agency goals and content—at least that rhetoric contained in the public documents available to researchers—does not vary in content over time. The lack of variation in policy statements makes the study of the relationship between statements and environment and between statements and actions pointless. And information about agency goals to be used in assessing policy results can be obtained without acquiring vast numbers of policy statements. Thus, the decision to delete policy statements from the framework was made.

2

Social Conditions and Policy Change

William M. Holmes

This chapter examines the relationship between change in social conditions and change in agency policy. The hypotheses address three questions concerning this relationship: (1) To what extent do different elements in the social environment of federal agencies influence policy changes in those agencies? (2) Is the effect of social conditions on policy change greater or less than the influence of changes in policy statements and agency maturity? (3) What factors increase or decrease the influence of social conditions on policy change?

Policy change is operationalized as change in agency expenditures. Four independent variables are examined: issue-related social conditions, general social conditions, change in presidential policy statements, and change in agency maturity. Data for 12 federal agencies were collected for the time span from fiscal 1952 through 1971. The analytical techniques employed included an historical trend analysis, a block variable path analysis, and a subsample test for interactive effects. The interactive effects of three factors were examined: policy issue area, level of agency maturity, and general state of society.

The findings of this study show that changes in policy actions are influenced by change in issue-related social conditions, change in agency maturity, and change in general social conditions, with issue-related social conditions having the most impact. Changes in both kinds of social conditions influence both change in policy statements and change in policy actions, but the impact is greater on changes in policy statements than on changes in policy actions. The findings suggest clinical possibilities for increasing the responsiveness of federal agencies to their environment by means of manipulating policy statements, agency maturity, and definitions or information concerning the state of society.

ALTHOUGH AGENCIES THEMSELVES may seem to endure, unchanging, over long periods of time, their policy actions are in a continual state of change. In fits and spurts, and with rationales that are not always entirely clear (perhaps even to themselves), policy-makers create, remold, and occasionally even terminate agencies' programs. Congress, the President, interest groups, clients, beneficiaries, and factors inside and outside the agency all contribute to changes in policy actions. Many of these influences will be examined in subsequent chapters in this volume, but the concern of the present chapter is with the effect that changes in external social conditions have on changes in policy actions. This concern has three aspects, which will be discussed in the succeeding sections: (1) the general relationship between social conditions and change in policy action; (2) the influence of social conditions relative to other independent influences on policy change; and (3) conditions that may enhance or depress the relationship between social conditions and policy change.

The Linkage between Social Conditions and Policy Change

The influence of social conditions on policy change is important for both pragmatic and theoretical reasons. Pragmatically, the extent to which changes in policy actions are influenced by social conditions is a measure of how responsive an agency is towards society. It is possible to tell whether an agency is being responsive to the elements to which it is supposed to be responsive by examining the influence of social conditions that are related to the goals of the agency on changes in the agency's policy actions. Examining the influence of social conditions also indicates whether an agency is influenced by conditions thought irrelevant to the goals of the agency. Such knowledge is important in holding agencies accountable for their actions and for pointing out potential areas for future policy change.

The relationship between social conditions and policy change is important on the theoretical level because there is little agreement about which forces control the magnitude and direction of policy change. The position taken in this volume is that policy changes are the result of a number of structural and environmental influences, including social conditions, on federal agencies. Domhoff (1970), Mills (1956), and Lundburg (1968) have argued that policy changes are controlled by a small, powerful elite. Davis et al. (1966), Fenno (1966), Sharkansky (1972), and Wildavsky (1964) have argued that policy changes are only modifications (or "increments") of previous policies.[1]

Social conditions influence policy change because of demands placed on actors in the policy arena by those conditions and because people in the arena become sensitized to developments related to their interests. Social science evidence indicates that people do tend to perceive changes in which they are interested (Hollander and Hunt, 1971; Kiesler et al., 1969). The greater the changes in one's environment, the more likely that they will be noted, even if a person is not interested in those changes (Hollander and Hunt, 1971; Kiesler et al., 1969). Any particular change may not force itself into the consciousness of all actors in the policy arena; but the greater the change in a social condition, the more likely that some actors will become aware of it. Social conditions affect policy by altering the habits, constraints of action, or perceptions of actors in the policy arena, who can become aware of the social changes through a variety of linkage mechanisms.

The principal conduits by which social conditions are conveyed to policy actors are public opinion, interest groups, Congress, the President, the courts, and information gathering mechanisms of the agency. The influence of public opinion is questionable at times, but letters, telegrams, phone calls, personal contacts, and public opinion polls do influence policy change on occasion, especially if the agency is in a financially vulnerable or politically sensitive situation. Interest groups abound in all areas of public concern, including the seven policy issue areas discussed later in this chapter. Their principal function is to influence change in policy actions in ways favorable to their interests. One way they do this is to provide policy actors with up-to-date information relating to their issue area—information that includes knowledge about changing demands and changing external pressures, including social conditions.

Information gathering mechanisms rest on the fact that agencies collect data to fulfill statutory requirements, for policy planning, budgetary allocations, and many other reasons. Whatever the reason for collecting social data, when the GAO, OMB, Congress, or the President ask the agency for evidence that it is responsive to public needs, it cannot entirely ignore the information it has gathered. If changes in social conditions are in a direction undesired by Congress, then congressmen may feel that legislation of some kind is necessary. Even the threat of legislation may cause an agency to change its policy. These same social changes may increase litigation concerning agency policies.[2] The FTC, ICC, NLRB, and FDA continually have cases before the courts. Other agencies litigate less often; but when a precedent is set contrary to agency policy, then policies must change. Whenever the President becomes concerned about social changes, policies are more likely to change. All these links are ways that changes in social conditions influence changes of policy in federal agencies.

THE RELATIVE INFLUENCE OF SOCIAL CONDITIONS

If the influence of social conditions on policy change is subject to debate among academicians, their influence relative to other independent factors is even more problematic. To assess effectively the relative influence of social conditions, one must simultaneously assess the contribution of other influences, since social conditions do not occur in a vacuum. For this study two other kinds of independent influences were studied—the policy statements made by actors and agency maturity. (It is assumed that other independent influences operate through these two variables, although this assumption is subject to future testing.) In addition, social conditions were divided into two categories—general social conditions and issue-related social conditions. General social conditions define the general state of society and have minimal direct impact on specific program activities. Issue-related social conditions impinge directly on a policy area and/or the program activities of the agency. These four concepts are elaborated in the discussion of variables used in the research design.

CONDITIONS AFFECTING THE RELATIONSHIP BETWEEN SOCIAL CONDITIONS AND POLICY CHANGE

A third aspect of the relationship between social conditions and agency policy actions is the role that outside factors may have in affecting the relationship. Dahrendorf (1959), Etzioni (1970), Gawthrop (1969), Rein (1970), Ripley et al. (Chapter 7), and Schultze (1971) have said that policy decisions may be unresponsive to the social environment of an agency on some occasions and responsive on other occasions. Dahrendorf (1959) has argued that the presence of interest groups results in governmental policy changes being more responsive to the wants and needs of the public. Etzioni (1970) has argued that the presence of "information feedback" can result in policy changes responsive to the public. Gawthrop (1969:188) found older agencies were more concerned with the techniques of their activities than with their policy towards their social environment. Rein (1970: 55, 174) has noted that agencies are more rigid in their policies when controlled by professionals and that agencies that have policy-making power residing in the local branches may have policy changes responsive to local concerns, even at the expense of achieving agency goals. Ripley et al. (Chapter 7) found the federal agency budgets of older agencies changed more slowly than younger agencies, that richer agencies made larger changes than poorer ones, and that service agencies changed more rapidly than regulatory agencies. Schultze (1971) has argued before Congress that the ability of agencies to change their policy in response to societal needs varies directly with the balance of federal revenues and expenditures.

The above arguments, findings, and assertions suggest a major caution that must be observed when talking about influences on policy change. One must always consider whether the influences hold for a limited situation or whether they hold for many different situations. Three conditions will be examined for their effect on the relationship between social conditions and policy change: 1) the effect of differing policy issue areas; 2) the effect of differing levels of agency maturity; and 3) the effect of differing states of society.

THE EFFECT OF POLICY ISSUE AREA

Agencies' policy statements and actions may deal with a number of different issue areas. Seven issue areas (issue areas are categories of issues that are closely interrelated) are examined in this chapter for their effect on the relationship between social conditions and policy change. The issue areas are: international involvement, economic–regulatory, social welfare–distributive, agriculture, civil liberties, natural resources, and labor. This is not an exhaustive list of all issue areas with which federal agencies deal, but several studies have shown that these are major issue areas (Clausen, 1973; Kessel, 1972; U.S. NSF, 1971).

Each of these seven issue areas has a number of dimensions. New facets of an issue continually arise and older ones may lose their importance. International involvement issue area concerns such things as defense, disarmament, world peace, and UN activity. Economic–regulatory concerns economic changes, consumer prices, unemployment, and balance of payments. The social welfare–distributive area deals with such things as health, income, social mobility, education, science, art, housing, and social insurance. Agriculture encompasses such problems as farm prices, retail price of food, and agricultural production. The civil liberties area has dimensions concerned with individuality, public order, equality, democratic economy, and free speech. The natural resources area is mainly concerned with pollution and production of raw materials. Labor issues tend to revolve around work stoppages and scientific manpower in industry. Since many of these issues overlap, it may be possible for an agency to change the definition of the issue area with which it is supposed to be concerned while continuing to address substantially the same problem. Shifting the issue area may result in an agency being more responsive to its environment (as the data will indicate).

THE EFFECT OF AGENCY MATURITY

Agency maturity includes manipulable as well as unmanipulable characteristics of federal agencies. There is little an agency can do about changing the number of years since it was established. There is much an agency can do regarding its size, the differentiation of organizational structure, characteristics of its personnel, and intra-agency communication. Chapters 6 and 7 present evidence that some of these dimensions influence the responsiveness of agencies to their environment. Subsamples of agency years for some of these dimensions (size and rate of change of agency personnel) will be examined to see if changing an agency's maturity will alter its responsiveness to changes in social conditions. If so, manipulating an agency's maturity may allow manipulating its responsiveness to social conditions.

THE EFFECT OF THE STATE OF SOCIETY

The ability of the federal government to manipulate or control the state of society is very problematic. On the other hand, Chapters 6 and 7 demonstrate that agency actions do change in response to environmental factors. During "good times" agencies may ignore social conditions since there is less pressure for federal intervention. During "bad times" there may be an increase in the demand that the federal government intervene in the situation, which would cause agencies to pay closer attention to their environment. Even if it is not possible to manipulate the state of society, it is possible to manipulate definitions of society. Changing society (when it is possible) or changing the criteria by which society is evaluated (when that is possible) may allow changing the way agencies respond to social conditions. This will be investigated by looking at subsamples of agency years for good and bad times, where the level of unemployment is used to determine the state of society.

Research Design

THE VARIABLES

In the preceding pages five principal variables were identified as important to the study of the relationship between social conditions and policy change—general social conditions, issue-related social conditions, policy statements, agency maturity, and policy actions. These variables and their operationalization will be discussed here before presenting the hypotheses and the research model. Note that two change measures were used for each variable to capture the dynamic aspects of the relationship between social conditions and policy change.[3] The magnitude of change measure revealed the amount of change, while the acceleration of change measure showed whether the rate of change was increasing or decreasing.

In operationalizing the variables, multiple indicators were chosen to achieve more accurate estimates of the relationship between every variable in the model than would have been possible using only single indicators. The indicators listed below were selected from a larger set of indicators on the basis of validity coefficients estimated by treating the variables as unobserved variables in a path model (for the details of this method, see Blalock, 1970; Hauser and Goldberger, 1971; and Heise, 1972). Redundant indicators were then deleted to reduce unreliability of estimates resulting from collinear indicators. Deleting invalid or redundant indicators insures maximum validity and reliability of the findings.

GENERAL SOCIAL CONDITIONS

Change in general social conditions is composed of magnitude and acceleration measures of change in social conditions that have a diffuse impact throughout all parts of the policy arena—they do not impinge directly on one policy area more than another. If the statements about program and agency goals made by federal agencies did not encompass the condition, implicitly or explicitly, it was termed a general social condition. Three indicators were selected by the criteria of maximizing validity and minimizing redundancy:

1. rate of change in the membership of religious groups having fewer than 50,000 members (generally, sectarian religions), .92
2. magnitude change in the percent of the total population not affiliated with a household ("unrelated individuals," according to the Census Bureau), .80
3. year (a linear trend variable acting as a surrogate measure of the general conditions not explicitly entered in the model), .68

ISSUE-RELATED SOCIAL CONDITIONS

Change in issue-related social conditions is composed of magnitude and acceleration of change in social conditions that fall in an issue area with which goals of a federal agency are concerned. Six indicators were selected that had the highest validity coefficients and lowest collinearity (redundancy) with indicators of other independent variables in the model. The indicators and their validity coefficients are:

1. total defense personnel, .82
2. unemployment rate, .75
3. magnitude change in unemployment rate, .70
4. magnitude change in the number of white collar workers, .78
5. magnitude change in the difference of white and nonwhite median income, .42
6. magnitude change in percent poor, .25

POLICY STATEMENTS

Policy statements are statements made by policy actors about the goals of the agency. Essentially, they are statements of intent, and subsequent policy actions can be compared to them. As was noted in Chapter 1, there are many empirical difficulties in working with policy statements, not the least of which is the massive task of collecting statements from numerous actors and analyzing those statements for their goal content. The use of policy statements in this study is limited to statements made by the President in his State of the Union messages from 1952 to 1971. The reason for this choice was one of expedience—a source of precoded statements was available to the author.[4] Thus, change in policy statements focuses only on the statements of one actor, the President, and only on the agency mentions and agency related statements contained in one set of his public messages. Indicators[5] and validity coefficients for this variable are:

1. factor loading for international involvement statements in Presidential State of the Union messages, .63
2. factor loading for civil liberties statements in Presidential State of the Union messages, .42

AGENCY MATURITY

Two aspects of agency maturity will be dealt with—agency size (total number of permanent positions in the agency) and change in agency personnel. The specific indicators and validity coefficients selected for this variable were:

1. magnitude change in the number of supergrades in the agency, .75
2. total agency personnel, .53

POLICY ACTIONS

Change in policy actions is concerned with magnitude change and acceleration in actions taken by the agency to achieve agency goals or to conform with previous policy statements. Among policy actions, changes in agency expenditures will be focused on, rather than rhetorical actions, planning actions, acquisitive actions, or other kinds of actions, because of their importance and their comparability.[6] Expenditures are undeniably important activities of an agency. Agency expenditures establish the latitude for most other kinds of actions. If an agency's expenditures don't change, it is difficult to change other actions of the agency. Unlike many other policy actions, expenditures occur in all agencies, and this common occurrence facilitates comparison among agencies. The indicators and validity coefficients for this variable are:

1. magnitude change in total agency expenditures, .59
2. rate of change in total agency expenditures, .53

CHOICE OF AGENCIES

Agencies were selected for each of the policy issue areas from a list of agencies for which data were available or could be collected from fiscal 1952 through 1971. The fit of issue area to agency was not perfect given multiple goals for many agencies. The agencies are not a random sample of all federal agencies, but findings similar to those reported here were found for other agencies (see Chapter 6), which suggests the findings may be generalizable. The agencies and their issue areas are:

1. International Involvement
   a. Agency for International Development (AID)
   b. United States Information Agency (USIA)
2. Economic–Regulatory
   a. Federal Trade Commission (FTC)
   b. Interstate Commerce Commission (ICC)
3. Welfare–Distributive
   a. Office of Education (OE)
   b. National Cancer Institute (NCI)
4. Agriculture
   a. Extension Service (ES)
   b. Commodity Credit Corporation (CCC)
5. Civil Liberties
   a. Equal Employment Opportunity Commission (EEOC)
6. Natural Resources
   a. Forest Service (FS)
   b. Bureau of Mines (BOM)
7. Labor
   a. National Labor Relations Board (NLRB)

ANALYTICAL TECHNIQUES

Three analytical techniques are used—path analysis, trend analysis, and subsample tests for interaction—to see whether the empirical findings support or oppose the hypotheses. The path analysis is used in evaluating support for the hypotheses concerning additive influences. The trend analysis looks at changes in agency characteristics and policy actions across time for social and historical influences on changes in policy actions. The subsample comparisons are used in examining the hypotheses concerning interactive influences on change in policy actions. These techniques are discussed in more detail in the Methodological Glossary at the end of the volume.

HYPOTHESES

It has been argued elsewhere (Holmes, 1974) that characteristics of agency maturity are influenced by changes in both general and issue-related social conditions. To help determine whether the indirect effect of social conditions (operating through agency maturity) reinforces or suppresses the direct effects of social conditions on policy changes, it is hypothesized:

H1. The greater the change in issue-related social conditions, the greater the change in maturity of the agency.

H2. The greater the change in general social conditions, the greater the change in maturity of the agency.

If we take into consideration that policy changes include policy statements as well as policy actions, then the additive effects of these influences can be summarized by:

H3. The less mature an agency's structure, the greater the change in policy statements.

H4. The greater the change in issue-related conditions, the greater the change in policy statements.

H5. The greater the change in general social conditions, the greater the change in policy statements.

H6. The less mature an agency's structure, the greater the change in its policy actions.

H7. The greater the change in agency policy statements, the greater the change in policy actions.

H8. The greater the change in issue-related conditions, the greater the change in agency policy actions.

H9. The greater the change in general social conditions, the greater the change in agency policy actions.

This chapter has argued that the impact of social conditions on an agency will vary for different issue areas, levels of unemployment, and different degrees of agency maturity. This implies three hypotheses concerning the interactive effects of these influences:

H10. Social conditions in an issue area will have a greater impact on change in policy actions of agencies in that issue area than for the average of all agencies.

H11. Change in policy actions of agencies with less mature structure will be more influenced by social conditions than change in policy actions of agencies with more mature structure.

H12. The influence of social conditions on change in agency policy actions will be greater during periods of high unemployment than in periods of lower unemployment.

The hypotheses are presented graphically in Figure 2–1 (p. 32), the basic research model. Figure 2–1 can be translated into two sets of general equations, one for the non-interactive model, and one for the interactive model. The equations and their symbols are presented in Table 2–1.

TABLE 2-1. General Equations for the Research Model

Noninteractive Model

$$M = a + b_1 I + b_2 G$$
$$S = a + b_1 M + b_2 I + b_3 G + u$$
$$P = a + b_1 M + b_2 S + b_3 I + b_4 G + u$$

Interactive Model

$$M = a + b_1 I + b_2 G + b_3 T*I + b_4 T*G + u$$
$$S = a + b_1 M + b_2 I + b_3 T*M + b_4 T*I + b_5 T*G + u$$
$$P = a + b_1 M + b_2 S + b_3 I + b_4 G + b_5 T*M + b_6 T*S + b_7 T*I + b_8 T*G + u$$

Symbols

S—change in policy statements
M—maturity of agency structure
I—change in issue-related social conditions
G—change in general social conditions
P—change in policy actions
T—interactive influence of agency maturity, issue area, and employment
b_i—regression weight of influence of the i'th variable
a—additive constant in equation
*—interactive relationship (an asterisk is used to denote interactive relationships because the nature of the interaction may be more complex than simple multiplication)
u—unexplained variation

FIGURE 2-1: DIAGRAM OF HYPOTHESIZED MODEL [a]

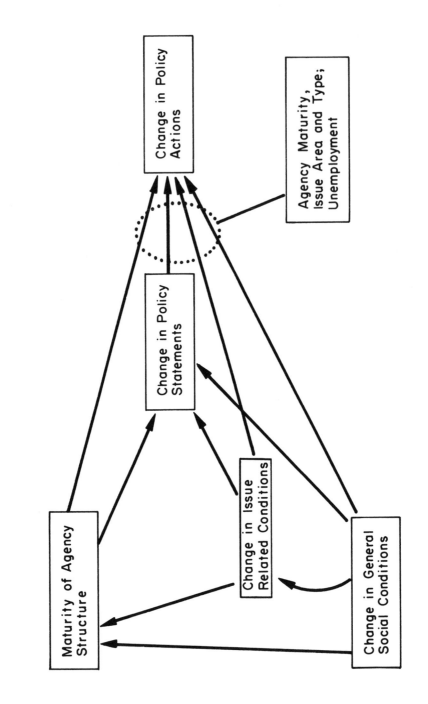

a. Curved lines indicate unanalyzed covariance of exogenous variables. Dotted line indicates possible interactive effect between agency age, issue area, and unemployment on change in policy action

Findings

RESULTS OF PATH ANALYSIS

The results of the block variable path analysis are presented in Figure 2–2. A summary statistical table for this model is included as Table 2–2 in the appendix to this chapter.

This model is very successful at explaining changes in policy statements (95% of the variance of changes in presidential policy statements). It does less well in explaining changes in budgetary actions (28% of the variance) and not very well in explaining changes in agency maturity (6% of the variance). There are several reasons for this latter inefficiency. The most important reason is that indicators that were correlated with agency maturity were deleted because they were collinear with other social conditions. The number of data points on the social conditions was simply not large enough to separate reliably the effects of the collinear variables, so they were deleted from the regression estimates. Had they been included, the "explained variance," multiple R-squared, would have been

FIGURE 2-2: RESULTS OF HYPOTHESIZED MODEL[a]

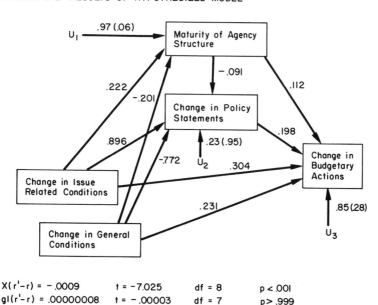

$$X(r'-r) = -.0009 \qquad t = -7.025 \qquad df = 8 \qquad p < .001$$
$$gl(r'-r) = .00000008 \qquad t = -.00003 \qquad df = 7 \qquad p > .999$$

a. Number in parentheses is amount of explained variance

50%, but this figure would have been inflated by the collinearity of the indicators. The 6% (as well as the 95% and 28%) is actually an underestimate of the true explained variance, but the choice was made not to include the collinear variables to avoid biasing the results in favor of the hypothesized relations. A more skillful analyst might generate a higher estimate of the true explained variance without including the inflation resulting from collinearity. In any case, the sheaf coefficients (multiple–partial, standardized regression coefficients) going into change in agency maturity are both statistically significant, so the conclusions are likely to remain unchanged.

The results of the path analysis support seven of the first nine hypotheses—*H1., H3., H4., H6., H7., H8.* and *H9.* Only two hypotheses (*H2.* and *H5.*) seem to be disconfirmed. Change in issue-related conditions does influence change in policy statements. Likewise, change in budgetary actions is influenced by change in agency maturity, change in policy statements, and change in issue-related conditions.

Hypothesis 2 was not supported. The negative effects of general social conditions mainly worked through influences represented by percentage of unrelated individuals and the rate of change in membership of sectarian religions. Increases in religious sectarianism and unrelated individuals both imply an increase in people in socially marginal positions. People in socially marginal positions do not participate very much in political activities (Milbrath, 1969). A growth in the number of people who don't participate means less pressure on agencies for change than there could be. As a result, less pressure for change means less change in policy statements. At the same time, the factors that produce an increase in marginality (alienation or unemployment, for example) may cause an agency to make adjustments to the situation. Their statements don't change because there is less pressure to change their goals. Their actions do change because an agency may perceive a need to change their means for reaching their goals.

This explanation is, of course, an *ex post facto* explanation. It would need confirmation using independent data before one could say the data supported this interpretation. It does, however, point out a potentially fruitful line of investigation. The search for non-issue-related social conditions that influence changes in policy actions may do better if it concentrates on looking at those general conditions that affect the levels of social and political participation in society. Since the latter are issue-related conditions, a general principle might be to look at general social conditions that influence issue-related conditions.

Hypothesis 5 also was not supported. General social conditions had a negative influence on change in policy statements. In fact, the influence of general conditions on policy statements is greater than its influence on change in budgetary actions. If it is true general conditions affect policy changes in terms of influences on rates of social and political participation, then the linkage from changes in general conditions to change in policy statements is understandable.

It is interesting that the regression slope from change in issue-related conditions to change in policy statements is also greater than that from change in issue-related conditions to change in budgetary actions, just as more of the variance of change in policy statements (95%) is explained by these social changes than that of changes in budgetary actions (28%). Clearly, the influence of social changes (issue-related or not) is greater on the rhetoric of a policy-maker (in this case, the President) than on the actual actions of the agency.[7] Agency maturity was the only variable whose impact was greater on actions than rhetoric, but in this case the influences were both of low magnitude and not greatly different from one another.

At the bottom of Figure 2–2 are various statistics that summarize the overall fit of the model with the observed relationships. Two tests of the overall fit are used, both based on estimating the zero order correlations between variables in the model using the path coefficients (Land, 1969; Duncan, 1969). One test involves computing the probability that the mean residual between the estimated and observed correlation is zero (using a paired sample t-test). For the model in Figure 2–2 the mean residual is -.0009, with a probability less than .001 of truly equalling zero (this is because a correlated sample test that was used is sensitive to small, but still significant, errors in prediction). Even though it is very likely the model underpredicts the observed correlations, the underprediction is not great (within one ten-thousandth of the true value). The other test involves computing the probability that the skewness of the distribution of residuals between estimated and observed correlations is zero. If the errors of prediction in the model are not random, but systematic, there is a strong likelihood that the distribution of residuals will be skewed as a result of the systematic under- or over-estimation. There is little chance the distribution of residuals in this case are skewed (greater than .999 probability of equalling zero).

To summarize the results of the path analysis, it can be said that changes in issue-related conditions have a major impact on changes in policy statements and budgetary actions. Changes in general social conditions and in agency maturity also affect changes in policy statements and budgetary actions. Changes in policy statements affect changes in budgetary actions more than changes in general social conditions or agency maturity, but less than changes in issue-related conditions. Generally, the influence of changes in social conditions has a greater impact on changes in policy statements than on budgetary actions.

RESULTS OF TREND ANALYSIS

On the whole, these twelve agencies became richer and larger during the fiscal 1952 through fiscal 1971 period. The average agency expenditure rose from $274,280,192 for the 1952–1961 period to $739,788,288 for the 1962–1971 period (the figures on which the analysis in this section is based are found in Table 2–3 in the chapter appendix). The average (mean) for the entire period was $515,900,000. The number of employees rose from 3,804 to 5,540, with an overall average of 4,722 persons employed per agency. These figures convey the impression that expenditures may have been rising faster than personnel for these agencies. This impression is strengthened by the fact that the spending-size ratio during the earlier period rose from $74,700 to $133,800 for the later period.

This success at getting more money and personnel has meant higher growth rates (magnitudes) of change during the later period. During the earlier period the average agency expenditure was declining at the rate of 10% per year, though differentially by agency issue area (some areas declined more rapidly than others, while some grew). Agency size for this period was growing at only 2.1% per year. In the latter half of this period the expenditures were growing at 40% per year and size at 6% per year.

What these growth rates mean is that the magnitude change in agency size and expenditures become much larger during this later period. It is hard to say when this "awakening" of federal activity occurred. Some agencies were actively changing throughout the entire period, for example, CCC, but most magnitude changes for agencies in this sample suggest fiscal 1957 as a possible starting point, with some agencies beginning as early as 1954 (ES, FS, and NCI) and others as late as 1961 (BOM, FTC, and OE). The tendency, however, is that the awakening began in the mid-fifties, with a slowdown beginning in the mid-sixties.

What factors could have contributed to the increased activity? Eisenhower reorganized the executive branch during this period. There was the Cold War and the race with Russia to orbit a satellite (and the jolt when their Sputnik was launched before our problem-laden Vanguard). This does not, however, explain why some agencies started their pattern of growth earlier than others. The differential growth between issue areas and for different degrees of agency maturity also influence the likelihood of agency growth. These influences will be discussed shortly.

This burst of activity that began generally in the mid-fifties appears to be slowing down. This is evidenced by the fact that the acceleration in change in agency size and expenditures is lower for the later period than the earlier period. During the earlier period, growth in size and expenditures was changing at -196% and 173%, respectively. During the later period, the figures had declined to 88.8% and 63%, respectively. For many of the agencies the percent change even became negative in the late-sixties.

There are a number of reasons that might explain the slowdown. Effects of the Vietnam war, agency maturation, and the change from a Democratic to a Republican president undoubtedly play a part. Rising inflation and unemployment would also contribute to this, since some agencies have reversals in the direction of their activity during high unemployment periods, as discussed in the following section.

SUBSAMPLE COMPARISONS

Three subsamples will be examined: agencies classified by issue area, agencies classified by degree of structural maturity, and years classified by high or low unemployment (greater than 5% versus less than 5%). Other interactive effects will also be discussed. Tables 2–3 and 2–4 in the chapter appendix offer statistical support for the figures mentioned.

ISSUE AREAS

In five of the seven issue areas, the issue-related condition for that area has a stronger influence on change in policy actions than the average for all agencies. This stronger influence did not occur in the economic–regulatory and labor subsamples, though it did hold for international involvement, social welfare–distributive, agriculture, civil liberties, and natural resources subsamples. This finding lends support to hypothesis 10 that issue area has an interactive effect on the relationship between social conditions and policy change.

Agencies in the agriculture issue area (CCC and ES) were more responsive to their social environment than agencies in any other area. Interest groups in this area are highly visible and active. Competition between these groups probably stimulates agriculture agencies to be responsive to changes in agricultural production and farm prices. The Department of Agriculture also has a very extensive information gathering system, not only concerning farm production and prices, but also concerning articulated wants of interest groups in this area. Both of these factors increase agency responsiveness in this area.

Natural resources agencies were the least responsive to social conditions. Two factors account for this. Until recently agencies in this area were dominated by special interest groups having common interests (rather than competing interests). The Forest Service has often been accused of being dominated by timbering interests (Davis, 1970:141; Reich, 1962:10). The Bureau of Mines has also been accused of domination by mining interests (Davis, 1970:11). Both of these agencies have slow rates of promotion, low rates of external recruitment of employees, and generally mature agency structure (Davis, 1970; Reich, 1962). All of these factors tend to decrease responsiveness of agencies in this area.

Agency Maturity

Comparisons were made for the agency maturity dimensions of size and magnitude change in size using cutting points of 2,500 for size and 20% increase or decrease for change in size. The findings related to the interactive effects of maturity on the relationship between social conditions and policy change were ambivalent.

Smaller agencies had smaller increases than larger agencies (13% versus 22% for magnitude increase in expenditures; 2% versus 6% for magnitude increases in size); but rapidly changing agencies had larger changes than more slowly changing agencies (80% versus 35% for increase in expenditures; 33% versus 2% for increases in size). On the other hand, the acceleration in expenditures was greater for smaller agencies than for larger ones (143% versus 89%), but vice versa for rapidly and slowly changing agencies (45% versus 118%). Generally, larger or more rapidly changing agencies are more influenced by their environment (have larger slopes) than smaller or more slowly changing agencies.

Two things may account for this, and both stem from the fact that comparisons are between zero order slopes, rather than partial slopes. The fact that larger agencies have greater changes in their budgets in response to their environment may be an artifact of larger agencies also being richer agencies ($1,009,744,128 average expenditure for larger agencies; $86,349,776 average expenditure for smaller agencies). This possibility can be tested by looking at the partial slopes between social conditions and budgetary changes while controlling for agency expenditures. When controls for agency expenditures are introduced, the evidence opposing Hypothesis 11 (smaller agencies being less responsive) may disappear. A second biasing fact is that historical trends have not been removed from the subsamples. Most agencies were larger during the later period than earlier, and many budgetary changes resulted from the Vietnam war, inflation, and unemployment during this period. The evidence contrary to Hypothesis 11 may also be an artifact of the historical trends. Controlling for these trends would allow testing this possibility. If introducing controls for agency expenditures and historical trends eliminates the possible association between agency size and increasing responsiveness, then hypothesis 11 would be confirmed. Otherwise, the evidence would be ambivalent and more work would need to be done on the measurement of agency maturity. If the evidence is favorable, then it may be possible to increase the responsiveness of federal agencies to their environment by lowering the maturity of these agencies.

GOOD TIMES VERSUS BAD

Hypothesis 12 posits that agencies are more responsive during high unemployment (bad times) than during low unemployment (good times). Comparisons were made between high and low unemployment subsamples (greater or less than 5% unemployment) to see if this was the case.

During low unemployment, agencies spent more and grew faster than during high unemployment ($532,380,160 versus $496,337,512 for average expenditures; 28% versus 2% for percent increase in expenditures). However, the acceleration in expenditures was greater during high unemployment than low (150% versus 82% and agency size was more subject to fluctuations than during low unemployment (1,345% versus 49%). This gives the impression of steady agency growth during good times, but many reversals in direction of change for agency behavior during high unemployment.

Reversal of policy during high unemployment is not uniform. Some influences on budgetary and structural changes reverse their influence and some do not. This pattern of federal agencies trying to go in many directions at once during bad times has regularities of social and political significance. High unemployment is likely to bring reversals in the direction of economic influences on budgetary behavior, but a strengthening of social welfare influences. The worse things get, the more likely an increase in unemployment or inflation will cause a reversal of budgetary decisions. By contrast, the worse things get, the more likely social welfare influences will push for an increase in the current direction of budgetary decisions.

This is not to suggest that one should wreck the nation's economy to make the federal agencies more responsive to their social environment. It does suggest that as more explicit criteria are developed for recognizing and documenting the presence of bad times, then agencies may be more responsive to such undesirable conditions when they occur.

Conclusions

These results generally support the hypotheses proposed concerning the influence of social conditions and other influences on change in policy actions for federal agencies. They also generally support a multi-explanatory variable approach to budgetary changes rather than a single explanatory variable approach. Previous budgetary changes played no significant role in explaining subsequent budgetary changes. Conditions in an agency's environment, especially changes in issue-related social conditions, play an important role in explaining change in policy actions. Even though changes in social conditions had a greater impact on changes in policy statements than on changes in policy action, social conditions had a greater impact on policy action changes than either changes in policy statements or agency maturity. The fact that only 28% of the variance of changes in policy actions was explained by these variables leaves questions about what additional variables influence policy change, but the influence of these variables cannot be doubted given the evidence in this case.

The examination of interactive effects of three factors (issue area, agency maturity, and level of unemployment) allows one to speculate about the possibility of increasing an agency's responsiveness to social conditions by manipulating those factors. Generally, variations in agency responsiveness to social conditions did occur for issue areas, degree of agency maturity, and how good or bad the times were. Manipulating issue areas of an agency implies agencies should consider examining the assumptions concerning which areas the agencies are supposed to be dealing with and to what extent different areas overlap. If the goals of an agency overlap several issue areas, that should be explicitly incorporated into the goals so that the agency may respond to all relevant states of society that influence its ostensible goal. The lack of such incorporation may prevent agencies from responding to factors that influence the success of their programs. Manipulating the maturity of an agency or its knowledgeability concerning its environment may also increase the responsiveness of federal agencies to the state of society and changes therein.

Notes

1. The incrementalist theory and the power elite theory of policy-making would be compatible if it were argued that incremental change serves the interests of a power elite—which it could, since incremental change (when it occurs) tends to favor the continuance of established policies. Incrementalists, however, have not taken this position. They tend to argue that incremental strategy is necessary for agency continuance by saying current policies must be continued to get the most money for an agency and, thereby, legitimate established policies.

2. For the numerous and complex ways that social changes can increase court litigation, the reader is referred to Friedman (1959), Goulden (1972), and Simon (1968).

3. A magnitude change measure was calculated by dividing a variable value in one year (t_0) by the value of the preceding year (t_1): (X_{t_0}/X_{t_1}).

   The acceleration change measure (rate) was calculated by dividing: $(X_{t_2} - X_{t_1})/(X_{t_1} - X_{t_0})$.

4. The data on the Presidential State of the Union messages was generously provided by Professor John H. Kessel, department of Political Science, Ohio State University.

5. Factor scores of a content analysis of the Presidential State of the Union messages for different issue areas are a measure of change in things emphasized in the messages because variations in the frequency of mentions for an area influence the total sum of squared deviations from the average number of mentions for an issue area, which influences the correlation of an issue area (the factor loading) with the year of the message.

6. The expenditure figures on which the change measures are based do not exclude salaries and expenses, but Chapters 6 and 7 indicate an extremely high correlation between total expenditures and expenditures minus salaries.

7. It seems likely that this is because policy statements are both easier and cheaper to change than policy actions. It may also be that, as in everyday reality, many people who want something (such as changes in policy actions) will settle for verbal attention, rather than push for specific behavioral commitments.

Appendix

TABLE 2-2. Estimated Correlations (Above Diagonal) and Observed Correlations (Below Diagonal) for the Research Model

	Gen. Cond.	Issue Cond.	Agency Matur.	Policy Stat.	Budg. Action
Gen. Cond.	1.0	.30	−.14	−.49	.21
Issue Cond.	.30	1.0	.16	.65	.54
Agency Matur.	−.14	.16	1.0	.16	.16
Policy Stat.	−.49	.65	.16	1.0	.30
Budg. Action	.21	.52	.16	.30	1.0

Equations and Standard Errors of Coefficients (in parentheses)

$$z_3 = -.207z_1 + .222z_2 + e$$
$$\quad (.083) \quad\quad (.077)$$

$$z_4 = -.772z_1 + .896z_2 - .091z_3 + e$$
$$\quad (.088) \quad\quad (.025) \quad\quad (.025)$$

$$z_5 = .231z_1 + .304z_2 + .112z_3 + .198z_4 + e$$
$$\quad (.162) \quad (.075) \quad\quad (.075) \quad\quad (.075)$$

Abbreviations Used in Table 2-2

Gen Cond.	Block influence of change in general social conditions
Issue Cond.	Block influence of change in issue-related social conditions
Agency Matur.	Block influence of agency maturity
Policy Stat.	Block influence of change in policy statements
Budg. Action	Block influence of change in budgetary actions

TABLE 2-3. Sample Means, Variances, N's

Sample	EXP Mean	EXP Var.	N	MAG.EXP Mean	MAG.EXP Var.	N	RATE.EXP Mean	RATE.EXP Var.	N	SIZE Mean	SIZE Var.	N	MAG.SIZE Mean	MAG.SIZE Var.	N	RATE.SIZE Mean	RATE.SIZE Var.	N
All	.5159E 9	.874E18	210	1.159	7.02	197	2.15	33.33	175	4,722	.292E 8	208	1.04	.018	196	−.76	822.57	184
Issue																		
Area																		
II	.9352E 9	.810E18	31	.808	2.58	29	2.82	13.12	27	9,987	.457E 7	28	1.00	.003	16	−10.50	3,824.20	14
Econ	.1556E 8	.640E12	40	.852	2.09	36	3.50	116.40	32	1,556	.417E 6	40	1.00	.004	36	4.68	450.60	34
Sw	.6928E 9	.140E20	40	1.310	1.39	35	1.17	27.50	31	1,301	.573E 6	40	1.04	.045	38	4.24	282.20	36
Agr	.1104E10	.140E20	40	1.690	23.32	36	1.59	12.71	32	3,107	.103E 8	40	1.09	.035	38	−1.54	177.40	36
Cl	.7701E 7	.240E14	7	1.340	.08	6	1.59	3.10	5	525	.101E 6	6	1.62	.151	5	1.47	.67	4
Nr	.1652E 9	.256E18	39	.940	7.02	35	1.56	3.46	31	10,696	.547E 8	39	1.07	.006	38	.98	18.50	36
Lbr	.1977E 8	.117E15	20	1.110	.02	19	1.19	10.36	18	1,817	.214E 6	20	1.06	.004	19	1.03	59.70	18
Ue																		
Low	.5324E 8	.960E18	114	1.280	7.34	109	1.82	36.81	89	4,690	.312E 8	114	1.12	.114	102	1.49	190.10	90
High	.4963E 9	.810E18	96	1.020	6.02	88	2.50	29.83	86	4,761	.271E 8	94	1.22	.179	93	−2.45	1,110.00	93
Agency																		
Matur.																		
Small	.8635E 8	.196E18	114	1.133	1.80	104	2.43	50.79	93	1,214	.499E 6	114	1.02	.064	97	2.37	260.90	99
Large	.1009E10	.144E20	93	1.220	13.82	83	1.84	14.90	74	8,976	.310E 8	94	1.06	.033	87	−4.51	1,494.60	81
Rapid	.6322E 9	.100E20	46	1.800	20.74	49	1.45	6.53	45	5,202	.236E 8	45	1.33	.116	14	−.09	6.87	11
Slow	.4056E 9	.556E18	137	1.350	8.08	136	2.18	41.98	122	4,887	.324E 8	135	1.02	.004	182	−.84	925.03	161
Time																		
Early	.2743E 9	.290E18	101	.900	4.81	92	2.73	42.62	83	3,804	.175E 8	98	1.02	.009	108	−2.96	3,119.80	96
Later	.7398E 9	.121E20	109	1.400	8.28	105	1.63	24.68	92	5,540	.385E 8	110	1.06	.029	87	1.89	237.70	83

TABLE 2-4. Slopes Predicting Change in Policy Actions (MAG.EXP.1)

					Independent Variables						
Samples	Il. Un.Bdg	Econ. Cpi	Econ. Ue	Mag. Sw.I.Pp	Cl. E.Nin	Mag. Agm.Sg	Rate. Stat.Cl	Mag. Stat.Il	Year	Year^2	N
All	.0100	.0189	-.2114	.336	4.0823	1.0768	.0058	-.2663	.055	.002	197
Issue Areas											
Il	-.5755	.0228	-.3650	3.128	-6.1304	-.0763	.0387	.1995	.063	.003	29
Econ	-.0654	.0196	-.1603	10.276	9.5543	-1.3256	-.0024	-1.3250	.052	.003	36
Sw	-.0346	.0066	.0909	6.275	2.0228	-.8235	.0096	-.8233	.032	.001	35
Agr	.2568	.0634	-.6493	-5.179	6.0846	5.9850	-.0346	-.3306	.181	.008	36
Cl	.0000	-.0161	-.1101	.000	-3.5623	-.4075	-.0044	.3437	-.073	-.002	6
Nr	-.0864	.0074	-.1993	-8.921	7.9691	2.3504	.0295	.3729	.006	.001	35
Lbr	-.0074	-.0021	.2072	-5.331	4.8101	3.6479	-.0040	.8780	.004	-.001	19
Ue											
Low	.0000	.0611	-.0612	-.868	3.2901	1.2003	-.0044	.0322	.058	.001	109
High	-.0001	-.1322	-.8319	1.905	4.2323	1.0838	.1402	-.3760	.024	-.002	88
Agency Matur.											
Small	-.0228	.0116	.0726	5.138	4.2384	.5366	-.0015	-.4780	.036	.001	104
Large	.0684	.0311	-.5564	-7.408	4.1636	1.4089	.0112	-.0090	.084	.004	83
Rapid	.1534	.0920	-.5406	-2.351	12.9097	.7838	-.0034	-1.2210	.225	.010	49
Slow	-.0408	.0098	-.1606	1.405	.6025	.7764	.0116	-.0483	.022	.001	136
Time											
Early	.0084	.0303	-.0619	.342	10.8123	1.2216	.0792	-.1220	.059	.006	92
Late	.0106	.0029	-.3181	-126.761	-.5542	.9372	-.0147	-.5655	.046	.001	105

44

3

A Nonincremental Perspective on Budgetary Policy Actions

William B. Moreland

This chapter explores the relationship between dimensions of agency maturity and budgetary policy actions in an attempt to construct an alternative to the standard incrementalist explanation of budget outcomes. Using 40 agencies within the Department of Agriculture over a time period from fiscal 1946 through 1971, a three stage time series analysis is conducted. First, various features of the "average" agency are examined and discussed. Second, a bivariate test of the research hypotheses is applied. And finally, a multivariate analysis is undertaken. The findings from this investigation show that many factors other than previous appropriations are important in explaining budget allocations. These factors include agency managerial capacity, agency size, and administrative experience of agency administrators and staff. The author concludes that an incrementalist approach is an inadequate explanation of budget outcomes.

THE GENERAL CONCEPTUAL SCHEME described in Chapter 1 contains an inherent challenge to the traditional explanation of budgetary outcomes that has come to be known as incrementalism. Briefly, the incremental explanation (which is grounded in the premises of a pluralist explanation of partisan conflict in the American political arena) argues that the amount of money an agency receives in a given time period is determined chiefly by the amount of money it received in the preceding time period. The conceptual scheme argues that policy actions (of which budgetary outcomes are one form) cannot be explained solely by previous policy actions. A variety of independent variables in addition to previous policy actions are asserted to be important, including administrative arrangements within the agency, coalitional activity, and environmental conditions. The disagreement between this scheme and the incrementalist perspective is clear: one position asserts that policy actions (budgetary outcomes) are explained chiefly by previous policy actions (budgetary outcomes), while the other position asserts that there are many explanatory factors.

Because acceptance of the incrementalist explanation of budget outcomes has been so widespread, and because the present effort is in direct conflict with that explanation, the following section comments on some of the principal empirical incremental studies and notes their shortcomings. The reader should note that despite its widespread acceptance, incrementalism does not mean the same thing to all people who use the word—in fact, one of its major problems is that it lacks a systematic and consistent definition. The works mentioned below are presented not because they represent independent and complete statements of incrementalism, but because they are among the most visible works on that subject.

An Incrementalist View of Budget Outcomes

DESCRIPTIVE INCREMENTALISM

Wildavsky's book (1964) was the first work to consider seriously the implications of an incremental explanation for the study of budget outcomes. Wildavsky (1964:15) asserts:

> Budgeting is incremental, not comprehensive. The beginning of wisdom about an agency budget is that it is almost never actively reviewed as a whole every year in the sense of reconsidering the value of all existing programs as compared to all possible alternatives. Instead, it is based on last year's budget with special attention given to a narrow range of increases or decreases. Thus, the men who make the budget are concerned with relatively small increments to an existing base. Their attention is focused on a small number of items over which the budgetary battle is fought.

Perhaps the most interesting feature of Wildavsky's discussion is the concept of a "budget base," defined as the total of those items in the budget that are noncontroversial or unchanging in successive budgets. The base is the core of an agency's defense of its budget. It is around this figure that new programs and activities are built (Wildavsky, 1964: Ch. 2). In support of his claim he offers a percentage breakdown of the change in final appropriations for 37 domestic bureaus over a 12-year period (1964:14). Wildavsky interprets the changes between successive budgets as marginal because a simple majority of the cases (53%) fall within a range of plus or minus 10%.

Fenno (1966:354) also presents tabular data in support of the idea that outcomes in budgetary decision situations are largely incremental. He argues that the norms of both agency officials and appropriations committee members produce marginal changes rather than comprehensive reprogramming of funds. The percentage changes portrayed in Fenno's tables suggest that aggregate dollars allocated to an agency by both OMB and Congress do not shift substantially from year to year. The inference is drawn that the largest determinant of an agency's budget is the final appropriation of the previous year. Fenno also discusses the budget base as a justification for the expectations of agency officials in budget hearings with the appropriations committees.

Unfortunately, the data presented by both Wildavsky and Fenno in support of an incrementalist description have little meaning for demonstrating or "proving" their point. It is one thing to demonstrate that marginal changes occur between successive budget allocations. It is quite a different thing to demonstrate that such changes are "caused" by the existence of the previous year's allocation. Moreover, in the absence of a commonly accepted definition of how much change constitutes incremental change, the choice of percentage breaking points for incremental versus nonincremental interpretations is arbitrary. Neither the reader nor a subsequent analyst of such data would necessarily have reached the same conclusions these authors provide. Their figures neither support nor refute the incremental argument.

ANALYTICAL INCREMENTALISM

Since the appearance of the descriptive studies of the budgetary process by Wildavsky and Fenno, several analytic models of a general budgetary process have been published. Articles by Davis et al. (1966), Sharkansky (1965), and Stromberg (1970) have developed mathematical representations of the process as a series of first difference or Markov equations. The theory proposed by Davis et al. (1966) has received considerable attention and will be discussed here as the leading example of these works.

Two important assumptions underlie the work of Davis et al. First, they believe that the complexity of the federal budget process requires the participants to adopt aids to calculation, the most important of which is the incremental method. Second, despite its complexity, they assert (1966:529) that "basic features of the [budget] process . . . can be represented by simple [mathematical] models which are stable over periods of time, linear, and stochastic."

The incremental method referred to by these authors is characterized by its marginal adjustments rather than revolutionary change; existing circumstances (the budget base) are taken as given with the expectation that only slight adjustments to an existing social reality will be attempted. Thus, the method of incremental political adjustment is posited as determining the strategies of the participants as well as describing the analytic budgeting process.

Eight equations are hypothesized by Davis et al. to explain the decision rules used by the participants in the budgeting process. The equations take the form of one- or two-variable regression models, with the independent variable(s) being either the magnitude of a previous appropriations request or a mean deviate in the form of a stochastic disturbance to a stable time-series trend. The major empirical findings of the Davis et al. study are derived from tests of the eight equations against congressional budget allocations for 56 federal domestic agencies across the time period from 1946 to 1963. The descriptive validity of the equations was confirmed in 86% of all congressional appropriations decisions—in only 55 instances would one of the eight equations fail to describe the appropriations decisions for the agencies.

The Davis et al. study reduces the budget process to empirically derived and tested mathematical models of the budget process, but these equations or models are merely descriptive, not explanatory. Smith (1967) noted that the Davis et al. theory does not account for the base points from which incrementalism proceeds. He writes (1967:150):

> The base points . . . are somehow supplied by exogenous forces, rather as an irritating distraction, so the authors can get down to the business . . . of modeling the incremental process . . . the type of behavior not considered within the framework of the model is mainly what the student of politics wants to know.

Smith's last point stems directly from the absence in the equations presented by Davis et al. of any explanatory variables other than the budget figure (or estimate) from a previous year. Davis et al. acknowledge the isolation of their explanation from external events only implicitly by discussing the reaction of the budget process to external events in terms of shift points. Defined formally as points in time where a regression coefficient becomes unstable, shift points represent occasions when incremental budgeting behavior was observed to change. Employing a common tactic among researchers, they note that these shift points can serve as a focus for future research (1967:152). But the presence of shift points is precisely the reason that incrementalism may be an inadequate explanation of budgetary processes and outcomes. The theory of incremental budgeting as formally proposed by Davis et al. (1966) and as discussed by Wildavsky (1964) and Fenno (1966) can always be shown to be true if the analyst uses two or more points in time that are sufficiently close together for comparison.

A point about the methodology of the Davis et al. study needs to be made. The equations in that study are reported without correction for a serious bias introduced by the presence of serial correlation among the independent variables. As Hibbs (1972) has shown, serious errors of interpretation may result if these biasing effects are not estimated and controlled. This methodological problem may well have impinged upon the results reported by Davis et al.

In sum, the incrementalist explanation of budget outcomes entails three main points: (1) agency budgets contain base points from which incremental budgeting proceeds; (2) these base points are the chief determinant of subsequent budget allocations; and (3) change from the base will be incremental, consisting of only small additions or deletions.

The Research Design

This chapter employs two concepts from the conceptual scheme introduced in Chapter 1—agency maturity and policy actions. The basic hypothesis in Chapter 1 asserted that a single inverse relationship exists between the concepts—greater maturity results in decreasing policy actions. The exception posited in the first chapter is that maturity in the sense of growing experience might push in the opposite direction. The present chapter begins with the expectation that not all of the indicators for maturity outlined in Chapter 1 would relate to policy actions in the same way. Specifically, a concept of administrative maturity is used here and is measured in terms of size, managerial capacity, and experience. This is a different concept of maturity from the more structurally based concept in Chapter 1. Increasing administrative maturity is expected to result in increasing policy actions. Five hypotheses were developed to explore the relationship between features of administrative maturity and agency policy actions.

H1. As agency size increases, the appropriations for the agency will increase.

A positive relationship is expected here not simply because more money is needed to pay for additional personnel, but because increasing agency size is an indication that agency program responsibility is also increasing. Although size is used as an indicator for structural maturity in other studies (see Chapters 4, 5, 6, and 7), it is also a compatible indicator for administrative maturity. Administrative maturity occurs when agency personnel master the administration of their programs and interact successfully with other parts of the government bureaucracy; administrative maturity is therefore helpful in increasing the agency's program responsibilities. (Agencies that are perceived as successful in implementing their programs are more likely to be successful in expanding their authority to new areas or in increasing their authority in existing program areas.) Increased program responsibility is related to increased agency size, which in turn is associated with increasing appropriations. Thus, a positive relationship between size and administrative maturity is likely to be present.

The indicator for agency size is the number of full-time permanent employee positions in the agency. The dependent variable is the amount of money the agency received annually in response to requests for appropriations, both regular and supplemental.

H2. As the managerial capacity of the agency increases, the appropriations for the agency will increase.

Managerial capacity is the agency's capability to take on new tasks and to increase program authority. The assumption is that agencies that are more administratively mature will have more managerial capacity. A simple indicator of this variable is the ratio of the number of supergrade personnel to the total number of personnel in the agency. Supergrades constitute the top-level managers of the agency. As the proportion of managers increases, it is likely that the agency will be more able to take on more tasks and will in fact expand its program authority. As that authority increases appropriations will also increase.

Supergrades are the number of GS 16's, 17's, and 18's (and their equivalents in salary terms) plus executive grade persons. Total size and appropriations are measured as in *H1*.

H3. As the cumulative administrative experience of the agency administrator increases, the appropriations for his agency will increase.

H4. As the cumulative administrative experience of the agency staff increases, the appropriations for the agency will increase.

H5. As the cumulative administrative experience of either the agency head or the agency staff increases, the budget success of the agency will increase.

Administrative experience simply means the experience of top agency personnel in working with the programs of that agency. It is especially important as a basis for congressional judgment about the agency. As developed by Fenno (1966:ch. 6), administrative experience is important during the interaction of congressmen and agency administrators at appropriations hearings. A large amount of administrative experience usually leads to favorable congressional perceptions of an agency representative's ability, preparedness, and amiability. Agencies with greater administrative experience are more administratively mature because the favorable perception by congressmen depends on qualities that are associated with administrative maturity, for example, the ability to administer programs successfully, and the ability to cope with other parts of the government bureaucracy. The rationale for these three hypotheses was the common sense expectation that agencies whose witnesses have rapport with the appropriations committee and who are well-perceived by them will receive better treatment budgetarily than agencies whose witnesses are not similarly regarded.

Direct measurement of the concept of administrative experience was not possible because of the difficulties of doing *post hoc* interviews with budgeting participants since 1946. However, an indirect measure based on the presence or absence of agency administrators and their staff and the number of consecutive appearances of these personnel before the House Appropriations Committee from 1946 to 1971 was used.[1] The assumption underlying the use of this kind of a continuity measure was that administrators and staffs who returned over a period of years to testify would be perceived by committee members as being more administratively experienced than witnesses whose appearances lacked continuity.

Appropriations are treated as in *H1.* and *H2.* Budget success represents the relationship between the amount of money an agency requested and the amount it actually received in percentage terms. A success measure was calculated for each agency for each of three decision points in the budget process: the agency-Department interactions, the agency-OMB interaction, and the agency-congressional interaction in the preceding fiscal year.

Examination of these hypotheses was conducted using 40 agencies of the Department of Agriculture as units of analysis over the time period fiscal 1946 to fiscal 1971. Figure 3–1 identifies the agencies used and the time spans of their various existences. The testing of the hypotheses consisted of a multi-staged effort: a descriptive profile of the

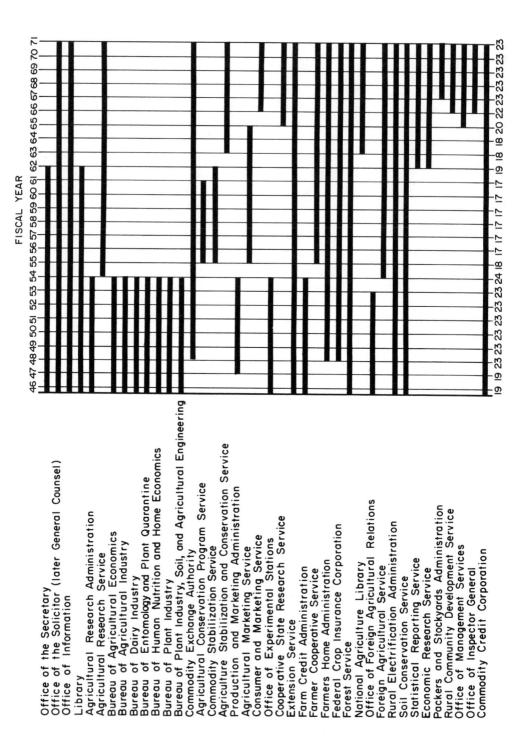

FIGURE 3 – I: LIFE - SPANS OF AGRICULTURE AGENCIES, 1946 – 1971

FISCAL YEAR

Office of the Secretary
Office of the Solicitor (later General Counsel)
Office of Information
Library
Agricultural Research Administration
Agricultural Research Service
Bureau of Agricultural Economics
Bureau of Agricultural Industry
Bureau of Dairy Industry
Bureau of Entomology and Plant Quarantine
Bureau of Human Nutrition and Home Economics
Bureau of Plant Industry
Bureau of Plant Industry, Soil, and Agricultural Engineering
Commodity Exchange Authority
Agricultural Conservation Program Service
Commodity Stabilization Service
Agriculture Stabilization and Conservation Service
Production and Marketing Administration
Agricultural Marketing Service
Consumer and Marketing Service
Office of Experimental Stations
Cooperative State Research Service
Extension Service
Farm Credit Administration
Farmer Cooperative Service
Farmers Home Administration
Federal Crop Insurance Corporation
Forest Service
National Agriculture Library
Office of Foreign Agricultural Relations
Foreign Agricultural Service
Rural Electrification Administration
Soil Conservation Service
Statistical Reporting Service
Economic Research Service
Packers and Stockyards Administration
Rural Community Development Service
Office of Management Services
Office of Inspector General
Commodity Credit Corporation

average agency was constructed, a bivariate analysis of the individual hypotheses was performed, and finally, a multivariate analysis encompassing all hypotheses was conducted.

The Average Agriculture Agency

No single agency in a group would conform to the statistical averages for all agencies in the group. Yet, a profile of the "average" agency can be useful for an understanding of the factors that influence budgetary politics in the department. Figure 3–2 displays the averages over time for six characteristics of the agencies: total number of personnel, number of supergrades, number of agency witnesses appearing at hearings, cumulative experience of agency administrators, cumulative experience of agency staff, and managerial capacity of the agency. Several trends are evident in the data.

The average number of personnel among agriculture agencies does not show extreme fluctuations, but there appears to be a cycle associ-

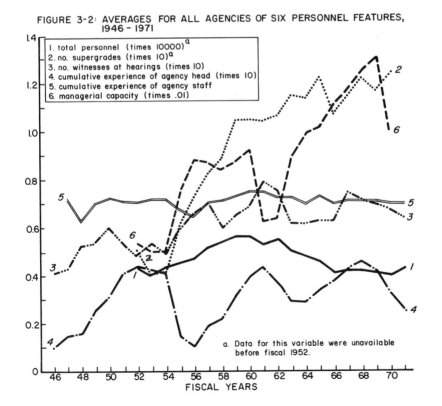

FIGURE 3-2: AVERAGES FOR ALL AGENCIES OF SIX PERSONNEL FEATURES, 1946 – 1971

1. total personnel (times 10000)[a]
2. no. supergrades (times 10)[a]
3. no. witnesses at hearings (times 10)
4. cumulative experience of agency head (times 10)
5. cumulative experience of agency staff
6. managerial capacity (times .01)

a. Data for this variable were unavailable before fiscal 1952.

FISCAL YEARS

ated with the change of presidential administration. A gradual increase in the average number of personnel begins in fiscal 1953, reaches a peak in fiscal 1960, and gradually declines to a relatively stable point beginning in fiscal 1966. The growth portion of the cycle appears to be concurrent with the Republican presidency of Dwight Eisenhower, and the decline portion concurrent with the Democratic presidencies of John Kennedy and Lyndon Johnson. This pattern is of particular interest since the peak growth years occur when the fewest number of agricultural agencies were in existence.

While the average size of the agencies remained relatively constant, the average number of managerial personnel (number of supergrades) grew dramatically. The increase of the average total size of an agency during the Eisenhower era is parallelled by an increase in the average number of supergrades that continued during the tenure of the Democratic presidents, reaching a peak in fiscal 1970.

Reflecting the increase in the average raw number of supergrades, the managerial capacity of the agencies shows a definite growth and decline, reflecting changes in presidential administration and reorganization of several agencies. The trend over time shows high growth for managerial capacity, that is, there were more supervisors for approximately the same number of employees.

No major shifts over time appear in the average number of agency personnel appearing at hearings, nor is there a tendency towards change concurrent with presidential turnover. The slightly increasing trend line could be indicative of a greater reliance upon staff, but that increase is small.

The graph of cumulative experience of the agency head appearing to testify at House Appropriations Hearings shows a definite cyclical pattern across time. This cycle is probably also presidentially linked, since turnover in party control of the presidency is often accompanied by many resignations and new appointments within the bureaucracy as the new president organizes his administration. The cycle of cumulative agency head experience conforms to this practice, with experience dropping after the inauguration of a new president (1953, 1961, and 1969) and growing during that president's term. The administrative staff of the agencies are apparently a more stable group than the agency heads—the graph of cumulative staff experience indicates little fluctuation in the level of experience.

Figure 3–3 presents the average budget request for agriculture agencies at each stage of the budget preparation cycle and their final appropriations in dollar amounts adjusted for inflation. The figures were adjusted to ensure that any growth observed would be due to factors other than inflation.

Rather dramatic changes are evident in Figure 3–3. From an overall standpoint, the level of budgetary support given to agriculture agencies

ADJUSTED FOR INFLATION, 1946-1971. (ALL FIGURES IN MILLIONS OF DOLLARS)

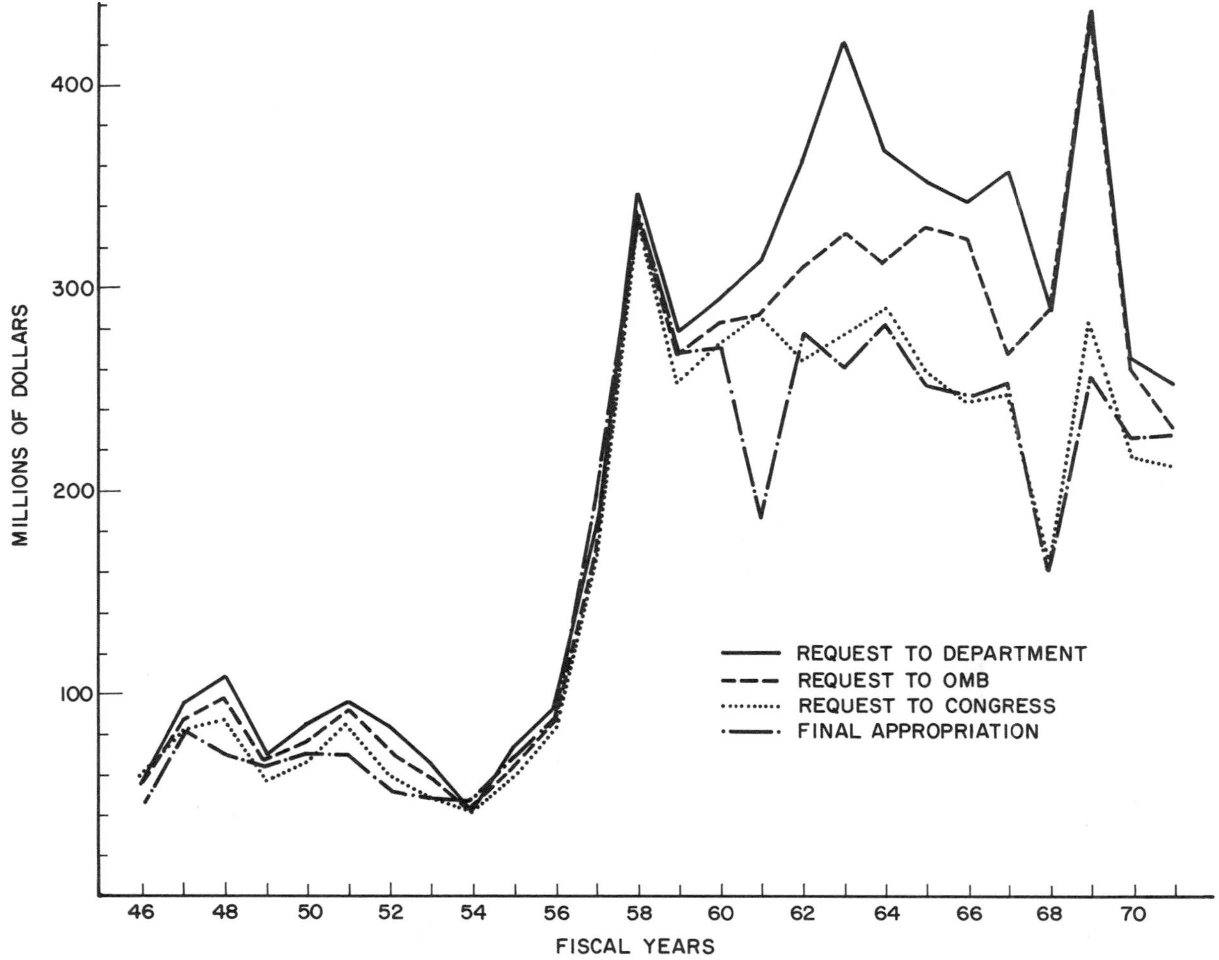

REQUEST TO DEPARTMENT
REQUEST TO OMB
REQUEST TO CONGRESS
FINAL APPROPRIATION

FISCAL YEARS

MILLIONS OF DOLLARS

400
300
200
100

46 48 50 52 54 56 58 60 62 64 66 68 70

55

up to fiscal 1957 is very much lower than the support given after that year. Prior to fiscal 1957 the average budget request at all stages seems to vary around an approximate level of $70 million. Beginning with the fiscal 1957 requests, however, rather dramatic upward requests are observed, reaching an approximate level of $300 million during the early 1960s. Moreover, the relative stability of the earlier period when only slight differences were observed between the average request levels is replaced by relative instability in the later period. These are not incremental changes!

Across the period it is evident that the OMB is the major critic of the average agency request. In every year the OMB request to Congress is below both the agency and department budget estimates. In a few cases the final appropriation exceeds the amount requested by the OMB. Congress appears to reinstate at least some of the funds cut by the OMB, justifying, perhaps, the claim that the Congress is in part a benefactor of agency programs (Fenno, 1966).

Concluding this descriptive section, Figure 3–4 presents the agencies' budget success at three different points, with OMB, with the department budget office, and with Congress. Figure 3–4 demonstrates convincingly

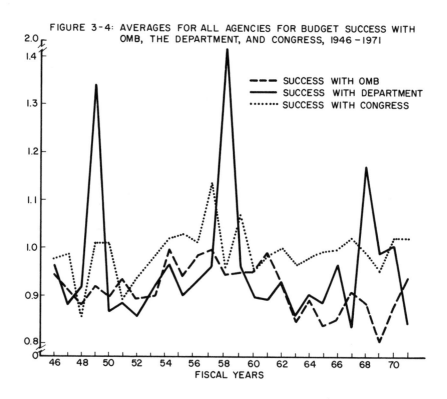

FIGURE 3–4: AVERAGES FOR ALL AGENCIES FOR BUDGET SUCCESS WITH OMB, THE DEPARTMENT, AND CONGRESS, 1946–1971

--- SUCCESS WITH OMB
——— SUCCESS WITH DEPARTMENT
········ SUCCESS WITH CONGRESS

FISCAL YEARS

that OMB rarely grants more than the requested amounts for agencies within the USDA. Indeed, since fiscal 1961 the OMB has approved an average agency budget in excess of 90% of requests only twice. During the earlier years (from fiscal 1954 to fiscal 1961) the OMB was much more likely to approve a request with only minor cuts. The immediate postwar era resembles the later period of the sixties.

The department budget office largely anticipates the actions of the OMB, except in fiscal 1949, 1958, and 1968. The Office of Budget and Finance within the department is apparently a formidable hurdle for agencies in the estimates stage. The department budget office frequently cuts the initial estimates more severely than subsequent OMB decisions.

Congress once again appears to be the benefactor more frequently than the wielder of the axe for agency budgets. The success ratio of agencies with the Congress may reflect, however, the restoration of budget cuts made by the OMB or the department.

Bivariate Analysis Findings

The results of the bivariate correlational analysis for hypotheses 1 to 4 are presented in Table 3–1. Two of the hypotheses receive modest support: *H1.* (as agency size increases, appropriations will increase) and *H4.* (as cumulative administrative experience of the staff increases, appropriations will increase). One of the hypotheses was disconfirmed and a relationship in the opposite direction from what was expected was discovered (*H2.*—as managerial capacity increases, appropriations will increase). And one of the hypotheses showed no relationship (*H3.*— as administrative experience of the agency head increases, appropriations will increase).

The lack of support for *H3.* may be due to the marked cyclical nature of administrative experience that was noted in the preceding section. The indicator for this concept (appearance of the agency head before a congressional committee) may be more reflective of the vagaries

TABLE 3–1. Bivariate Correlation Results for Hypotheses 1 to 4 (corrected for autocorrelation)

	Hypothesis	Final Appropriation$_t$
H1.	Agency Size$_{t-1}$	0.2033
H2.	Managerial Capacity$_{t-1}$	−0.1162
H3.	Cumulative Experience of Agency Administrator$_{t-1}$	0.0593
H4.	Cumulative Experience of Agency Staff$_{t-1}$	0.3062

of administrator turnover due to political factors than it is of congressional perceptions of agency personnel, especially since the same measure when applied to an apparently more stable group (agency staff) did show a positive relationship with appropriations.

The negative relationship between managerial capacity and appropriations is related to a finding reported in Chapter 6 of this volume, where the effects of supergrades on appropriations are examined, while controlling for other factors including agency age and relative size of budget. Supergrades were found to have a positive effect on appropriations for poor agencies (which are usually younger), but a negative effect for rich agencies (which are usually older). Thus, the effects of agency age might explain the unexpected relationship in *H2*. Another explanation might be that the indicator chosen to measure managerial capacity is not actually measuring that concept. In other chapters in this volume, the proportion of supergrades is used to measure hierarchical complexity, a dimension of structural maturity that is negatively related to policy actions. The finding in *H2.* may be reflecting a component of structural maturity rather than administrative maturity as was intended.

The relatively low magnitude of the linear correlation coefficients may be due to the cyclic nature demonstrated by several of the independent variables (see Figure 3–2 and its discussion). Agency size, managerial capacity, and administrative experience of the agency head all demonstrate various types of cycles. Only cumulative staff experience seems to be free of any cyclical effects, and that is the variable showing the highest correlation with final appropriations.

Although they are not dramatic, the correlation coefficients in Table 3–1 lend support to Fenno's observations (1966) that congressmen on the Appropriations Committee are sensitive to the administrative arrangements within an agency. Further, the finding linking agency size with appropriations is consistent with findings reported in Chapter 6.

The results of the bivariate analysis for *H5.* are presented in Table 3–2. The correlation coefficients in the table offer strong support for the hypothesis. A clear relationship exists between experience and budget success at each stage of the production of a budget. An agency with a relatively experienced administrator *or* staff will receive more of its budget requests at every stage of budget preparation. Conversely, the relatively

TABLE 3-2. **Bivariate Correlation Results of Hypothesis 5 (corrected for autocorrelation)**

Cumulative Experience	Agency Budget Success$_t$ with:		
	Department	*OMB*	*Congress*
Administrator$_{t-1}$	0.1989	0.3225	0.3345
Staff$_{t-1}$	0.5398	0.8490	0.8991

inexperienced agency (both in staff and administrator) will be less likely to receive what they ask for. The effects of experience are most pronounced at the congressional stage and are relatively less important at the other stages. Fenno's (1966, 1959) discussion of congressional respect for thorough and confident presentation of budgetary arguments on the part of agency administrators and staff before congressional committees is supported. Apparently, a similar effect is evident in agency relations with the OMB, supporting the observations of Davis and Ripley (1967) and Freeman (1955).

Multivariate Analysis Findings

The analysis discussed in the preceding section dealt with the variables only in a simple bivariate fashion and did not attempt to assess the specific effects of the budget allocation in a previous year. The support found for the bivariate hypotheses suggests that a more complete elaboration of factors affecting budgetary decisions might be productive.

Using a technique suggested by Hibbs (1972) and Malinvaud (1970), multivariate generalized least squares (GLS) estimates for the variables used in the previous discussion were formed. Table 3–3 presents the results of the regression on final appropriations of the nine independent variables after correcting for autocorrelation.

Eight of the nine independent variables in Table 3–3 are significant to an explanation of the agencies' final appropriations, although the effect of managerial capacity was not in the expected direction. The only variable that does not appear to affect the final appropriations is the cumulative experience of the agency administrator.

Of the eight variables the three budget success measures are, perhaps, the most interesting and surprising. The sign of the partial correlation coefficient indicates an inverse relationship: as budget success decreases in one fiscal year the magnitude of the final appropriation in the following year increases. These findings appear to be anomalous, since budget success has been linked with an increase in the size of a budget (Wildavsky, 1964). Yet, the inverse relationships are supported by Sharkansky's (1965) and Fenno's (1966) observations that budgetary aggressiveness may result in larger budget cuts (lower success), but relatively speaking, agencies that request more get more. [See LeLoup (1973) for a discussion of budgetary aggressiveness.]

Continuity of agency staff appearance before congressional appropriations subcommittees, both yearly and cumulatively, has a positive influence on final appropriations. Holding other factors constant, as the stability of appearances increases, final appropriations increase. A 10% increase

TABLE 3-3. Generalized Least Squares Estimates for Selected Relationships with Final Appropriations (after correction for autocorrelation)

Independent Variable	Parameter Estimate[a]	Standard Error	Partial Correlation
Final Appropriations$_{t-1}$	0.4350	0.0337	0.5888
Number of Agency Witnesses at Appropriations Hearings$_{t-1}$	383.809E+5	29.672E+5	0.5920
Agency Managerial Capacity$_{t-1}$	−21486.43E+5	5321.19E+5	−0.2235
Agency Head Present at Appropriations Hearings$_{t-1}$	3591.698E+5	416.132E+5	0.4400
Cumulative Staff Experience$_{t-1}$	5100.848E+5	545.652E+5	0.4693
Cumulative Experience of Agency Head$_{t-1}$	20.159E+5	32.039E+5	0.0357
Success of Agency with Department$_{t-1}$	−482.643E+5	156.984E+5	−0.1719
Success of Agency with OMB$_{t-1}$	−3789.168E+5	484.833E+5	−0.4057
Success of Agency with Congress$_{t-1}$	−6049.587E+5	547.648E+5	−0.5314

R Squared	F Statistic	df
0.8521	198.38	(9,310)

a. These regression estimates are based upon data for the fiscal year period 1952–1971 only, because personnel data for the period prior to 1952 were not available.

in stability of staff appearances results in over a \$5 million increase in the final budget allocation. The observations of Fenno (1966), Horn (1970), and Wildavsky (1964) suggesting the positive effects of staff experience are supported by this finding. Congressmen, apparently, do make decisions about budget allocations based upon judgments of administrative experience.

The presence of the agency administrator during appropriations subcommittee hearings is positively related to the amount of the final allocation. The magnitude of the parameter estimate, however, should not be interpreted to mean that the administrator's absence would result in the loss of \$359 million in the amount finally appropriated. Of a total of 473 possible appearances by an agency head only thirteen absences occurred across the period. Moreover, of the thirteen absences, nine were associated with a change of administration following an agency reorganization or the appointment of an administrator during the startup phase of a new agency. For practical purposes this factor has little effect on the amount of funds appropriated to the agency (it acts as a constant and does not affect the outcome). The estimate may predict, however, the initial start-up funding for the agencies that came into existence during the period.

The effect of managerial capacity was not in the expected direction, although the partial correlation coefficient is stronger than that in the bivariate analysis. Again, this finding may be a reflection of the effect of agency age as reported in Chapter 6.

The size of the agency contingent appearing before an appropriations subcommittee is so highly correlated with the number of personnel in the agency $(r = 0.63)$ that it is hard to say that simply increasing the number of people available for testimony will increase the final appropriations. The estimates contained in Table 3–3 suggest, however, that an increase of one person in the staff appearing before the committee will increase the final appropriation by close to \$40 million. A more inclusive explanation, perhaps, would distinguish why a large contingent of agency staff would be associated with a large agency (or vice versa). The number of programs, or beneficiaries, or geographic dispersion readily come to mind as possible sources for growth of both the agency and its administrative staff.

The regression estimate for the effect of the final appropriation in year t–1 on the allocation for year t provides clear evidence in refutation of an incrementalist explanation of budget outcomes for the agencies in this study. For every dollar appropriated in year $t - 1$ an agency can only depend upon receiving 44 cents in the budget for a subsequent fiscal year. When considered with the time-series graphs of the average budget requests and allocations presented in Figure 3–3, this finding is not surprising. Severe changes occur in fiscal 1957 (upward), 1959 (downward), and 1968 (downward), to name only three examples. As the partial correlation coefficients in Table 3–3 clearly show, factors other than previous appropriations directly influence final appropriations.

The only variable in Table 3–3 that does not have an effect on final appropriations is cumulative experience of the agency head. Two factors may vitiate this finding, however. The strong cyclical trend of this variable evidenced in Figure 3–2 adversely affected the linear correlation. Second, the average tenure of agency administrators across the period was only 3.1 years. Although the recruitment process was not specifically investigated, one possible source of new administrators is the experienced staff of the agencies. Credible staff experience may carry over in subsequent appointments.

Conclusions and Implications

This chapter has outlined a time-series perspective for the analysis of budget decisions for agencies within the U.S. Department of Agriculture.

The final appropriations of agencies were related to a variety of measures that tapped the general concept of agency maturity. The final appropriations in one year were shown to affect a subsequent year's budget allocation, but only as one element in a relatively complex multivariate explanation. The validity of these findings suggests that other variables may affect decisions at different stages of budget preparation.

As the partial correlation coefficients in Table 3–3 demonstrate, many factors directly influence the amount appropriated. Last year's budget is not the chief determinant of this year's budget, contrary to Davis et al. (1966). The important point, however, is neither the specific ranking of other variables in explanatory power nor the magnitude of the estimated effect of any single variable. The most important conclusion supported by the evidence in Table 3–3 is that final appropriations for the agencies are dependent upon a number of factors and not just the mechanistic addition to or subtraction from a base allocation.

Among the more interesting results of the multiple regression are those associated with staff stability and budget success. These measures, perhaps more than any of the others, are directly controlled by the agency administrator. The staff the administrator takes with him to congressional hearings is a matter of personal choice, a choice that can have a significant impact on the outcome of the hearings. An additional inference that seems warranted suggests that the stability of staff is important at other stages of the budget process. As Davis and Ripley (1967) point out, the experience of agency, as well as OMB staff, may have an impact on program decisions. It is also possible that staff experience and low turnover will influence the growth of program related authority. Indeed, if the results reported here apply to other action measures as well, it is very possible that new authorizing legislation as well as new executive authority will be affected by staff considerations.

The general indication that can be derived from the various findings associated with the success ratios argues strongly for aggressiveness in budget style. The administrator who rapidly increases the size of budget requests may find that his budget is cut more deeply than his conservative colleagues in other agencies. But as Sharkansky (1965) points out, the agency may receive a relatively larger budget for its troubles.

Likewise, the agency administrator and staff who are aggressive in developing a program of new activity for the agency and who are persuasive in their relations with two of the three other decision-makers may find themselves turned down occasionally. Relatively speaking, however, the aggressive agency will expand old programs and add new ones more often than a more passive bureau.

What can be said concerning the variables used to measure the concept of administrative maturity, and of that concept itself? Two of the variables worked in the predicted direction and in that sense supported the concept. Both agency size and administrative experience of the staff were positively correlated with greater appropriations. Administrative experience of the agency head did not correlate well, but this fact may be due to the decided cyclical and political nature of the variable. When the same measure was applied to staff members less subject to cyclical turnover it showed a good correlation with the dependent variable.

The surprising negative relationship between managerial capacity and appropriations may be a reflection of effects that were not controlled for in this study (for example, agency age or size of agency budget). Or it may be that the indicator for managerial capacity is not appropriate and reflects a component of structural rather than administrative maturity.

Overall, however, it seems clear that administrative maturity is separate from structural maturity and that it has a different relationship to policy actions. Kinds of maturity will be discussed further in the concluding chapter.

In terms of the general research model, it is not asserted here that maturity is the only concept that is important in explaining policy actions. Many concepts not dealt with here, including coalition activity, political party behavior, public opinion, and congressional leadership would be important in a multivariate model explaining policy actions.

The advantage of the multivariate approach, as Smith (1967) noted, is that the beginning points of a budget allocation can be traced. An incrementalist perspective on budgets inherently precludes examination of factors other than previous budgets—explaining budget bases in terms of external factors is not possible.

Furthermore, the causative agents of change, and not the change itself, become the units of explanation in a multivariate approach. The focus used here is not principally concerned with "small" or "large" change, for such judgments are frequently subjective. It is pointless to argue over whether change is small or large. The analyst's attention should be directed at the factors that can explain the observed change, regardless of its size.

Note

1. The measures for administrative experience were calculated for both agency administrator and agency staff on an annual and a cumulative basis. The source of the data for these measures was the House Appropriations Hearings for the Department of Agriculture, from 1946 to 1971.

   Cumulative experience of the agency head was the number of consecutive annual appearances of the agency administrator before the Appropriations Committee. The annual experience measure for the agency head was a simple presence or absence measure—either he was present or he was not.

The cumulative staff experience measure was formed as a ratio between the number of people who repeat in presenting testimony at hearings and the number of people who *could* have repeated. For instance, if five people return for testimony in the second year of an agency's existence from a total of ten people who gave testimony the previous year, then the cumulative ratio would be $5/10 = 0.50$. Suppose the third year the same five people returned, then the ratio would be $10/15 = 0.67$, reflecting a higher level of experience and stability. The yearly ratio was formed in a similar manner, but in this case the measure reflects *only* the amount of stability from year to year. For instance, in successive years suppose that ten, seven, and eight people appeared on behalf of the agency. In the second year suppose all seven people who appear were present during hearings in the previous year. The ratio that would result would be $7/7 = 1.0$. Now suppose that in the third year all eight people who appear have never been before the committee. The ratio would be $0/8 = 0$. Annual and cumulative staff experience were correlated at the 0.62 level, suggesting that relatively the same people showed up for testimony both from year to year *and* over time.

4

Agency Policy Actions: Determinants of Nonincremental Change

Lance T. LeLoup

This chapter seeks to identify systematic sources of change in agency appropriations. It criticizes the standard incrementalist perspective on budgeting for emphasizing stability of appropriations and for defining change as random, because both of these approaches preclude examination of regular determinants of change.

In the analysis, a variety of sources of change are developed from two concepts introduced in the theoretical framework of Chapter 1—agency structural characteristics and agency political environment. The dependent variable used is percent change in agency appropriations, but preliminary findings suggested that percent change in agency budget requests should also be examined as a dependent variable. The hypothesized relationships are tested using bivariate and multivariate analyses and recursive path estimation on a data base for eight "politically salient" agencies from 1960 through 1971.

The findings show that percent change in appropriations is determined primarily by percent change in requests. This indicates the relatively greater importance of the Executive branch compared to Congress in affecting change in agencies' budgets. The level of presidential attention and support, and changes in agency size were found to be important determinants of change in requests. Contrary to the incremental view, the change in requests and appropriations have little relationship to previous change.

The findings are important in showing that systematic factors explaining change exist and in revealing a major potential for political actors to cause agency budget change. The results suggest that expansion oriented agencies should not be concerned about the incremental strategy of moderation, but rather should seek to increase their size, support from the President, and requests to Congress in order to expand appropriations.

ATTAINING A DESIRED SHARE of the annual allocation of federal revenues is a concern of paramount importance to all agency officials. Unlike a private firm, most federal agencies depend solely on the response to the yearly request for appropriation of funds for their existence. Virtually all agency goals, strategies, and actions are contingent on the outcome of the budgetary process.

In the last decade, political scientists have contributed substantially to our understanding of this crucial dimension of federal policy-making. About thirty years after V. O. Key lamented the "lack of a budgetary theory" (1940), political science indeed has a theory of budgeting: incrementalism, or incremental budgeting. As a type of administrative decision-making, incrementalism was popularized by Charles Lindblom (1959) in both descriptive and prescriptive terms. Application of an incremental viewpoint to the budgetary process in the United States was most notably accomplished by Wildavsky (1964), Davis et al. (1966), and Fenno (1966).

According to the incremental view, because of the complexity of issues and the cognitive limitations of participants, budgeting is characterized by relative stability and by small incremental change. "Incremental calculations proceed from an existing base" (Davis et al., 1966: 530); appropriations are based primarily on the previous year's appropriation. The simple and consistent calculations made by participants can be translated into linear decision rules represented by several simple stochastic equations (Davis et al., 1966). An agency decision rule might be to ask for slightly more than needed but not too much (thus, confidence in them is not lost). A congressional decision rule might be to cut an agency request a certain percentage almost automatically. In general, the "striking regularities in the budgetary process" (Davis et al., 1966: 529) are indicative of the stability of the process and of the decision rules employed by the participants.

Of particular interest to this study are the sources of change in appropriations. Davis et al. (1966:531) define change as "random shocks to an otherwise deterministic system." Change does occur periodically but often is manifested by changes in decision rules. Other differences between predicted and actual observations are the result of "disturbances" and "special circumstances." They assume that the rate of appropriations change is fairly constant from year to year, subject to periodic adjustment (shift points) and that deviations from this stable pattern represent random error. This error is assumed to be normally distributed over time for agencies.

The incremental explanation of budgetary outcomes has important implications for research. It focuses heavily, almost exclusively, on the stability of the process from year to year. This emphasis of necessity forecloses attention to change in the outcomes or to factors that contribute to change when it is observed. In addition, by defining change as a random occurrence, incrementalists forego the analysis of factors within the budget process that may have a systematic, regular effect on the allocation of funds. Thus, working within the confines of incrementalism severely limits the scope of the analyses undertaken.

Incrementalism, despite its general acceptance in the discipline as a theory of budgeting and its widespread use in political science texts and research (see, for example, Sharkansky's work on state and federal budgeting, 1969), has nonetheless generated some negative reactions. Moreland (1973) has criticized the methodology of incrementalism, suggesting that the strong relationships were caused by not controlling for serial correlation in the time-series data. Natchez and Bupp (1973) looked at changes in the distribution of funds *within* an agency in attempting to demonstrate changes in priorities masked by incremental analysis.

Aware of the research limitations imposed by an incremental perspective and based on a belief that change in appropriations is not simply a random event, this chapter undertakes to demonstrate that regular, identifiable, nonrandom causes of change in appropriations do exist. This chapter does not purport to be a direct theoretical and empirical refutation of the theory of incremental budgeting (for example, it will not attempt to refine prediction of total appropriations). It does question, however, the incrementalists' assumptions of stability and random error. The empirical foundation of incrementalism rests primarily on the lack of deviation between appropriations and requests in the next year and the corresponding strong correlation between total appropriations in consecutive time periods. This paper suggests that substantial change from year to year is not as infrequent as supposed and has been deemphasized because of the dominance of the incremental view.

The Research Design

The focus of this study will be to identify regular sources of change in agency appropriations. The primary dependent variable used is percent change in appropriations (from the previous year's appropriations). The use of a percentage change figure has three things to recommend it: it facilitates analysis with agencies combined [rather than resorting to developing single-agency models as in Davis et al. (1966)]; it allows comparison between agencies despite magnitude differences in absolute appropriation levels; and there is evidence that percentage change figures are important to participants in the budgetary process [for example, Davis et al. (1966: 350) and also Chapter 6 of this volume].

EXPLANATORY CONCEPTS

Two major concepts from the framework introduced in Chapter 1 were explored for their systematic effect on percent change in agency appropriations—agency structural characteristics and agency political environment. These concepts are discussed below. Their relationships to the dependent variable are summarized in the research hypotheses presented at the end of the section.

AGENCY STRUCTURAL CHARACTERISTICS

Bailey and Mosher (1968), Downs (1967), Simon (1953) and others have linked characteristics of agency structure to policy actions and results. This body of literature suggests that certain types of agencies tend to behave in certain ways. Agencies that are more traditional, closed, mature, rigid, or conservative tend to be less active and less oriented towards expansion than agencies that are nontraditional, open, immature, flexible, assertive, or acquisitive.

One of the basic hypotheses in Chapter 1 suggests that agencies that are less rigid in their personnel structure will be more likely to try to increase their level of activity. One identifying characteristic of an expansion oriented agency is the desire to seek additional employees. Some agencies actively seek expansion, some passively seek it, and still others are content to remain stable. While agencies are constrained in their ability to increase the size of their personnel force by a number of external factors, they retain some discretion in requesting more positions. Since both internal and external factors are reflected in changes in the size of an agency, it can be said that changes in size reflect the desire to change, the ability to change, or both. In any case, changes in size indicate flexibility, and it is hypothesized that these agencies are more likely to have larger increases in funding. Because it is possible that change in size may be a function of the previous years' appropriations, it will be necessary to test for spuriousness in any relationship between change in size and change in requests and appropriations.

Another indicator of rigidity in agency structure is the amount and rate of change in the hierarchical structure of an agency. Each agency at any point in time has a certain ratio of supergrades to middlegrades to lowergrades. Although again subject to external constraints, change in the distribution of personnel within an agency (such as an increase in the hierarchy at the top marked by a jump in the percentage of supergrades) is reflective of the agency's flexibility.

It is suggested, then, that agencies with a less rigid personnel structure will be characterized by increases in size and increases in the ratio of supervisory personnel and that these agencies will tend to have a greater increase in their percentage change in requests and appropriations.

THE POLITICAL ENVIRONMENT

While there are many relevant dimensions of an agency's external environment, two dimensions of the political environment—presidential attention and support, and congressional conflict and partisanship—were judged to be the most proximate, regular features likely to affect the agency. While much literature has focused on the process of budgeting in Congress and the Executive branch, this chapter represents an attempt to look at the effect of features of the two branches on agency appropriations in a systematic manner. Underlying this attempt is the assumption that the political environment differs for agencies in a given year: some receive a great deal of attention and support from the President while others receive little. There are also variations in the level of conflict and partisanship in Congress generated by different agencies and their programs.

Why should these environmental factors affect change in requests or appropriations? The Office of Management and Budget (OMB) and the President are of great importance in determining what request figure for an agency is ultimately sent to Congress. Budget officials send out preliminary guidelines and negotiate with agencies on their budget requests. The President's direct role in budgeting is obviously limited by the scope of presidential responsibility and duties (Sharkansky, 1969:62). Presidential time and attention are scarce commodities, and Presidents must sample selectively the issues and agencies with which they become involved (Polsby, 1965:2). Agencies and programs with a higher presidential priority are likely to receive larger increases in appropriations.

Some indication of presidential priorities is essential to get a sense of the environment agencies face in the presidency. One measure of this environment is references concerning an agency or its programs made by the President in his public speeches and statements (presidential attention), and the positive or negative content of those references (presidential support).

Given the vast scope of the federal bureaucracy, an agency receiving public attention and support from the President would seem to be more likely to experience major changes in its appropriations. Receiving presidential attention and support, an expansionist agency may have the opportunity to request more, and even a nonexpansionist agency may be directed to increase its budget and programs. In sum, an agency receiving high levels of presidential support and attention relative to other agencies is more likely to increase its percentage change in requests and appropriations in a positive direction.

Agencies also face differing environments in Congress. Some agencies are controversial; they tend to stimulate partisan conflict and generate close roll call votes where many amendments are offered. Other agencies are noncontroversial, and their budgets and programs face relatively little conflict in the House and Senate. The norms of Congress are to resolve conflict, particularly over appropriations, at the committee and subcommittee level (Fenno, 1966). This not only facilitates the smooth conduct of legislative business but protects the prestige and reputation of the committee. Conflict and partisanship over an agency's programs and budget represent a level of saliency sufficient to violate the norms of conflict resolution. The probable impact of this environmental factor on agency appropriations is less clear than presidential attention and support. While high conflict and partisanship may sometimes result in an increase in appropriations, it seems more likely that this will have a negative effect on percentage change in appropriations. Conflict may also serve as a constraint in the formulation of future budget requests. The fact that an agency engendered a great deal of conflict in the previous year may have a moderating effect on the amount of appropriations change requested.

LEVEL OF REQUESTS

The preceding discussion of the congressional and presidential dimensions of an agency's political environment raises the question of the relative impact of Congress and the President on appropriations change. Central to this question is the degree to which Congress goes along with executive branch requests. How much is the percentage change in requests used as a cue by congressional decision-makers? The relationship between percentage change in requests and percentage change in appropriations will give an indication of the use of this cue. If this relationship is strong, it will indicate the relative importance of the executive branch in affecting appropriations change and may suggest that change in requests rather than change in appropriations is the most important variable to be explained. Anticipating a strong relationship, the hypotheses have been worded to include percent change in requests as a dependent variable.

PREVIOUS CHANGE IN APPROPRIATIONS

The theory of incremental budgeting stresses the relative stability of the calculations made by participants, at least over the short run. This would imply that an important determinant of one year's percentage change in appropriations is the previous year's change in appropriations. To find a strong relationship between these variables would support the incrementalist position. To find little or no relationship would tend to support the contention that percentage change in appropriations is not simply a function of previous budgetary experiences and patterns.

HYPOTHESES

H1. Increases in percentage change in requests tends to relate highly to increases in percentage change in appropriations.

H2. Increases in size and hierarchy tend to increase the percentage change in requests and appropriations.

H3. Increases in presidential attention and support tend to increase percentage change in requests and appropriations.

H4. Increases in the level of congressional conflict and partisanship tend to decrease percentage change in appropriations; increases in past levels of congressional conflict and partisanship tend to reduce percentage change in requests.

H5. Previous year's percentage change in appropriations does NOT tend to have a strong effect on percentage change in requests or appropriations.

The relationships to be explored among the concepts are presented graphically in Figure 4–1.

DATA BASE AND METHODOLOGY

The test of the model in Figure 4–1 is based on data collected for eight federal agencies over the time period from fiscal 1960 through 1971. These agencies are Veterans Administration (VA), Atomic Energy Commission (AEC), National Aeronautics and Space Administration

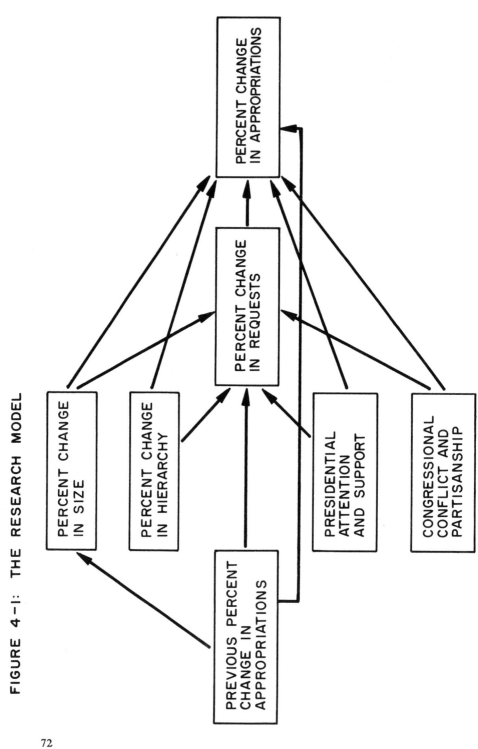

FIGURE 4-1: THE RESEARCH MODEL

(NASA), Commodity Credit Corporation (CCC), Agency for International Development (AID), Army Corps of Engineers (ACE), Federal Aviation Agency (FAA), and Office of Education (OE). This group of agencies is in no way presented as a random sample of all federal agencies. In fact, selection of the agencies depended upon their political salience—to be included in the sample, an agency must have had some specific roll call votes in Congress and must have received some attention from the President during most of the years of the study. Such purposeful selection does not necessarily bias the sample toward change. As the following section shows, some agencies underwent substantial change in appropriations while others experienced practically none. While this kind of sample limits the ability to generalize to all federal agencies, the findings do have implications for a universe of "politically salient" agencies.

The appendix to this chapter details the operational measures of the concepts. In some cases, multiple indicators were used and combined into indices (for example, presidential attention and support, congressional conflict). In other cases, one of several indicators was chosen (for example, hierarchy measures).

The methodology used in this analysis is purposely different than the single-agency, time-series regression employed by Davis et al. (1966). The eight agencies over 12 years provide a maximum of 96 cases for the multivariate analysis of change. While this sacrifices the ability to make specific statements about the temporal development of a single agency's appropriations, combining agencies allows the examination of the relative impact of differences in the independent variables across agencies and across time. Combining agencies allows the examination of many more potential determinants of change. Lagging the data allows assessment of the impact of percentage changes in appropriations in the previous year. The data for all the variables are lagged to approximate, as closely as possible, the actual sequence of the budgetary process. (Time lags are discussed in the chapter appendix.)

Recursive path estimation is used to test the relative impact of the suggested independent variables on percentage change in appropriations. Recursiveness (one-way causality) is justified primarily because of the time sequence of the data. Since one variable is measured prior to another, it is reasonable to draw a causal arrow in just one direction. Recursive path analysis has a number of advantages. Causal models not only specify relationships between independent variables and the dependent variable but can also make explicit the relationships among prior variables (Van Meter and Asher, 1973). It allows the examination of alternative causal paths as well as allowing estimation of both direct and indirect effects. Recursive path estimation using standardized coefficients allows one to compute the percentage of variance explained as well as the magnitude of the residual (unexplained) variance (Wright, 1960).

The use of this technique requires that certain assumptions be met: these include system closure, interval level data, uncorrelated residual terms, and linear and additive relationships (Land, 1969). These assumptions are satisfactorily met by this analysis.[1] Path coefficients are estimated from a series of complex equations determined from the variables included in a model and the direction of causality assumed. The actual values of the path coefficients can be estimated from multiple regression of all variables having a direct effect on a given variable. The path coefficients presented here are estimated in this manner; the structural equations from which these coefficients are derived are not presented.[2]

Recursive path estimation using agencies combined is not the only methodology that could have been used. An alternative might have been to analyze residuals from linear regression equations like those of Davis et al. (1966). The technique used here, combining agency data, seems to be an optimal one at this stage of research for assessing differences across agencies, in comparing the relative impact of past percentage changes in appropriations with the hypothesized structural and environmental determinants, and in meeting the assumptions of recursive path estimation.

Findings

APPROPRIATIONS CHANGE AND INCREMENTALISM

Simple graphs and tables can quickly reveal a great deal about a set of data. To obtain an initial understanding of the nature of these agencies' appropriations, the raw appropriations were graphed over time. These data are presented in Figure 4–2. In addition, the percent change from the previous year's appropriation for each agency for each year was calculated, and it is summarized in Table 4–1 (see p. 76).

Figure 4–2 shows that a variety of patterns of growth (and shrinkage) in appropriations were present among the agencies. Certainly there is no uniformity in pattern, nor does stability, much emphasized by incrementalists, seem to be a dominant characteristic. Table 4–1 shows that over half of the cases of change in appropriations (53.5%) were greater than ±10%, and almost one-third (30.3%) were greater than ±20%.

To test the possibility that this sample of agencies might possess an unusual distribution, the figures were compared to a similar distribution using Fenno's sample of 36 agencies (1966). Table 4–2 (see p. 77) compares Fenno's figures for House Appropriations Committee decisions with the figures presented in Table 4–1.[3] The figures for the distribution of the larger sample are quite close to the distribution of the eight agencies, with 47% being changed more than ±10% by the House Appropriations Committee.

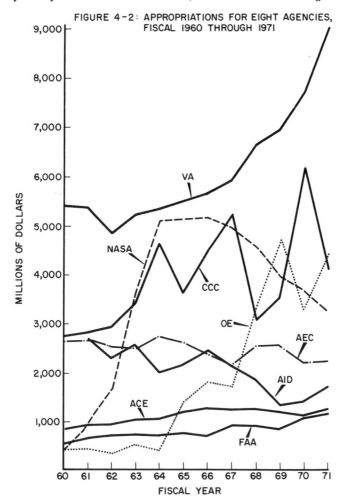

FIGURE 4-2: APPROPRIATIONS FOR EIGHT AGENCIES, FISCAL 1960 THROUGH 1971

Fenno's description of his own data is interesting. He asserts: (1966: 355) "A frequency distribution of committee decisions relative to the previous year's appropriation reveals, again, a basic incrementalism." Yet, no firm definition of incrementalism is offered. One might have looked at the same data and concluded that the figures show a surprising amount of change given a supposed pattern of "basic incrementalism." This suggests that incrementalism may well be at least partially in the eye of the beholder.

Using an arbitrary criterion for incrementalism of ±10%, the eight agencies in this study are equally divided between incrementally and nonincrementally dominated patterns. Four agencies change more than

TABLE 4-1. Distribution of Percent Change in Appropriations for Eight Agencies, 1960 to 1971 (figures in percentages)

Intervals of Change	FAA	AEC	ACE	CCC	NASA	AID	VA	OE	All Agencies
0.0 – ± 10%	64%	60%	82%	18%	50%	18%	73%	9%	46.5%
±10.1 – ± 20%	9	30	18	27	10	46	27	18	23.2
±20.1 – ± 50%	27	10	0	46	10	36	0	55	23.2
over ± 50%	0	0	0	9	30	0	0	18	7.1
Totals	100%	100%	100%	100%	100%	100%	100%	100%	100.0%

TABLE 4-2. Comparison of the Distribution of Appropriations Change for Two Samples of Agencies (figures in percentages)

Change Interval	36 Agencies[a] (1947–1962)	8 Agencies (1960–1971)
0.0 – ± 10%	53.2%	46.5%
± 10.1 – ± 20%	21.9	23.2
± 20.1 – ± 50%	19.8	23.2
over ± 50%	4.9	7.1
Totals	99.8%	100.0%

a. These data were adapted from Fenno (1966:356, Table 8.1). The figures do not add to 100 due to rounding.

±10% a majority of times (NASA, OE, CCC, and AID), and four agencies change less than ±10% a majority of times (ACE, FAA, AEC, and VA). In combining all eight agencies, a variety of appropriations change patterns are to be explained in the bivariate and multivariate analyses.

APPROPRIATIONS CHANGE AS THE DEPENDENT VARIABLE

THE BIVARIATE RELATIONSHIP WITH CHANGE IN REQUESTS

The use of percentage change in agency requests as a cue to Congress is important to this analysis, and it has implications for the agency's political environment. The stronger the relationship between change in requests and change in appropriations, the less important congressional action or committee action would appear to be. This statement is made with full recognition of the integral role of Congress and the appropriations committees in the appropriations process. In terms of the causes of change, however, Congress may not be nearly as important as the Executive branch, suggesting that the incremental explanation of the decision-making processes may be most applicable to Congress.

Table 4–3 presents the bivariate relationship between change in requests and change in appropriations. The relationship for this sample of agencies combined is quite strong ($r = .93$). This relationship implies that most of the variance in appropriations change can be explained by how requests differed from last year's appropriations. As the wide range of correlation coefficients for individual agencies shows, Congress has a more important role in determining appropriations change for some agencies than for others. Only for the Agency for International Development do changes in requests have no impact on appropriations outcome. Congress has taken a particularly negative view of foreign aid in contrast to the strong and continued support from the Executive branch in this period.

TABLE 4-3. The Bivariate Relationship between Percent Change in Requests and Percent Change in Appropriations

Agency	r
NASA	.99
AEC	.98
OE	.98
CCC	.91
ACE	.87
VA	.81
FAA	.53
AID	−.01
All Agencies	.93

With this exception, it appears that in seeking a better understanding of budget change, percentage change in requests, not percentage change in appropriations, is most interesting and important as an independent variable.

BIVARIATE RELATIONSHIP WITH ALL INDEPENDENT VARIABLES

Table 4–4 presents a number of interesting relations between the independent variables and percent change in appropriations. Size, presidential attention and support, and congressional conflict all have significant relationships with change in appropriations. Of particular interest is the lack of any substantial relationship between appropriations change and the previous year's change. This finding tends to confirm the hypothesis that, contrary to the incremental view, past levels of change in appropriations are not the crucial determinant of change. Changes in the hierarchial structure and the level of partisanship also show no significant relationships in the bivariate case. (The lack of relationship between these three

TABLE 4-4. Bivariate Correlations between Independent Variables and Change in Appropriations

Independent Variables	Percent Change in Appropriations
Percent Change in Requests	.93
Presidential Attention and Support	.49
Congressional Conflict	−.29
Partisanship	.14
Percent Change in Size	.44
Percent Change in Hierarchy	.07
Change in Previous Year's Appropriations	.09

variables and the dependent variable was confirmed in the multivariate test, although these results are not reported here.)

MULTIVARIATE RELATIONSHIP WITH INDEPENDENT VARIABLES

The path model presented in Figure 4–3 shows the simultaneous effects of the independent variables on percent change in appropriations. Estimation of the path coefficients in this model reveals that the impact of size, presidential attention and support, and congressional conflict observed in the bivariate analysis is substantially reduced in the multivariate case. The impact of size is totally negated and the impact of presidential attention and support fell from $r = .49$ to $p = .13$; congressional conflict was reduced from $r = -.29$ to $p = -.14$. This indicates that there is still a slight direct relationship between presidential attention and support and percentage change in appropriations and that the level of conflict in Congress retains a slight tendency to reduce appropriations change.

CHANGE IN REQUESTS AS THE DEPENDENT VARIABLE

BIVARIATE RELATIONSHIP WITH INDEPENDENT VARIABLES

Table 4–5 presents the bivariate relationships between the independent variables and change in requests. The variables relating most strongly with change in requests are presidential attention and support and

FIGURE 4–3: PATH MODEL SHOWING DIRECT EFFECTS ON PERCENT CHANGE IN APPROPRIATIONS

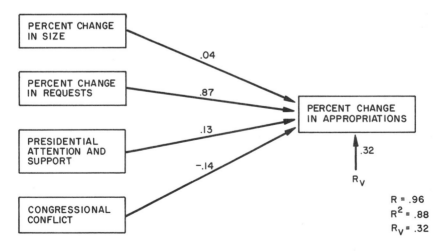

TABLE 4-5. **Bivariate Correlations between Independent Variables and Change in Requests**

Independent Variables	Percent Change in Requests
Presidential Attention and Support	.52
Congressional Conflict[a]	−.10
Partisanship[a]	.01
Percent Change in Size	.41
Percent Change in Hierarchy	−.05
Change in Previous Year's Appropriations	−.01

a. This variable was lagged one year.

change in agency size. The previous year's levels of congressional conflict and partisanship do not appear to have much effect on changes in the level of requests. Again, notably missing is the linkage between the previous year's change in appropriations and change in this year's requests. This further reinforces the findings that agency budget change is not contingent on the past rate of change.

MULTIVARIATE RELATIONSHIP WITH INDEPENDENT VARIABLES

Figure 4–4 presents a multivariable path model showing the principal explanatory variables for change in requests. The explanatory power of size and presidential attention and support is retained in this model. One

FIGURE 4-4: PATH MODEL SHOWING DIRECT EFFECTS ON PERCENT CHANGE IN REQUESTS

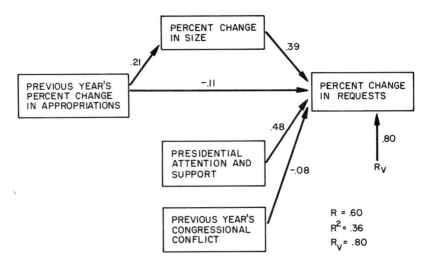

important question with respect to the impact of change in size is whether there is an independent effect on requests change. That is, changes in the number of agency personnel may be a function of previous appropriation changes. This can be tested in this model and as Figure 4–4 shows, change in size is affected by previous appropriation change, but it is not a pervasive determinant ($p = .21$). This implies that whether internally or externally directed, increases in agency size tend to increase agency requests.

DISCUSSION OF FINDINGS AND HYPOTHESES

Figure 4–5 represents a merging of Figures 4–3 and 4–4. The path coefficients in this model make it possible to evaluate the research hypotheses.

H1. The findings show clearly the predominance of percentage change in requests in explaining percentage changes in an agency's appropriations.

As mentioned earlier, this implies that Congress relies heavily on requests, particularly the percentage change figure, as a guide to their action. The conclusions of Davis et al. (1966), Fenno (1966), and other incrementalists may be applicable to congressional decision-making. The point is, whatever their decision calculus, it does not make much difference in explaining budget change. The exception of AID was noted earlier as a case in which changes in appropriations were very much dependent on congressional action. With the politically salient agencies studied here, this seems clearly to be the exception. If AID were dropped from the analysis, the requests-appropriations change relationship would undoubtedly be even stronger. This finding identifies the Executive branch as the more important source of appropriations change and implies increased importance to explaining changes in the level of requests.

H2. Changes in agency's hierarchial structure did not show any relationship to percentage changes in requests or appropriations. A second characteristic of agency structure, percentage change in size, did show a relationship.

The multivariate analysis shows that the effect of changes in an agency's size operates on appropriations change indirectly through requests change. This suggests that agencies can improve their appropriations position through growth in the previous time period. While the analysis here necessarily simplifies very complex relationships concerning personnel, the results suggest that deeper, more careful probing of agency characteristics, structures, processes, and their effect on policy actions, may be important.

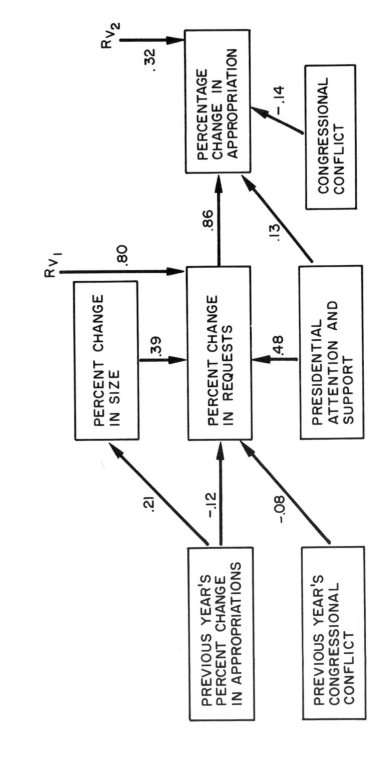

FIGURE 4-5: AGGREGATE PATH MODEL SHOWING DETERMINANTS OF PERCENT CHANGE IN APPROPRIATIONS

The findings of this study are fairly consistent with those presented in Chapter 6, although subsamples of large and small agencies were not considered.

H3. Presidential attention and support, as shown in Figure 4–5, is an important determinant of percentage change in requests (p = .48).

Figure 4–5 shows that the level of attention and support an agency receives from the President has both a direct and indirect effect on change in appropriations. The indirect effect of (.48) × (.86) = (.39) added to the direct effect (.13) results in a total positive effect on percentage change in appropriations of (.52).[4] Presidential attention and support was measured independently of budgetary politics; it is an indicator of presidential concern and priorities. That a general interest on the part of the President can be partially translated into budget change is an important addition to our understanding of budgetary politics.

The exception of AID is relevant to this discussion of presidential attention and support as well. While it is not possible to present all the data on individual values of the environmental variables, it is worth noting that AID received relatively high levels of attention and support but had a slightly declining appropriations pattern. This serves to reduce the magnitude of the relationship found here. What is of interest is that looking at AID separately, the relationship between presidential attention and support and appropriations change is $r = .40$. This means that even though high presidential priority for foreign aid did not result in budget growth, appropriations change from year to year for AID did relate to variations in presidential interest. This finding suggests that in the case of AID, high support from the President prevented even more serious cuts from taking place, if not the eradication of the program altogether.

H4. The congressional environment, as measured here, did not appear to have a significant impact on either requests or appropriations change.

Partisanship was found to have no impact at all. The relative levels of congressional conflict occurring during appropriations deliberations did have a slight tendency to reduce the percentage change in appropriations $(p = -.14)$. This may be enough of an effect for agencies to want to minimize conflict during consideration of their programs and budgets. The level of conflict and partisanship in the previous year did not appear to be a constraint on the executive managers in formulating requests to Congress. While some generalizations can be made, the relationships are not strong enough to inspire a great deal of confidence in them. Individual agencies develop their own relationships with Congress. A relatively conflictual or partisan environment does not seem to have a consistent impact on appropriations change. In any case, the findings tend to minimize the importance of Congress, except in the case of AID, as a major source of change in the distribution of funds.

H5. Finally, the proposition that change in requests and appropriations are NOT a function of previous percentages of change was confirmed.

Previous appropriations change actually has a slight negative effect as shown in Figure 4–5 ($p = -.12$). This would indicate a weak moderating tendency; agencies with a relatively larger change in the previous year may be less likely to have as great an increase in requests. Of course, the findings show this to be a very slight tendency. The lack of a strong relationship is an important finding concerning sources of appropriations change and the incremental theory of budgeting. If change is fairly consistent from year to year, as the incrementalists assert, one would have expected this relationship to be strong.

Conclusions and Implications

Combining data for all agencies has the advantage of facilitating the study of numerous possible sources of appropriations change, and it allows one to develop general budget strategy advice for agencies, subject to individual variations. Application of such strategies to specific agencies is enhanced when additional information about a particular agency is available.

An important variable to consider in this regard is the general internal goal-orientation of the agency, that is, whether it is inclined toward growth and expansion or toward stability. Agencies interested in expansion might well focus on achieving budget growth (large positive percent change in appropriations), while conserving agencies might focus less on growth and more on achieving high budget success (large percent of requests appropriated) (LeLoup, 1973). Based on the findings reported in this chapter and on this categorization of agency goals, the following strategies are offered for expansionist agencies.

1. Concentrate efforts on building supportive groups and coalitions in the presidency and executive branch.
2. Be as assertive and convincing as possible with OMB managers to allow the maximum amount of increase in requests to Congress.
3. Actively seek favorable public attention and support from the President.

4. Attempt to increase agency size by hiring the maximum number of people allowable under current requirements and by seeking to expand hiring authority.

5. Attempt to minimize the level of conflict in Congress by downplaying any controversial aspect of programs.

Individual agencies could vary from the "normal expansionist strategy," according to particular situations and needs.

There are some important differences in these strategies and the strategies implied by the incremental theory of budgeting. Wildavsky's discussion of agency strategies (1964: Ch. 3) seems to concentrate on Congress and the necessity of agencies' "developing a clientele," "building confidence," and "playing it straight," whereas strategy 1 suggests that agencies should concentrate their efforts on the Executive branch rather than on Congress. Strategy 2 also represents an important change from incremental advice. Wildavsky stressed that agencies must not request all the money they feel they could use (1964: 21). Davis et al. (1966: 530) also stress moderation.

The findings presented in this chapter suggest that larger increases in requests to Congress result in greater appropriations growth than moderate increases. This conclusion is reinforced by previous research (LeLoup, 1973), confirming Sharkansky's (1966) proposition that assertive agencies have a smaller percent of their requests appropriated but have greater overall growth. While there are reasonable limits to the amount an agency can request, perhaps the incremental theorists have overemphasized the importance of moderation.

One way to receive large increases in requests seems to be to have public support from the President. While an agency may do what it can to solicit support, attention and support may come without agency efforts. Presidential interest and executive branch initiative may, in effect, force expansion on a reluctant agency. The history of the Office of Education in the 1960s is suggestive of this kind of pattern (Bailey and Mosher, 1968).

Agency assertiveness, as measured by size of agency requests to the OMB, may be another important cause of budget change. These data were not available for the agencies in this study, but their inclusion would represent an important addition to the analysis. Since presidential attention and support and agency size only partially explain change in requests, agency requests to the OMB may be an important link.

The main task of this study was to test for the existence of systematic determinants of budget change. The findings suggest that the dominant theory of incremental budgeting is overly restrictive. Recognizing that some stability and incremental change are present in budget development, the emphasis on stability has prevented an adequate understanding of the forces of change. It has been shown that, for this group of agencies, percentage change in appropriations is a variable that is empirically related to changes in agency structure and environment. These are regular, not special, circumstances. These findings demonstrate the need to expand the boundaries of relevant questions as defined by the incremental theory. The model of appropriations change presented here constitutes a supplement to the incremental theory and, along with other work stressing nonincremental aspects of budgeting, it should mark the beginning of a more balanced theory of budgeting and budget change.

If the findings here give rise to doubts about the incremental view, it is with respect to the potential for political actors to affect change in the distribution and allocation of funds. The results illustrate the usefulness of the conceptual framework presented in Chapter 1 for improving our understanding of public policy-making and indicate the importance of structural and environmental variables for the analysis of policy actions.

Notes

1. These assumptions are satisfactorily met. System closure is probably violated in every social science application. Enough independent variables, some not reported here, were included to cover a wide range of determinants. While more could always be included, the system can be assumed to be closed.

   The data for almost all the variables and indices are interval level, including: personnel size, dollars, percentages, mentions, roll call votes, etc.

   Uncorrelated disturbance terms, as required by assumption 3, means that no excluded variable can have an impact on two variables included in the model. If this were the case, it would mean that the relationship between the two variables would be a function of some third, unmeasured variable. Since many variables not reported here were included in earlier research, findings indicate that this assumption is met.

   When considering percentage change in appropriations separately, linearity is more of a problem with agencies combined. Earlier research indicated some possible interaction between environmental variables, but the model reported here showed no signs of interaction.

   Serial correlation (multicollinearity) could have been a problem if the relationship between appropriations change in consecutive time periods was stronger. Since the findings revealed that the relationships are weak, multicollinearity is not a problem.

2. The path coefficients (standardized regression beta coefficients) were established using the MULTR program in the PSTAT package. T tests, degrees of freedom, and error variance were inspected.

3. While House Appropriations Committee action is not exactly comparable to the data on final appropriations, it was the closest comparison available

since Fenno did not present data comparing either Senate action, conference committee decisions, or final floor actions with the previous year's appropriations. Based on Fenno's findings, House committee actions should be a conservative figure with respect to final action and underestimate the amount of nonincremental change.

4. Indirect effects of variables can be computed by the product of the simple paths that compose a compound path. The total effect of one variable upon another can be computed as the sum of the direct and indirect paths (Stokes, 1971:70–92).

Appendix

OPERATIONAL MEASURES

PERCENT CHANGE IN REQUESTS

This measure was derived by finding the percentage of an agency's budget request to Congress divided by its appropriation in the previous year (request to Congress$_t$/appropriations$_{t-1}$). Raw data for this measure were collected from the annual Senate document *Appropriations, Budget Estimates, Etc.* and excluded amounts for supplemental appropriations.

PERCENT CHANGE IN APPROPRIATIONS

This measure was derived by finding the percentage of an agency's appropriation divided by its appropriation in the previous year (appropriation$_t$/appropriation$_{t-1}$). The raw data came from *Appropriations, Budget Estimates, Etc.* and excluded amounts for any supplemental appropriations. Figures used represented final congressional action.

AGENCY STRUCTURE

Agency size represents the total number of full-time, permanent employee positions within an agency. These data came from the *Appendix to the U.S. Budget.*

Two measures of hierarchy were used, the ratio of supergrade employees to agency size, and the ratio of middlegrade employees to agency size. Supergrades are the number of employees with a ranking of GS 16, 17, or 18, plus their equivalents in salary terms, plus any executive level employees. Middlegrade employees represent the number of GS 13, 14, and 15 employees plus their equivalents in salary terms.

Percentage change for each of these three measures was simply calculated by dividing a year's value by the value of the preceding year (X_t/X_{t-1}).

PRESIDENTIAL ATTENTION AND SUPPORT

Raw data for each of the following measures was collected from the *Public Papers of the President.*

A. *Mentions:* the number of times the President mentions an agency in his public statements in a given year.

B. *Policy Statements:* a listing of policy statements made concerning the agency and its programs in:
1. State of the Union address
2. Budget Message
3. Economic Report of the President
4. Press conferences
5. Special messages
6. Any statement containing an agency mention

C. *Tone:* Each policy statement was given a score for its favorability to the agency and its programs:
'   0 negative, nonsupportive
1 neutral
2 positive, supportive
The scoring included intercoder reliability tests.

D. *Mean Tone:* average tone scores for all policy statements made in a given year

E. *Index of Presidential Attention and Support:* (Number of mentions + number of policy statements) × (mean tone)

CONGRESSIONAL CONFLICT AND PARTISANSHIP

Raw data for these measures were collected from the roll call votes reported in *Congressional Quarterly Almanacs* that related to an agency or a major program uniquely identified with the particular agency.

A. *Amendments:* the total number of amendments offered on the respective floors of both houses (all types of votes included)

B. *Mean Vote split:*

$$1 - \left[\frac{\dfrac{yea_1 - nay_1}{total_1} + \dfrac{yea_2 - nay_2}{total_2} + \ldots \dfrac{yea_n - nay_n}{total_n}}{n} \right]$$

C. Congressional Conflict was measured using the index: (Number of roll calls) (Mean vote split).

D. Partisanship was measured using a Mean Index of Likeness which represents the complement of the difference between respective percentages voting "yea" in the Republican and Democratic groups. The measure is computed by:

1 − [% yea (Republicans) − % yea (Democrats)]

and is meaned over all the roll calls in a given year.

TIME LAGS

Figure 4–6 is presented to help clarify the temporal relationships among the variables. The specific time lags used were as follows:

1. -Percentage Change in Requests (requests submitted in early January): change from (FY_{-1}) to (FY).
2. -Percentage Change in Appropriations: change from (FY_{-1}) to (FY)—Previous Year's Percentage Change in Appropriations: change from (FY_{-2}) to (FY_{-1}).
3. -Percentage Change in Size: change from (FY_{-2}) to (FY_{-1})
   -Percentage Change in Hierarchy: change from (FY_{-2}) to (FY_{-1})

FIGURE 4-6: TEMPORAL RELATIONSHIPS

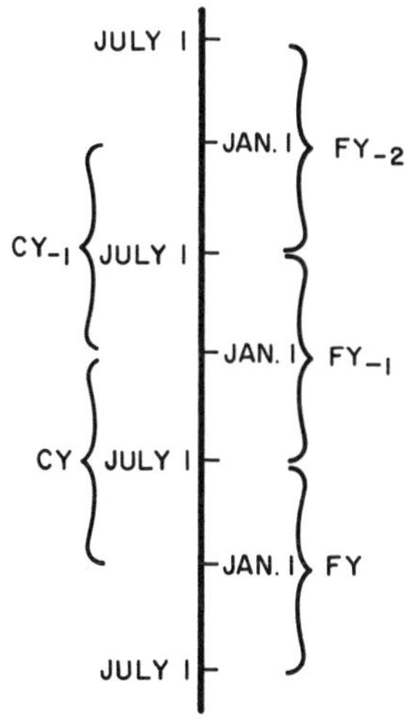

FY = FISCAL YEAR
CY = CALENDAR YEAR

(during fiscal year just prior to administration formulation of requests).

4. -Presidential Attention and Support: measured in (CY_{-1}) (in calendar year before and during formulation of requests).

5. -Congressional Conflict and Partisanship: measured in (CY) (during congressional deliberations).

 -Previous Year's Congressional Conflict and Partisanship: measured in (CY_{-1}).

5

The Relationship between Budgetary and Functional Policy Actions

Steven A. Shull

This study initiates research in the previously unexplored area of nondollar measures of agency policy actions, which are labelled functional actions. These functional actions are measures of what an agency is doing out in the field as it implements its programs— in effect, they are the substantive content of agency policy. Because much previous policy research has assumed that functional or implementing actions are simply an outgrowth of agency budgetary resources, the principal research hypothesis of this study focused on the relationship between budgetary and functional policy actions. It asserted a direct, positive connection between budgetary actions as the independent variable and functional actions as the dependent variable.

The study used data for eight federal agencies over a time span from fiscal 1960 through 1971, and data analysis methods included univariate analysis, bivariate correlation, and multivariate regression analysis. The findings of the study showed that there was only moderate support for the research hypothesis. The relationship between budgetary and functional actions was not always positive, nor was it particularly strong. In general, agencies appeared to have considerable freedom from budgetary constraints as they shaped their functional actions.

MUCH OF THE RESEARCH in policy-making to date (as well as that within this book) has measured policy as a dependent variable and has relied only on fiscal measures of policy, such as size of appropriations or expenditures. While these budgetary policy variables are retained in this study, they are treated as an intermediate step, rather than the end result of agency policy-making. Budgetary variables are used as predictors of the substantive activities of agencies in the field, which are called functional policy actions. Functional actions are concerned with the policy content of agency policy actions, and encompass tangible measures of what the agency is doing to implement its programs.

Although budgets certainly serve as a profile of agency activities, it has long been assumed (perhaps because of the unwillingness to look beyond the relatively accessible dollar measures) that agency programs depend entirely on dollars as the limits of program expansion. What are defined here as functional actions of agencies have been taken for granted or have been assumed to be largely the result of an agency's budgeting experience. This assumption appears in much of the literature on agency activities (see, for example, Rourke, 1969:25). Although ultimately the common sense argument that an agency cannot do anything unless it has a budget is irrefutable, the assumption that dollars define programs seems deserving of empirical testing, especially since some scholars have evidence that level of spending is only one of a number of factors that affect agency services (Sharkansky, 1969:168; LeMay, 1973).

This study departs from previous policy research traditions in two important ways: first, it treats budgetary variables as independent rather than dependent variables in the research model; and second, it initiates a systematic typology of substantive policy content that is comparable across agencies. Whether agencies have any flexibility beyond the budgetary stage, or whether their functional actions are determined wholly by budgetary factors will be the focus of the present study.

Research Design

The general hypothesis to be tested in this study concerns the relationship between two dimensions of policy actions: budgetary actions and functional actions. A direct, positive relationship between the two types of policy actions is posited.

H1. The greater the change in agencies' budgetary actions, the greater the change in their functional actions will tend to be.

Support of the hypothesis will confirm the position that dollars are related to agency program activities. A weak relationship would indicate that dollars serve only as an outer constraint on program activities, and that agencies have internal latitude in shaping their activities.

While the hypothesis is worded to suggest that "greater" is equivalent to an increase in budgetary and functional actions, this is not always the case. In respect to percent change measures, greater refers only to magnitude of change, which may be positive or negative.

CONCEPTS AND OPERATIONALIZATION

BUDGETARY POLICY ACTIONS

Dollars have long been used as measures of agency policy actions [see, for example, Key (1949), Lockard (1959), Dawson and Robinson (1963), Dye (1966), Hofferbert (1966), Sharkansky (1970, 1968), and Fry and Winters (1970)]. The indicators of budgetary policy actions used in this study consist of several measures derived from agency appropriations and expenditures. Although expenditures are considered to be a budgetary variable, it is argued that they differ from appropriations (even though raw values of the two are highly correlated) in that expenditures are less subject to coalition pressures (Wildavsky, 1964:123–125). Expenditures also occur at a later and less visible stage of the policy process than do appropriations. Presumably, the agency (as well as other executive institutions) has more latitude in shaping expenditures than appropriations, although one could argue that agency involvement in the appropriations process differs considerably as some agencies take far more initiative than others [see Sharkansky (1969) on agency assertiveness]. This characteristic of greater agency influence (or latitude) on expenditures compared to appropriations makes the expenditures variable similar to functional actions [see Weidenbaum and Larkins (1972: Ch. 5) for a more involved discussion of agency expenditures].

The indicators of budgetary actions used in this study were the percent change in appropriations (from the previous year), the percent change in expenditures (from the previous year), budget success (appropriations as a percent of the amount requested by the agency from Congress), and agency expenditures as a percent of the total federal budget. The latter two variables were used only in the regression model to provide an additional dimension of budgetary actions and to provide four independent variables in the regression.

Although expenditures occur at a later stage in the budget process, and although they include sources other than regular appropriations, examination of the data indicated that change in appropriations and expenditures could be compared in the same fiscal year. Very little difference occurred in their correlations, whether they were lagged or not.[1] In addition, a data point is retained when they are treated in the same year, an important consideration since the number of years in the time frame is small.

FUNCTIONAL POLICY ACTIONS

Functional actions are nondollar measures of agency policy activity that occur subsequent to the budget process. These actions are literally the activities the agency pursues as it implements programs. Because the activities are so disparate, and because this is an entirely uncharted area of policy research, three general classes of functional actions were developed to guide data collection and analysis. The three classes of activities are acquisition of physical resources, delivery of benefits, and target beneficiaries served.

The acquisition of physical resources encompasses activities that expand or maintain an agency's physical resource base. Physical resources include such things as specialized equipment, land, raw materials, and field units (offices, bases, special outposts). Two measures of physical resources were selected for use—the number of field installations an agency possessed and beneficial facilities of the agency.

Delivery of benefits is used in a broad sense to mean performance of services by the agency, where services are defined by the agency's mission. Two measures of service performance were used, activities performed (these included agency-specific activities) and number of field personnel used by the agency in performing its services.

Target beneficiaries measure the recipients of agency activities. Primary beneficiaries are groups that receive some agency service, and potential beneficiaries are populations that could receive services at some future time. Indicators for both of these measures are agency-specific.

Although beneficiaries no doubt will be used in the study of policy results in future research, the use of beneficiaries under the rubric of policy actions is not out of order here. One of an agency's principal activities is the cultivation of clientele groups, whose support is useful as the agency seeks to promote itself and its programs throughout the bureaucracy. While primary beneficiaries may be the more immediate barometer of agency clientele, potential beneficiaries is expected to indicate the prospects of the agency to attract beneficiaries in the future.

The specific indicators used for each of the six measures of functional policy actions are identified in Table 5–2. Even a brief glance at these indicators shows that functional actions present a major data collection problem. While budgetary measures of actions (dollars) are innately comparable, and while functional actions *variables* are at least theoretically comparable, the indicators for a particular measure of functional activity are almost always unique to the agency, when such indicators can be located at all. The existence of data on nondollar measures of agency activities is limited, and there is no general source for such information. It is left to the agencies to publish information about their activities, and the agencies' reports vary widely in both amount and quality of data reported. The upshot of the current state of nondollar data for policy actions is that one is left with no choice but to use differing indicators to measure the same functional action. Sometimes the indicators fit the concept very well, other times an indicator may be only tangentially related, and other times there may be no data at all. While the validity of this approach may be challenged, the exploratory nature of the study and the state of the data allowed no choice.

One might argue that a different indicator for each agency makes comparability impossible and limits the researcher to doing a series of case studies. That position is not accepted here. While individual differences among the agencies will be studied, the principal focus is on developing general patterns of agency activity. Standardized measures of functional action variables were used for that purpose.

The two standardized measures used were a growth measure and a percent change measure. The growth index measured change in the raw variable value against a base year value of 1.0. The percent change measure measured change from the value of the previous year. The growth index reflects a true standardization in that each agency starts from the same level (1.0) and thus comparison between agencies is facilitated. The growth measure also illustrates the actual yearly (or cumulative) increments undistorted by large variations in percent change values. In this way the growth measure is more similar to the raw data but has the advantage of being in standardized form. It also has the advantage of indicating direction of change—a value greater than 1.0 represents an increase, while a value less than 1.0 indicates a decrease. The percent change measure is more reflective of annual changes in variable values than the growth measure, and it also conveys directionality of change.

DATA BASE

This study covers a time period from fiscal year 1960 through 1971 and focuses on eight federal agencies as the units of analysis. The eight agencies are: Veterans Administration (VA), Army Corps of Engineers (ACE), Commodity Credit Corporation (CCC), Atomic Energy Commission (AEC), National Aeronautics and Space Administration (NASA), Agency for International Development (AID) (the first year for this agency was 1961), Office of Education (OE), and Federal Aviation Administration (FAA).[2]

This selection of agencies is in no way claimed to be a random sample. Care was taken to insure that the agencies differed both from each other and over time on the variables used in this and a related study (Shull, 1974). In addition, the agencies include both those in departments (ACE, AID, FAA, OE, CCC) and independent agencies (AEC, VA, NASA). This distinction of agency type is one way of including agencies that have been statutorily granted different structures and missions.

METHODOLOGY

DATA ANALYSIS TECHNIQUES

A variety of techniques were employed in this study, ranging from comparison of agencies on a single variable to multivariate analysis.[3] Although the agency is the unit of analysis, the research is conducted both for agencies individually and for all agencies aggregated.

Comparison of agencies on a single variable allows the researcher to detect patterns of change among agencies as well as between variables. Thus, the use of single variable analysis can be a useful adjunct to hypothesis testing. One should be aware, however, that when mean and range values are used (as in Figures 5–1 and 5–2, pp. 98, 99), they can be masking a greater amount of variance that is occurring year to year.

The bivariate analysis utilized simple product-moment correlation coefficients that were computed at both levels of aggregation. When agencies are aggregated, the number of data points is at its maximum, and thus confidence in the correlation coefficients should be high. However, the disadvantage of this approach is that a low correlation may mask considerable variation within agencies. To detect differences among agencies, bivariate correlation coefficients were also computed for each agency separately. While confidence in analysis based on such a small number of data points (10 or 11 depending on the agency) must be limited, propositions can be tentatively tested by the direction and magnitude of the correlation values.

Multiple regression was used to examine the relative importance of each budgetary action holding the others constant. Because the degree of freedom limitation is further aggravated by the introduction of a greater number of explanatory variables, regressions were computed only for agencies combined. The results of regression analysis will appear in two forms: standardized beta coefficients and the amount of variance explained in a dependent variable by all four independent variables.[4] Standardized betas control for the effects of other standardized independent variables in a particular regression "model," and suggest the relative contributions of different variables to the total explained variance (R^2). Thus, standardized betas have similar properties to partial correlation coefficients.

CONFIRMATION OF THE HYPOTHESIS

Correlation and regression analysis were used to test the research hypothesis. In terms of magnitude of correlation values, the arbitrary cutting point of $\pm.20$ was selected as the "significant" value. In evaluating the findings, the following criteria were applied:

—A correlation value equal to or greater than $\pm.20$ tends to confirm the hypothesis (assuming the coefficient is in the predicted direction).

—A correlation value less than .20 suggests no relation exists.

It should be emphasized that the value of $\pm.20$ is an arbitrary level for which no special importance is claimed. It is not intended to imply statistical significance. Individual agency correlations can be compared to this standard by listing the number of agencies that tend to confirm or disconfirm the hypothesis or that show no relationship. The results of regression analysis will be more indirectly related to the hypothesis testing, but should more clearly show which independent variables are more closely related to, and explain most of the variance in, the dependent variables being analyzed.

Findings

To gain some insight into the nature of the policy actions of the agencies in this study, the first parts of this section provide a descriptive look at the agencies' budgetary and functional policy actions. (Although raw values of functional actions are presented and discussed, only standardized measures for these variables were used in the subsequent analyses.) The results of the bivariate and multivariate analysis of the relationship between budgetary and functional actions are presented in the concluding portion of this section.

A DESCRIPTIVE LOOK AT BUDGETARY ACTIONS

Figures 5–1 and 5–2 present the highest, lowest, and average figures for percent change in appropriations and expenditures by agency. The patterns of greatest and least change are similar for both variables. CCC,

FIGURE 5–1: LEAST, GREATEST AND MEAN PERCENT CHANGE
IN APPROPRIATIONS FOR EACH AGENCY

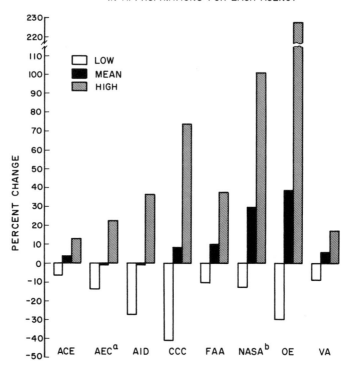

a. Data for fiscal 1962 to 1971 only
b. Data for fiscal 1961 to 1970 only

FAA, NASA, and OE showed instances of greatest percent change in expenditures, while the same agencies plus AID showed greatest change in appropriations. The *average* percent change in appropriations exceeded ±10% (an arbitrary cutting point) for two agencies, OE and NASA, while the average percent change in expenditures exceeded ±10% for four agencies, OE, NASA, FAA, and CCC. Although the figures make it clear that every agency (except the AEC) experienced nonincremental change (greater than ±10%) in appropriations and expenditures at least once from 1960 to 1971, the fact that the number of agencies with an average percent change in expenditures greater than ±10% was greater than the number of agencies experiencing nonincremental change in appropriations might be indicative that agency administrators feel less bound by an incrementalist perspective as they spend funds than congressmen do as they make appropriations.

Table 5–1 offers some evidence contrary to this speculation, however. The total number of times each agency experienced a nonincremental

FIGURE 5-2: LEAST, GREATEST, AND MEAN PERCENT CHANGE
IN EXPENDITURES FOR EACH AGENCY

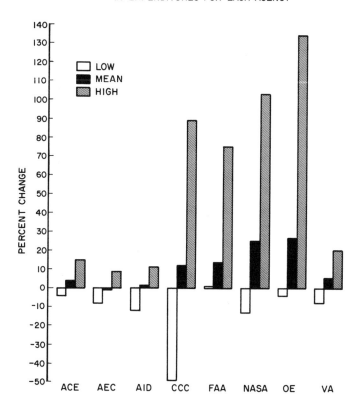

TABLE 5-1. **Number of Times Agencies Experienced Nonincremental Change in Appropriations and Expenditures**[a]

| Agency | Percent Change in: | | (N) |
	Appropriations	*Expenditures*	
OE	10	8	11
CCC	9	8	11
AID	9	3	11
NASA	5	7	10
AEC	4	0	10
FAA	4	3	11
VA	3	3	11
ACE	2	2	11
Totals	46	34	86

a. Nonincremental means percentage change equal to or greater than ± 10%.

change in appropriations and expenditures is summarized in the table for the period 1960–1971. Individually, some agencies experienced non-incremental change in both variables (OE, CCC), and some agencies experienced primarily incremental change in both variables (FAA, VA, ACE), while there is no clear relationship between the variables for the remaining agencies (NASA, AEC). Overall, the number of nonincremental cases for appropriations is much greater (53.5%) than it is for expenditures (35.9%). This may suggest that agencies are more cautious in making their expenditures.

DESCRIPTIVE LOOK AT FUNCTIONAL ACTIONS: A COMPARISON OF RAW DATA AND STANDARDIZED INDICATORS

Table 5–2 identifies the indicator and the raw data values for the beginning year and the ending year of the six functional policy actions used in this study. The purpose of these two values is to show the magnitude of the development of the particular activity from the beginning of the study to the end (usually a span of twelve years). The presentation of these widely disparate raw data values is made, not because there is great confidence in comparing different indicators for different agencies, but because it was believed essential to have some feel for the initial data if one is to assess the policy ramifications of particular agency activities. The fact that indicators of a particular variable differ widely tends to confirm the initial judgment that the standardized values have greater legitimacy in terms of bivariate and multivariate data analysis. Nevertheless, one should not lose sight of what the original data look like, particularly if one hopes the fruits of the research effort will have some utility to agency decision-makers in the real world.

The two standardized measures of functional actions, growth and percent change, are also presented in Table 5–2. The following paragraphs briefly discuss the standardized measures for each agency. (The interrelationship of growth and percent change of each functional action is summarized in Table 5–8 in the appendix to this chapter.)

There was too little information about the CCC to have much confidence in understanding its relative standing in the functional actions, since data were available for only two of the six variables. For those two variables (activities performed and potential beneficiaries), however, the agency tended to have a fairly low rank, and to have experienced a decline from its earlier years.

NASA, and to a lesser extent OE, were agencies that tended to experience greater average change than their overall growth would lead one to expect. This is because of a leveling off (or even a decline as for

TABLE 5-2. Raw and Standardized Data Values for Functional Policy Actions

Agency	Indicator Name	Raw Data 1960 (or) Initial Figure	Raw Data 1971 (or) Final Figure	Standardized Index of Growth	Standardized Average Percent Change
Acquiring Physical Resources[a]					
1. Field Installations					
ACE	# buildings owned	5,196	6,598	1.3	2.4
AEC	# buildings owned	7,026	6,048	.86	-1.0
AID	# regional bureaus + # program offices + # management offices	14	19	1.4	6.9
CCC	Missing Data				
FAA	# regional offices and/or # major field organs	6	12	2.0	7.0
NASA	# field installations	10	11	1.1	1.1
OE	# staff offices + # service elements	7	19	2.7	19.7
VA	# buildings owned	7,565	5,211	.69	-3.3
2. Beneficial Facilities					
ACE	volume of reservoir storage (in millions of acre feet)	162	231	1.4	3.3
AEC	square feet of buildings owned	73,115	76,414	1.05	.42
AID	Missing Data				
CCC	Missing Data				
FAA	# aircraft towers licensed	139	281	2.0	7.4
NASA	# applications satellites	6	5	.83	4.1
OE	# classrooms provided for by PL81-815 funds	1,818	7,866	4.3	44.5
VA	square feet of buildings owned	114,719	109,305	.95	-.43

TABLE 5-2. Continued

			Raw Data		Standardized	
Delivery of Benefits	Agency	Indicator Name	*1960 (or) Initial Figure*	*1971 (or) Final Figure*	*Index of Growth*	*Average Percent Change*
3. Activities Performed	ACE	amount of hydroelectric power generated (billions KWH)	28	68	2.5	8.7
	AEC	# nuclear power plants under construction	11	76	6.9	21.2
	AID	# surveys authorized by AID	1	11	11.0	348.4
	CCC	quantity of commodities pledged in CCC loan program (bushels of corn)	571,960,000	323,320,000	.56	-1.2
	FAA	# aircraft handled by FAA air-route traffic control centers	9,437,900	21,571,000	2.3	9.7
	NASA	# spacecraft launches obtaining earth orbit or beyond	16	30	1.9	12.1
	OE	# students housed under PL81-815 funds	63,039	46,717	.74	39.4
	VA	# loans dispersed	146,000	284,000	1.9	8.9
4. Field Personnel Utilized	ACE	Missing Data				
	AEC	# contract employees	104,612	99,207	.95	-.42
	AID	# direct hire personnel overseas	2,900	2,800	.97	.56
	CCC	Missing Data				
	FAA	# non-Washington field employees	36,341	44,557	1.2	2.4
	NASA	employment at major installations other than headquarters	8,963	30,460	3.4	14.6
	OE	Missing Data				
	VA	# employees in Veterans Benefits Office	17,374	16,426	.95	-1.6

TABLE 5-2. Continued

Target Beneficiaries	Agency	Indicator Name	Raw Data		Standardized	
			1960 (or) Initial Figure	1971 (or) Final Figure	Index of Growth	Average Percent Change
5. Primary Beneficiaries	ACE	public attendance at recreation areas	109,000,000	300,000,000	2.8	9.7
	AEC	# nuclear powerplants licensed to operate	2	21	10.5	34.6
	AID	# participant trainees	8,121	7,198	.89	-1.0
	CCC	Missing Data				
	FAA	# airmen certificates held (pilot)	348,060	733,000	2.1	7.9
	NASA	# patent waivers granted	9	8	.89	115.6
	OE	# eligible applicants for PL81-874	3,797	4,628	1.2	1.8
	VA	# patients treated in VA hospitals	111,410	84,002	.75	-2.5
6. Potential Beneficiaries	ACE	Missing Data				
	AEC	# contractor & construction design employees	11,199	8,554	.76	-1.6
	AID	# less developed countries participating in investment insurance programs	55	91	1.7	7.5
	CCC	total farm population (thousands)	15,635	9,425	.60	-4.5
	FAA	# all airports/airfields recorded with FAA	6,426	11,261	1.8	5.3
	NASA	Missing Data				
	OE	enrollment in public institutions of higher education	2,100,000	6,200,000	2.9	10.3
	VA	# living veterans	24,000,000	28,000,000	1.2	1.7

a. The acquisition of physical resources was assumed to occur later in time than other functional actions. Data for these functional actions were therefore lagged one year behind data for delivery of benefits and target beneficiaries (which were assumed to occur in the same fiscal year as budgetary actions).

NASA) of the very rapid growth the agencies experienced in the earlier years of the study. Because the magnitude of this early growth was considerable, the agencies (particularly OE) still appear in a relatively favorable position in terms of functional actions.

The FAA and ACE are fortunate agencies in experiencing positive yearly change and overall growth on every functional action measure. While their yearly changes were less dramatic (more stable) than those for NASA, they generally experienced greater overall growth. The AEC also experienced a degree of stability, but unfortunately for the agency, the results were mixed on each of the three categories of functional actions. While the AEC generally experienced incremental changes similar to FAA and ACE, they tended to be moderately negative, resulting in overall decline in the agency's functional actions.

AID exhibits moderately positive change and growth on acquisition of physical facilities but mixed behavior on delivery of benefits and target beneficiaries served. Its substantial growth in activities performed and potential clientele may assist AID in its relative position in the future.

The VA experienced yearly decreases and overall decline in both types of physical resources. While the same pattern exists for field personnel utilized, the agency is making a greater effort in activities performed. The VA also had a conflicting experience on the two measures of beneficiaries served, with growth experienced for potential beneficiaries and decline for primary clientele. This increase in the number of living veterans may be more a function of health patterns rather than increasing numbers of entrants into the military. If this proves to be the case, then the eventual impact on the agency will not be as favorable as the figures on potential beneficiaries first appear.

THE RELATIONSHIP OF BUDGETARY AND FUNCTIONAL ACTIONS

BIVARIATE ANALYSIS

Table 5–3 presents the correlations for percent change in appropriations with functional actions and percent change in expenditures with functional actions for agencies combined. These figures certainly do not provide conclusive support for the assumed relationship between budgetary actions and functional actions. Only eight of the 24 relationships meet the confirmation criterion, and many of the 24 relationships are negative (only 16 were in the proper direction). Both of the measures of budgetary actions seemed to have the same effect on the dependent variables in terms of number of confirmations—there were four significant relationships

TABLE 5-3. Correlations Between Budgetary Actions and Functional Actions for All Agencies Combined

	Percent Change in:	
Functional Actions	*Appropriations*	*Expenditures*
Change in:		
Field Installations	.37*	.19
Beneficial Facilities	−.08	.45*
Activities Performed	.07	.01
Personnel Utilized	.71*	.69*
Primary Beneficiaries	−.07	−.13
Potential Beneficiaries	.23*	.14
Growth in:		
Field Installations	.10	.07
Beneficial Facilities	−.16	.09
Activities Performed	−.14	−.10
Personnel Utilized	.12	.23*
Primary Beneficiaries	−.14	−.22*
Potential Beneficiaries	.23*	.21*
Total Number of Confirmations[a]	4	4

a. An asterisk (*) indicates a "significant" correlation coefficient, but not necessarily a confirmation. To confirm, the coefficient must have had the predicted sign and be greater than .20.

between percent change in appropriations and functional actions measures, and four between percent change in expenditures and the functional actions measures. Neither of the budgetary measures seemed to relate more to either the growth or change measures of the functional actions. Overall, the number of significant relationships is smaller than expected, and the magnitude of the significant relationships is also less than expected. However, the figures in Table 5–3 do support the statement that there is a tendency for budgetary actions (as measured by percent change in appropriations and expenditures) to be positively correlated with change and growth in functional actions.

This tendency is only slight, however, especially since the strongest observed relationships may be due to other factors. For example, the largest coefficients exist between both of the budgetary measures and personnel utilized. There is obviously a relationship between agency size and number of personnel utilized, and it has been shown in other chapters that agency size is related to budgetary actions.

The figures in Table 5–3 might be challenged by one who argues that the use of standardized measures of budgetary actions is distorting a relationship between dollars and functional actions. To test this possibility, correlations between the raw values of appropriations and expenditures with the 12 measures of functional actions were computed. These correlations showed that the raw values of budgetary actions were even less related to functional actions than the standardized measures—only five of the 24 relationships were significant ($\geq$.20) and these were of low magnitude.

The general conclusion to be drawn at this point in the discussion is inescapably that there is only a minimal relationship between budgetary and functional actions, at least when agencies are combined. A few more specific statements can be made, however. There does appear to be a positive relationship between both budgetary variables and field installations, between expenditures and beneficial facilities, and between both measures and potential beneficiaries. Even though the coefficients are small, there is a consistent negative relationship between budgetary measures and primary beneficiaries. Although this was not expected, it may be the result of agencies making a greater effort to acquire clientele support when they are experiencing budgetary stability.

Do the low correlations in Table 5–3 mask variation between individual agencies? The correlations between budgetary and functional actions were calculated for each agency separately and are presented in Tables 5–4 and 5–5 (see p. 108). These tables indicate that there is a considerable amount of variation in the correlations for individual agencies, but no pattern among agencies or variables is apparent. The principal features of the data in these tables are summarized in Table 5–6 (see p. 109). This table shows, for each independent variable, the number of cases (agencies) that confirmed, disconfirmed, or showed no relationship to the research hypothesis.

As is evident in Table 5–6 (and also Tables 5–4 and 5–5), the relationship between budgetary actions and functional actions is not improved when agencies are disaggregated. Neither percent change in appropriations nor percent change in expenditures showed a consistent relationship to the measures of functional actions. Overall, there were more disconfirming cases than confirming cases for each independent variable. Neither variable came close to having a majority of confirming cases, although percent change in expenditures had more such cases (30 out of 78) than percent change in appropriations (18 out of 78). Both variables showed more confirming cases with respect to the change measures of functional actions than with respect to the growth measures.

Some specific findings deserve mention. The independent variables both tend to be positively related to change measures of delivery of benefits, but negatively related to growth in acquisition of physical resources and primary beneficiaries served. Thus, agencies experiencing high magnitude budget changes seem to increase their activities and personnel and therefore their capability to deliver benefits. Agencies demonstrating budgetary stability (low magnitude change) appear to retrench themselves into acquiring physical resources and in seeking additional (immediate rather than future) clientele support.

TABLE 5-4. Correlations between Percent Change in Appropriations and Functional Actions

| Agency | Acquisition of Physical Resources | | | |
| | *Field Installations* | | *Beneficial Facilities* | |
	Change	Growth	Change	Growth
ACE	−.16	−.32*	.51*	−.35*
AEC	.23*	−.08	−.00	−.25*
AID	.55*	.18	MD	MD
CCC	MD	MD	MD	MD
FAA	−.14	.08	.10	−.00
NASA	.73*	−.56*	.29*	−.45*
OE	.38*	.02	−.31*	−.30*
VA	−.03	−.61*	−.10	−.47*

| Agency | Delivery of Benefits | | | |
| | *Activities Performed* | | *Personnel Utilized* | |
	Change	Growth	Change	Growth
ACE	.11	−.26*	MD	MD
AEC	−.25*	−.04	.38*	.05
AID	.40*	.10	.05	−.45*
CCC	−.08	−.12	MD	MD
FAA	−.04	−.15	.19	.02
NASA	.60*	−.31*	.87*	−.91*
OE	.54*	−.16	MD	MD
VA	.09	.48*	.28*	.31*

| Agency | Target Beneficiaries Served | | | |
| | *Primary Beneficiaries* | | *Potential Beneficiaries* | |
	Change	Growth	Change	Growth
ACE	.10	−.31*	MD	MD
AEC	−.09	−.22*	.33*	.37*
AID	−.03	−.39*	.08	−.31*
CCC	MD	MD	−.42*	.02
FAA	−.03	.15	.08	−.05
NASA	.09	−.25*	MD	MD
OE	−.15	−.15	.67*	.01
VA	−.33*	−.64*	−.09	.53*

* indicates coefficients achieving the arbitrary criterion of significance (± .20).
MD indicates data were not available for the variable.

MULTIVARIATE ANALYSIS

Multiple regression analysis was used to determine whether the relationships observed during bivariate analysis persisted when several budgetary variables were simultaneously related to functional actions. Two additional budgetary action variables (appropriations success and agency expenditures as a percent of the total federal budget) were included in the analysis to see if other budgetary variables would also have a small re-

TABLE 5-5. Correlations between Percent Change in Expenditures and Functional Actions

Agency	Acquisition of Physical Resources			
	Field Installations		*Beneficial Facilities*	
	Change	Growth	Change	Growth
ACE	−.42*	−.32*	.54*	−.23*
AEC	−.20*	−.31*	−.55*	−.63*
AID	−.17	−.21*	MD	MD
CCC	MD	MD	MD	MD
FAA	−.14	.38*	−.23*	.33*
NASA	.84*	−.10	.21*	−.42*
OE	−.14	−.60*	.59*	.02
VA	−.61*	−.70*	−.30*	−.67*

Agency	Delivery of Benefits			
	Activities Performed		*Personnel Utilized*	
	Change	Growth	Change	Growth
ACE	−.13	−.15	MD	MD
AEC	.06	−.04	.22*	−.04
AID	.55*	.37*	.45*	−.31*
CCC	−.17	.43*	MD	MD
FAA	−.44*	−.23*	.29*	−.54*
NASA	.51*	.05	.72*	−.71*
OE	−.15	−.13	MD	MD
VA	.35*	.50*	.79*	.59*

Agency	Target Beneficiaries Served			
	Primary Beneficiaries		*Potential Beneficiaries*	
	Change	Growth	Change	Growth
ACE	.28*	−.18	MD	MD
AEC	.24*	−.46*	.64*	.51*
AID	.44*	.16	.38*	−.60*
CCC	MD	MD	.22*	.07
FAA	−.39*	.40*	−.23*	.29*
NASA	−.31*	−.35*	MD	MD
OE	−.29*	−.25*	−.21*	−.03
VA	−.53*	.68*	−.01	.59*

* indicates the coefficient achieves the arbitrary criterion of significance (± .20).
MD indicates that data were not available for the variable.

lationship to functional actions. These new variables were statistically unrelated to percent change in appropriations and expenditures and thus were believed to measure different dimensions of budgetary policy actions.

Table 5–7 (see p. 110) presents the results of the regression analysis. It was expected from the bivariate correlation coefficients that the two budgetary change variables generally would contribute a larger share of the variance in the model. The figures demonstrate that the relative im-

TABLE 5-6. Confirmation of the Research Hypothesis: Summary of Individual Agency Correlations between Budgetary and Functional Actions

	Percent Change in Appropriations					Percent Change in Expenditures				
	Confirm[a]	Dis-confirm[b]	No Relationship[c]	No Data	(N)	Confirm[a]	Dis-confirm[b]	No Relationship[c]	No Data	(N)
Change in:										
Field Installations	4	0	3	1	8	1	3	3	1	8
Beneficial Facilities	2	1	3	2	8	3	3	0	2	8
Activities Performed	3	1	4	0	8	3	1	4	0	8
Personnel Utilized	3	0	2	3	8	5	0	0	3	8
Primary Beneficiaries	0	1	6	1	8	3	4	0	1	8
Potential Beneficiaries	2	1	3	2	8	3	2	1	2	8
Subtotal	14	4	21	9	48	18	13	8	9	48
Growth in:										
Field Installations	0	3	4	1	8	1	5	1	1	8
Beneficial Facilities	0	5	1	2	8	1	4	1	2	8
Activities Performed	1	2	5	0	8	3	1	4	0	8
Personnel Utilized	1	2	2	3	8	1	3	1	3	8
Primary Beneficiaries	0	5	2	1	8	2	3	2	1	8
Potential Beneficiaries	2	1	3	2	8	3	1	2	2	8
Subtotal	4	18	17	9	48	11	17	11	9	48
Total	18	22	38	18	96	29	30	19	18	96

a. A case was counted as confirming if the sign of the correlation coefficient was in the proper direction and the magnitude was equal to or greater than .20.

b. A case was counted as disconfirming if the sign of the coefficient was not in the proper direction and the magnitude was equal to or greater than .20.

c. No relationship was said to exist if the magnitude of the coefficient was less than .20 regardless of the sign.

TABLE 5-7. Regression Model for Budgetary and Functional Policy Actions (Standardized Beta Coefficients)

Functional Actions	% Δ App	% Δ Exp	Success	% Federal Budget	$R^2 =$ Variance Explained
Change in:					
Field Installations	.32	.10	−.19	−.15	20%
Beneficial Facilities	−.28	.56	−.17	−.05	29%
Activities Performed	.06 ·	.01	−.17	−.01	4%
Personnel Utilized	.55	−.08	.21	.48	79%
Primary Beneficiaries	−.02	−.12	.01	.11	3%
Potential Beneficiaries	.19	.08	−.03	−.17	9%
Growth in:					
Field Installations	.04	.08	−.21	−.28	14%
Beneficial Facilities	−.24	.19	−.22	−.14	12%
Activities Performed	−.17	.00	−.43	−.07	21%
Personnel Utilized	.07	.18	.04	.21	9%
Primary Beneficiaries	−.08	−.20	.05	−.13	7%
Potential Beneficiaries	.16	.17	−.04	−.19	11%

portance of a particular budgetary variable depends to a considerable extent on the functional action to which one is referring. Percent change in appropriations and expenditures each contribute the preponderance of variance to change in particular functional actions, and in each instance the relationship is positive. Specifically, percent change in appropriations is related to field installations and personnel utilized, and percent change in expenditures to beneficial facilities. Expenditures as a percent of the total federal budget and budget success were generally negatively related to functional actions, most prominently with both change and growth in field installations and potential beneficiaries for the former, and field installations and activities performed for the latter.

It is evident from the table that even the four variables combined explain little variance in functional actions. In those instances where at least a minimal threshold of variance is explained (20%), the variables generally are better at predicting change rather than growth measures.

In conclusion, results of regression analysis are not very different from correlation in finding that budgetary actions are generally not highly related to functional actions. The inclusion of two new and unrelated budgetary variables lends even further confidence to this statement. In only one instance do the four budgetary actions explain more than 30% of the variance in functional actions, and in this instance the close relationship of the functional action (change in personnel utilized) to the structural variable agency size may be partially responsible for this high figure.

Summary and Implications

This study has shown that the relationship between agency budgets and their functional actions is not as strong or extensive as has been commonly assumed. The findings indicate that there is generally a small, positive relationship between budgetary and functional actions. Agencies experiencing large budget change tend to increase delivery of benefits, while agencies experiencing budget stability tend to acquire physical resources and serve primary beneficiaries.

In addition, the relatively large proportion of cases in which change in agency budgets was greater than ±10% suggests that the standard assumptions about the incremental nature of agency budgeting need to be reexamined. The instances of nonincremental change occurred both for appropriations and expenditures, although expenditures were found to be more incremental than appropriations. (Chapters 3 and 4 explore the incrementalist treatment of budgeting in more detail, as does Shull, 1974.)

In terms of functional actions, it has been shown in this chapter that many of the activities in which agencies engage are interrelated. More specifically, agencies tend to acquire physical resources to enable them to deliver benefits or services to particular clientele groups in society. In spite of this similarity among many of the functional actions when agencies were combined, considerable differences exist when agencies are considered separately.

IMPLICATIONS FOR AGENCIES

Overall, agencies that experienced the greatest change in appropriations and expenditures also showed the greatest change and growth in functional actions. However, because this relationship is not particularly strong (at least for this sample of agencies), the advice to agency personnel based on this finding must be guarded. In general, although seeking high budgetary change may entail risks, in the long run the agency that does so is likely to experience development in its functional actions.

A need exists in policy research to direct attention to variables that are manipulable by policy-makers (Williams, 1971:14, 54). Common sense indicates that certain factors are more subject to influence and control by agency personnel than others. In Figure 5–3 I have presented some impressionistic judgments about the controllability of a variety of concepts used here and in another study (Shull, 1974). This figure is useful not only for its placement of one concept relative to another, but also because

FIGURE 5-3: MANIPULABILITY OF VARIABLES BY AGENCY PERSONNEL

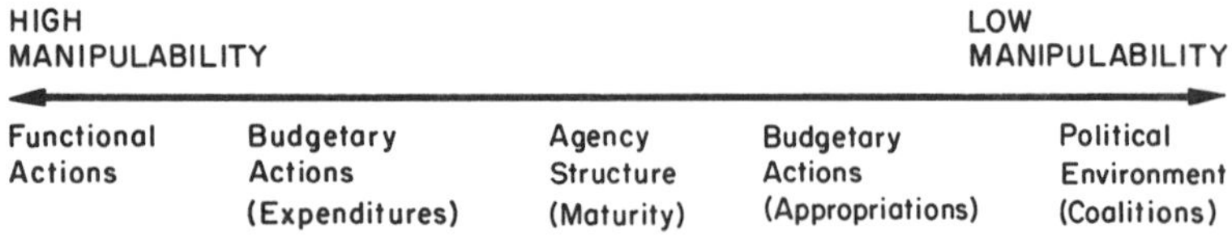

HIGH MANIPULABILITY				LOW MANIPULABILITY
Functional Actions	Budgetary Actions (Expenditures)	Agency Structure (Maturity)	Budgetary Actions (Appropriations)	Political Environment (Coalitions)

it lends support to the notion that many of the widely researched areas in public policy to date have dealt with concepts least subject to control by agency personnel. Roherty (1970) may be right in saying that social scientists are not sympathetic to the constraints under which decision-makers operate.

While the placement of concepts on the scale in Figure 5–3 is somewhat arbitrary, it is not without some theoretical and empirical rationale. (For a fuller justification of the ranking, see the findings reported in Shull, 1974.) Since budgetary decisions (appropriations) involve governmental actors other than the agency, the agency appears to be more at the mercy of these outside institutions than it is in subsequent program (or implementing) decisions. Fritschler (1969) demonstrated that the bureaucracy has been delegated considerable authority by Congress. The President is also largely removed from questions of administrative policy (Truman, 1969). Ripley (1972a, 1972b) has shown that presidential and congressional influence in bureaucratic policy-making is greatest at the same stage—in policy decisions rather than subsequent program choices. This literature lends some confidence to the assertion of greater agency control in later stages of policy-making (functional actions).

The rankings in Figure 5–3 are not rigid, and within a given concept there are different degrees of control. For example, expenditures and appropriations rank differently even though they are both budgetary policy actions. This is primarily because expenditures are less encumbered by influences from other institutions (Wildavsky, 1964: 123–125).

This study has shown that agency ability to manipulate functional actions is not greatly constrained by their budgetary experiences. Thus, functional actions are ranked higher than budgetary actions. This does not mean, however, that agencies have unlimited flexibility in their activities subsequent to budget actions. It has been shown elsewhere (Shull, 1974) that other factors (agency maturity and governmental coalitions) do constrain agency activities both in terms of budgeting and functional activities.

IMPLICATIONS FOR RESEARCH

The principal contribution of the present study to the policy research framework developed in Chapter 1 has been the exploration and testing of nonbudgetary indicators of agency policy actions. These functional (or implementing) policy actions provide insight into the nature and scope of agency activities that goes beyond mere size of agency budgets and simple dollar measures of those activities. Naturally, a complete test of the entire research framework using functional actions was beyond the scope of this chapter, but a fuller exploration of the relationship of functional actions to a variety of independent variables is available elsewhere (Shull, 1974).

Attention to the functional actions of agencies is important because these are the activities over which the agency has greatest control, and because they have a direct effect on the lives of citizens, both beneficiaries and nonbeneficiaries. Attention to functional actions is imperative if one is to evaluate the societal impact of agency programs (policy results). Thus, analysis of functional actions is a prerequisite to the assessment of policy results.

Notes

1. The relationship between percent change in appropriations and percent change in expenditures in the same year is $r = .34$; when expenditures is lagged one year after appropriations, the relationship is $r = .30$.
2. Why is the agency level used rather than focusing on the department or the program? Natchez and Bupp (1973) make a persuasive case for programs rather than agencies as units of analysis. It is true, as they point out, that "program" budgets aggregated to the agency level may mask a great deal of variation that is occurring within an agency. Thus, they contend that the appearance of stability and incrementalism of agency budgets is far less in reality than it appears. The same argument could be made for aggregating agency budgets to the departmental level, and it is clear that agencies within a department (just as programs within an agency) may fare very differently in budgeting. However, it is argued here that decision-makers (particularly congressmen and the President) think more in agency than in department terms, and that the department (with the exception of Defense) has little influence or effect on agency budget success. Although the program level might better explain nuances in budgeting, the data sought for this research were primarily available for the agency level only.
3. The correlational and regression techniques incorporated here both assume a linear relationship among the variables. It is likely, however, that some of

the relationships are not linear, and more extensive use of nonlinear techniques is contemplated for future research.

4. Cursory examination of standard error in the regression models demonstrated that error was generally smaller than the standardized betas and thus was probably minimal.

Appendix

TABLE 5-8. Intercorrelation of Standardized Functional Policy Actions

	Change in:						Growth in:					
	FI	BF	AP	PU	Pr.B.	Pot.B.	FI	BF	AP	PU	Pr.B.	Pot.B.
Change in:												
FI	—											
BF	.54*	—										
AP	-.23*	-.22*	—									
PU	.25*	.30*	.06	—								
Pr.B.	-.16	-.03	-.04	.11	—							
Pot.B.	.19	.09	.11	.14	-.12	—						
Growth in:												
FI	.65*	.32*	-.09	.11	.01	.17	—					
BF	.51*	.60*	-.40*	.00	.24*	.06	.75*	—				
AP	.07	-.08	.19	.08	-.06	.21*	.10	.04	—			
PU	-.03	.11	-.08	.23*	.40*	.11	.34*	.54*	-.12	—		
Pr.B.	-.19	-.11	-.06	-.12	.32*	-.12	-.18	-.03	-.19	-.02	—	
Pot.B.	.59*	.39*	-.04	.18	-.08	.51*	.76*	.45*	.05	.61*	-.35*	—

FI   — Field Installations
BF   — Beneficial Facilities
AP   — Activities Performed
PU   — Personnel Utilized
Pr.B. — Primary Beneficiaries
Pot.B. — Potential Beneficiaries

An asterisk indicates coefficient meets criterion of "significance" (±.20).

115

6

Structure, Environment, and Policy Actions: An Empirical Exploration

Randall B. Ripley, Grace A. Franklin,
William M. Holmes, and William B. Moreland

This chapter relates four kinds of independent variables—agency maturity, partisan strength in the electorate, economic conditions, and previous policy actions—to budgetary policy actions as the dependent variable. Data for ten federal agencies varying widely in number of employees, size of budgets, and range of programmatic activities were collected for the time period from fiscal 1952 through 1971. The longitudinal analysis involved three separate tests: a trend analysis, a subsample test for interactive effects, and a path analysis. The findings from this study show that all of the categories of independent variables have explanatory power; all of the research hypotheses are generally supported. The findings also support the concept of a life cycle of agencies: while agencies are younger, their policy actions (and the latitude for action) are increasing. The relationship reverses as agencies get older ("senile"), and shrinking of policy actions sets in. In middle age agencies experience stability in their policy actions and latitude for actions at a high level.

117

THIS CHAPTER uses three different analytical techniques (longitudinal trend analysis, a subsample test for interactive effects, and longitudinal path analysis) in a limited test of four hypotheses—three of which are discussed in Chapter 1 and one of which is treated as an assumption in Chapter 1.

The Nature of the Empirical Test

HYPOTHESES

H1. **The less mature an agency, the greater the changes in its policy actions—usually in the direction of increasing government activity. (The more mature an agency, the less the changes in its policy actions.)**

H2. **As the Democratic party gains strength in the electorate, changes in policy actions coming from agencies are greater, usually in the direction of increased government activity. (As the Democratic Party loses strength in the electorate, changes in policy actions coming from agencies are less, including some changes in the direction of decreased government activity.)**

H3. **As economic conditions change more rapidly, changes in policy actions coming from agencies are greater. (As economic conditions change less rapidly, changes in policy actions coming from agencies are less.)**

H4. **Changes in policy actions cannot be explained solely on the basis of previous actions.**

OPERATIONALIZATION

The preceding hypotheses require that four concepts be operationalized: agency maturity, partisan strength, economic conditions, and policy actions. Table 6–1 summarizes the indicators used for each of these concepts and also includes abbreviations for each of them. The following paragraphs discuss the concepts in detail. Specific indicators chosen for operationalizing these concepts are also discussed.

AGENCY MATURITY

This concept encompasses numerous dimensions that have been explored in a great range of literature about organizations (see, for

TABLE 6-1. A Summary of Indicators for Concepts[a]

Concept	Indicator
1. Agency Maturity	a. Number of years since creation of agency (AGE)
	b. Number of employees in the agency (SIZE)
	c. Number of supergrade employees in the agency (SG)
	d. Number of middlegrade employees in the agency (MG)
2. Partisan Strength	a. Percent of the two-party vote for all Democratic candidates for the House of Representatives (DV)
3. Economic Conditions	a. Percent unemployed civilians in the labor force (UE)
4. Policy Actions	a. Annual appropriations to the agency (APP)
	b. Annual expenditures of the agency (EXP)

a. Abbreviations for the indicators that are used throughout this text are contained in parentheses.

example, Blau and Scott, 1962; Blau and Schoenherr, 1971; Weber, 1946; Downs, 1967). A central notion in that literature is that as agencies mature they get more complex, more stable, more experienced, and better able to cope with their environment. It is also asserted that at some point in time organizational senility sets in.

We selected indicators (admittedly crude ones) to measure three of the dimensions of maturity mentioned in Chapter 1 (age, size, and hierarchical complexity).

We have defined agency age in a strict calendar sense as being the number of years elapsed since the agency's creation. (Data for this indicator come from the *Government Organization Manual* and the *U.S. Codes.*)

Agency size has been defined as the number of employees in an agency (more specifically, the number of permanent full-time positions in an agency). (Data for this indicator were collected from the *Appendices to the Budget of the U.S. Government* or from materials supplied by the budget or personnel offices of the agencies themselves.)

To begin to explore the concept of hierarchical complexity, we used two separate indicators: the number of middlegrade employees in an agency and the number of supergrade employees in an agency. (Middlegrades are employees with a rank of GS 13, 14, or 15 plus their equivalents in salary terms; supergrades are employees with a rank of GS 16, 17, or 18 plus their equivalents in salary terms. Data on the number of middlegrades and supergrades were collected from the *Budget Appendix* or from materials supplied by the agencies.) Our assumption was that as the numbers of middlegrades and supergrades increases, the hierarchical complexity of the agency was likely to be increasing.

Because of data limitations, we did not attempt to measure functional complexity or administrative experience. For the same reasons we did not attempt to combine the indicators of the other three concepts to form a single index of maturity. Each indicator was treated separately in the tests; the question of whether or not they were jointly tapping the dimension of maturity was left unexplored.

PARTY STRENGTH

Partisanship both in society and in the government is important in explaining public policy (see, for example, Downs, 1957; Dye, 1966; Rossiter, 1960; Campbell et al., 1960; Sundquist, 1968; and Key, 1949, 1966). In this empirical test we chose to look only at partisan strength in the electorate. Key (1966) has demonstrated that voters make choices based on their own policy preferences. Both Key and Scammon and Wattenberg (1970) have also shown the size of the vote for a party's candidate for President is related to voter acceptance or rejection of the policies proposed and/or pursued by the parties.

For our purposes a measure that taps this policy-related behavior of the electorate is preferable to the alternative of forming aggregate scales derived from dispositional items (partisanship or issue area feeling of a respondent) in national opinion surveys. The mean percent of the Democratic party vote for the House of Representatives was chosen for this reason. The Democratic party vote is defined as the mean district vote for all Democratic candidates for the House of Representatives. (Data for this indicator were calculated using information gathered from the *Congressional Directory*.)

ECONOMIC CONDITIONS

A widespread appreciation of the importance of economic conditions to the nature of governmental policy exists in the literature on policy (see, for example, Burns, 1956; Donovan, 1967; Ripley, 1972a; Sundquist, 1968; Dye, 1966), and, partially as a result of this attitude, economic conditions are extensively monitored and statistically mapped by many agencies of the government. There exists a wide range of indicators on economic conditions in both the theoretical and empirical literature. The percent of the unemployed labor force is one of the most popular measures because of the availability of data and the fit between this indicator and economic health (see, for example, Flax, 1972; Sundquist, 1968). The decision to use this indicator was influenced by our findings in attempting to construct an aggregate scale of economic conditions for other purposes. Percent unemployment, number of new housing starts annually, personal income saved, private investment as a percent of GNP, and per capita income were found to be intercorrelated at a fairly high level, thus we felt justified in using percent unemployed as a rough index of economic conditions. (Data on unemployment were collected from the monthly publication of the Council of Economic Advisers, *Economic Indicators*.)

POLICY ACTIONS

There are numerous ways to measure policy actions, many of which involve extremely complicated data collection problems. For this test we chose two fairly accessible measures of policy actions; annual agency appropriations and expenditures. Despite the importance of Congress in determining both figures (appropriations more directly than expenditures), it is both customary and appropriate to use these as measures of agency actions (see, for example, Fenno, 1966; Wildavsky, 1964). Agencies, after all, need not merely await congressional action passively; the level of their own aggressiveness also helps determine the amount of money available to them (Sharkansky, 1965). We chose appropriations and expenditures not only because the data problems were less severe, but also because these budgetary items represent broader allocative and priority decisions.

The figures collected for agency appropriations represent only the amount found in the agency's "regular" annual bill. No supplemental, special, or deficiency appropriations were included [except for two years in which the regular appropriation bill for an agency (the AEC) was stalled and the agency received its regular funds in a supplemental bill]. The data on expenditures for the agencies represent all federal funds expended (this figure excludes expenditures from trust fund accounts as well as expenditures for salaries and expenses). The appropriation data were collected from the *Congressional Quarterly Almanac* and the *Appropriations, Budget Estimates, Etc.,* an annual Senate document. The expenditure data were collected from the *Budget of the U.S. Government*.

We realize that there are some objections to using raw dollar values rather than a standardized value to measure agencies' policy actions. However, we adhere to the use of raw dollar values for part of our analysis for two reasons. First, developing a standardized value comparable between agencies and across time is beset with almost as many problems as using the raw values alone. Second, the substantive interest of the study is in explaining actual dollar appropriations.

Problems of developing an adequate standardized measure are numerous. If the standardizing transformation does not have clear theoretical meaning, then the interpretation of the standardizèd score is confused. A transformed appropriation figure may have a very different meaning than the raw appropriation figure. In fact, bias can be introduced into the results if all of the theoretical implications of a transformation are not clear. Since a major reason for transforming data is to eliminate bias in the data, one would have to be relatively certain that the standardized score eliminated the suspected bias and did not introduce biases of its own. The authors have not found a standardizing transformation that has theoretical interpretability, that eliminates bias between different agencies, and that does not introduce bias of its own. In the absence of any good standardizing transformation raw values are used.

Raw dollar values also happen to be a principal variable to be explained by this study. If we want to know what causes raw dollar values, we must study raw values. Also, since most of the "incrementalist" studies of appropriations use raw dollar values, our findings would not be comparable to theirs unless we use raw figures. In challenging the methodology and findings of the previous studies, the use of raw dollar values is necessary to show what happens when different methods are used.

CHANGE MEASURES

Early in this study it became evident that in addition to dealing with the simple raw values of indicators, change measures for these indicators could and should be employed, especially for the dependent variables. (The literature on budgeting, especially on the incremental nature of budgeting, supports the contention that federal managers are very sensitive to changes in the size of their agency and their budget, and they think as much in terms of percent differences from a baseline as they do in terms of raw numbers of dollars and people.)

Three dimensions of change are of general interest to us: the direction of change (increasing to decreasing), the magnitude of change (large to small), and the rate of change (fast to slow). Numerous measures of these dimensions are available and include percent differences, raw differences, ratios, acceleration functions, and residual deviates from predictions among others. (See Bohrnstedt, 1969, Duncan et al., 1961, and Harris, 1963, for general discussions of different change measures.) For the present paper we have chosen two measures that both have relatively few statistical biasing problems (when compared to other possible measures) and also allow us to focus most clearly on the policy questions that interest us.

The first measure is a lagged ratio value: the value of a variable in a given year (t_1) is divided by the value of the variable in the preceding year (t_0). We call this measure the *magnitude of change* (MAG) and express it as X_{t1}/X_{t0}: If X_{t1} is less than X_{t0}, then the ratio value will be less than one. If X_{t1} is greater than X_{t0}, then the ratio will be greater than one. The possible values of the ratio range from zero to infinity. The ratio value can be converted to a percentage figure by subtracting one from it. The direction of change in the raw value of X_t from some previous value of X would ordinarily be apparent from the sign of the change associated with the raw values. Using MAG, a decrease in relative value is indicated by a value of less than one, and an increase is indicated by a value greater than one.

The second measure is a lagged difference ratio. The difference in variable value in a base year (t_1) and the succeeding year (t_2) is divided by the difference in variable value in the base year (t_1) and the preceding year (t_0). This measure reflects the *rate of change* (RATE) and can be expressed as $(X_{t2} - X_{t1})/(X_{t1} - X_{t0})$. The rate of change measure has a range from negative infinity to infinity. Negative values mean the variable is reversing its previous direction of change. Zero values mean that changes in the variable occur at a constant rate with no acceleration, deceleration, or reversals of direction. Positive values mean that increases or decreases occur more rapidly than before.

We have selected these two measures for three reasons. First, the different information offered by the two allows us to speak with more confidence about the problems that interest us than would the use of either alone.

Second, we avoided raw value change measures (such as gain scores and residual deviates from prediction) because they generally produce unreliable statistical estimates. The unreliable estimates basically result from the high autocorrelation of variables frequently used in longitudinal policy studies. In this study we found autocorrelation among agency appropriations, expenditures, and size.[1]

Third, the two measures selected are most congenial to the questions we are posing about agency budgets. MAG measures how large the change is relative to the raw value of the previous year. Since we are interested in whether changes from base figures are large or small, this relative magnitude of change measure is appropriate.

RATE measures how rapid or slow change is in a given direction (acceleration or deceleration as distinguished from a reversal in direction of change). Since we are also interested in whether change in a policy is continuing to accelerate or decelerate at a constant rate or whether the direction of change is reversing, this measure is appropriate to our study.

For the present study we have limited the application of change measures to four variables (SIZE, SG, MG, and APP) in the subsample test for interactive effects. In Chapter 7 we expand the use of change measures to include more variables and additional techniques, including path analysis.

DATA BASE

Time-series data spanning fiscal years from 1952 through 1971 were collected for ten agencies of the federal government. Those agencies were: Rural Electrification Administration (REA) within the Department of Agriculture; the National Cancer Institute (NCI) and National Institute of Mental Health (NIMH), both within the Department of Health, Education and Welfare; the U.S. Information Agency (USIA; 1955 is the first year of the study for this agency) within the State Department; and six independent agencies: Veterans' Administration (VA), Federal Aviation Administration (FAA; prior to 1959, data for the Civil Aeronautics Administration were used); Civil Aeronautics Board (CAB); Federal Trade Commission (FTC); Interstate Commerce Commission (ICC); and the Atomic Energy Commission (AEC).

These agencies were selected for a variety of reasons—intrinsic interest, variability in work force and size of budget (the range of total employment is from less than 1,000 to more than 170,000 and the range in budget authority is from about $3 million to more than $9 billion), variability in substantive concerns, and availability of good data. We do not claim that these agencies represent a probability sample of all federal agencies. A probability sample was not used because there would be disagreement among specialists in bureaucracy on the nature of the universe from which to draw a sample. Because we have found similar results using other agencies, we have a high degree of confidence that the findings using any ten or more federal agencies (with any consistent definition of agency) would not vary significantly from what we have found. However, the latter assertion is, of course, subject to empirical testing. But until that testing can take place, we realize that scientific enterprises always produce tentative findings; nevertheless, the importance and utility of the findings in hand need not be dismissed because of their tentativeness.

Methodology

Methodologically, we have focused on time-series (or longitudinal) analysis. This focus was chosen because of both the nature of our hypotheses and the methodological advantages of the orientation. We chose three specific applications of longitudinal analysis: (1) trend analysis, (2) a subsample test for interactive effects, and (3) path analysis. These techniques are discussed in the Methodological Glossary.

In our hypotheses we are broadly concerned with the effects of organizational "maturation" and environmental conditions upon change in policy actions. Time-series analysis is important in the study of what happens to Executive branch agencies as they mature. We do not assume that the variables that affect an agency remain stable over time, but rather that they vary systematically with the "environmental" conditions—including social and economic conditions. A cross section of time for the environment will have key variables constant for all agencies. While this is useful for controlling the effects of the environment, it is not good for studying the effects of environment on public policy. The only way one can study the effects of some environmental conditions is by use of time-series data. The methodological advantages of time-series analysis have been widely discussed. In addition to permitting a study of "environmental effects," time-series analysis can help to separate systematic error from random error in the prediction equations (Coleman, 1968; Heise, 1970). It allows measuring the proper time lags between variables that do not affect each other instantaneously (Bohrnstedt, 1969) and provides information on the directionality of effects between variables when this may be in doubt (Bohrnstedt, 1969; Heise, 1970). Campbell and Stanley (1963) have noted that a longitudinal design can be used as a quasi-experimental design subject to fewer problems than a static group comparison. This advantage is especially important if one wants to study the results of policy action when it is not possible to set up an experimental design. Longitudinal information can also be used in relating historical analysis to quantitative studies.

One problem with time-series analysis is that the data acquired seem subject to an insoluble sampling problem. One can do a systematic across time sample for finite time segments (such as every year for a 20-year period), but cyclic phenomena may introduce systematic bias in the sample. Events unique to the time segment sampled may also have a biasing effect. Yet, it is impossible to do a probability sample of the universe across time since many data are only reported annually and sometimes not at all. This, however, mainly affects the external validity of the study. We cannot generalize about all U.S. Executive branch agencies for all time. We can generalize about the agencies under study for the period involved; and we can continue collecting data for other agencies and expand the generalizability of the findings to an indefinite (but not infinite) degree.

Findings and Interpretation

A. LONGITUDINAL TREND ANALYSIS

The inspection of regression equations was used for the basic purpose of examining the effects of organizational aging on policy actions and on other attributes of maturity. The literature insists that aging is important (see, for example, Downs, 1967), and we wished to look at the matter empirically. Some clear findings emerged (see Table 6–4 in the appendix to this chapter for the statistics supporting these findings).

A–1. As agencies get older they get richer in terms of both appropriations and expenditures. This certainly is an expected finding. It simply means that agencies in general grow budgetarily over time. It also implies that the range of agency actions in general grows with age. Since the governmental budget itself was growing constantly during the period under study, it would be surprising if another finding emerged, unless the period had also been one of an extraordinary number of creations of new agencies and phasing out of old agencies. This finding suggests that no such pattern existed from 1952 through 1971 (an inspection of materials such as *Congressional Quarterly Almanac* and the *Government Organization Manual* lends support to this statement).

A–2. As agencies get older, the magnitude of change in appropriations decreases. This simply means that the size of increases or decreases in appropriations gets smaller over time. This finding supports the notion that age brings relative budget stability to agencies—and this budget stability is likely to mean stability for all kinds of policy actions. This finding cannot be attributed to an increase in the appropriations base on which the change figure is computed. Appropriations do not increase uniformly over time, nor do they significantly co-vary with change measures of appropriations. If the decreasing magnitude were attributable to an increase in the appropriations base, then there should be a negative correlation between raw appropriations and change measures of appropriations. The correlations between raw and change measures for the variables mentioned here and below are all less than .09. When these correlations are adjusted downward for sample size inflation, almost all of these correlations become zero. Thus, none of our findings for change measures can be caused by variations in the base on which the change measure is computed.

A–3. As agencies get older, the rate of change in appropriations moves from a period of oscillation to a period of acceleration. This suggests that youthful agencies change their patterns of policy actions rapidly and sporadically but that more mature agencies settle into a pattern in which the rate of change in their actions moves in a rather predictable and steady direction.

A–4. As agencies get older, they also get larger (in terms of total personnel, supergrades, and middlegrades). This supports the view that our indicators of maturity do in fact move together and that perhaps a composite index can be developed in the future. It also supports the notion that as agencies get older their activities can increase because increasing numbers of personnel (including the managerial types included in middlegrades and supergrades) are necessary—although not sufficient—to support increasing nonbudgetary policy actions.

A–5. As agencies get older, the magnitude of change in total personnel, number of middlegrades, and number of supergrades decreases. This finding again supports the view that a composite index for maturity based on our indicators is possible. This finding also supports the notion that age in an agency brings stability—both in its personnel and budget and, by implication, in its programs.

A–6. As agencies get older, the rate of change in total size moves from a period of oscillation to acceleration (paralleling the movement in appropriations), but the rate of change in middlegrades and supergrades moves from a period of acceleration to a period of oscillation. The finding with regard to total size supports the point that young agencies may be groping for their mission by changing their actions with some rapidity (and this would also both be necessitated and facilitated by flexibility in their total work force). The findings with regard to middlegrades and supergrades are not contradictory; in fact, they are supportive. To make basic program decisions young agencies need relatively large numbers of managers (middlegrades and supergrades); once they are on board and basic programmatic decisions are made, then the rate of change in their numbers can become more sensitive to a variety of budgetary, economic, and political pressures, and the rate of change as a result oscillates.

These findings on rate of change do not suggest that an index of maturity cannot be constructed. Most of the evidence supports our position regarding the effects of maturity. The evidence suggests that the effects of the numbers of middlegrades and supergrades are not well understood, and these measures may not be strongly related to maturity.

B. SUBSAMPLE TEST FOR INTERACTIVE EFFECTS

This technique was used to explore the effects of party strength on policy actions, agency maturity on policy actions, policy actions on subsequent policy actions, and party strength and economic conditions on agency maturity.

Agencies are dichotomized into relatively rich agencies (those with more appropriations) and relatively poor agencies (those with less appropriations) and into relatively large agencies (those with more employees) and relatively small agencies (those with fewer employees). Most of the large agencies were also rich and most of the small agencies were also poor, but the fit between the two dichotomies was not perfect so that the two subsamples were used separately. A variety of intriguing findings emerged (see Table 6–5 in the chapter appendix for statistical support of these findings).

B–1. As Democratic strength in the electorate increases, small and poor agencies get relatively more appropriations than rich and large agencies. This suggests that agencies ignored when Republican strength is relatively high will see their fortunes increase when Democratic strength is relatively high. The implication is that there are "Democratic" agencies and "Republican" agencies that systematically are favored or disfavored with respect to appropriations depending on the distribution of partisan strength. This gives substance to the notion that there are very real and meaningful policy differences between the parties.

B–2. Large agencies have higher magnitude decreases in appropriations than small agencies. This suggests that large agencies are more vulnerable in budget cutting periods mainly because they present a larger target. Their actions in general are also more likely to be more severely curtailed in such situations. Size is also shown to be important in that an increasing rate of change in size for rich agencies (and also for large agencies) will decrease appropriations, whereas an increasing rate of change in size for poor agencies (and also for small agencies) will increase appropriations. If small and poor agencies can manage to grow rapidly, then their budgetary position will improve and they will have less severe restraints on their latitude for action.

B–3. In rich agencies the number of supergrades has a negative effect on appropriations. But in poor agencies supergrades have a positive effect on appropriations. One implication for federal managers is that those in poor agencies should work particularly hard for additional top-level managers because the addition of such people will increase the latitude for policy action.

B–4. The number of middlegrades has a more positive effect on appropriations in rich agencies than in poor agencies. This implies that the growth of middlegrades in an agency already rich is probably a sign of vitality and a sign that the support necessary for continuing to get richer is present. If a poor agency cannot even manage to grow at the middlegrade level, it is probably relatively bereft of the support it needs to improve its overall budgetary fate.

B–5. Age increases appropriations for the rich agencies (and also for the large agencies) and decreases them for the poor agencies (and also for the small agencies). Poor and small agencies that are also aging are probably dying in terms of their appropriations and therefore in terms of their latitude for action. They can, however, offset a bleak future by increasing their supergrades or by increasing the rate of change in their total size (see *B–2. and B–3.*).

B–6. Agencies already rich have a decreasing rate of change in appropriations; poor agencies have an increasing rate of change in appropriations. Rich agencies also have a higher magnitude of decrease in appropriations than poor agencies. At a theoretical level, these findings give a hint that a simple incrementalist view of appropriations (that is, that one year's appropriations can be almost totally explained by the previous year's appropriations) is not very explanatory; other factors can and do intervene so that change in appropriations varies significantly from agency to agency (see Davis et al., 1966, on the incremental nature of budgeting and appropriations. Chapter 3 of this volume focuses directly on the incrementalist perspective).

At a practical level these findings suggest a mixed message for the managers of poor agencies. They may have a number of factors working against them (as indicated in previously discussed findings), but at least the magnitude of their decreases is smaller than those suffered by richer agencies. And, if their appropriations are increasing, the rate of change in those appropriations is a pattern of increasing growth. On the other hand, even though cuts, when they come, may be of a smaller magnitude than those for richer agencies, those cuts may be very disruptive in a program that is already small, or perhaps even marginal.

B–7. As Democratic strength in the electorate increases, large and rich agencies increase in total size. Small agencies also increase, but less rapidly than large agencies. Poor agencies decrease in size, supergrades, and middlegrades as the percent of the Democratic vote increases. Compared to *B–1.* this suggests that size and appropriations really are separable variables, and that although there may be "Democratic" agencies in terms of appropriations (including the small and the poor under Republicans), there may be other, more nonpartisan forces that lead to the continuing decrease in size, middlegrades, and supergrades of relatively poor agencies. It is also possible that Democrats favor poor agencies whose programs involve a high ratio of spending to personnel, whereas they are less supportive of poor agencies with a "service" orientation (that is, a low ratio of spending to personnel). Democrats may, in effect, try to push agencies into a "spending" stance; Republicans may push in the opposite direction. In any event, poor agencies may either gain or lose as the Democrats gain, depending on other characteristics of specific agencies.

B–8. As unemployment increases, the size of the rich agencies increases and the size of the poor agencies decreases. The size of both large and small agencies will increase, but more for large agencies than for small agencies. This suggests that in troubled economic times relatively small and poor agencies are more vulnerable, than large and rich agencies. Intuitively, the budget and program proposals of President Nixon in 1973 confirm this view. His proposals would have left the large, rich departments like Defense and HEW in relatively good shape; but the smaller, poorer parts of the government, such as the Model Cities Administration in a small Department (HUD), the Office of Economic Opportunity, or the Economic Development Administration in another small Department (Commerce) were all slated for extinction.

C. PATH ANALYSIS

This analysis began with the conviction that a simple incremental view is not sufficient to explain the policy actions of agencies, even when those actions are measured by appropriations. In the present test we sought to analyze the relative explanatory power of structural variables (SIZE, MG, SG, AGE) and previous actions (APP and EXP) on actions (APP). Models involving three-year time lags were used.

Our belief that appropriations in year t_1 could not explain everything of importance about variations in year t_2 was also supported by statistical reasoning. Bartlett (1935) demonstrated that autocorrelation in time-series data inflates the correlations and standard errors. Bohrnstedt (1969) has shown that traditional approaches to estimating parameters with longitudinal data produce unreliable results. Thus, if the data used by incrementalists have self-correlation, as the incrementalists argue, the estimates of the effect of previous year's value will both be inflated and unreliable. Hibbs (1972) has given examples where the estimates have been spuriously inflated. Hibbs also shows that Ordinary Least Squares (OLS) estimation of parameters for one's model produces inconsistent estimates; and he recommends using a complicated procedure using Instrumental Variables (IV), OLS regression, Correlogram Analysis, and Generalized Least Squares (GLS) regression—or at least using IV regression prior to OLS regression. To do otherwise seriously biases the estimates of the previous year's appropriations on subsequent years—and the bias is in a direction favorable to the incremental position. In short, the procedure used by incrementalists in demonstrating the importance of the previous year's appropriations on subsequent year's appropriations is both unreliable and inflates the estimated effects in favor of their thesis.

We decided to test the effects of agency structure on policy actions by evaluating a causal model that assumed such variables had an effect. The model presented in Figure 6–1 was our starting point. MG was subsequently dropped because it was so collinear with SIZE that it appeared they both tapped the same dimension. Including MG makes the estimates of the path coefficients more unreliable than dropping this variable (unless one is doing block variable analysis, which we were not). After preliminary analysis, agency expenditures (EXP) was added as an explanatory variable. The link between EXP and APP can be justified, since expenditures may be used as a guide to what an agency

FIGURE 6-1: INITIAL MODEL FOR PATH ANALYSIS

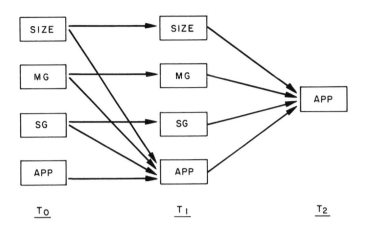

needs by the agency administrators in their appropriations request and since most expenditures, ultimately, come from appropriated monies. After rounds of evaluating, trimming, and reevaluating the model, two competing models appeared as plausible explanations of reality. They are presented in Figures 6–4 and 6–5 in the appendix to the chapter. Ultimately, they were rejected in favor of the "best" path model, which is presented in Figure 6–2. The reasons for choosing this model over the other two are also dicussed in the appendix. A number of specific findings emerge from an analysis of the best path model. (Table 6–6 in the chapter appendix provides statistical support for the following statements.)

C–1. There is clear support here for the common notion on the part of administrators that they should spend all the money they have before the end of any given fiscal year. Even though expenditures data are not used explicitly in making appropriations requests, they in fact help explain change in appropriations in a statistical sense. In general, the large path coefficient between EXP in t_1 and APP in t_2 (and a similar relationship between t_0 and t_1) suggests that the more an administrator spends in one year the more appropriations his agency will get in a subsequent year. (The main caveat that an administrator must observe is, of course, that he should not spend money on some purpose that outrages the Office of Management and Budget or Congress.)

C–2. Previous appropriations do explain subsequent appropriations, but are not as important as expenditures and are not a great deal more important than size. A common belief about the simple incremental nature of budgeting (that is, that appropriations at t_2 are almost wholly explained by appropriations at t_1) is called into question by this finding. And, given the substantial dollar differences between the amounts of

FIGURE 6-2: THE BEST PATH MODEL

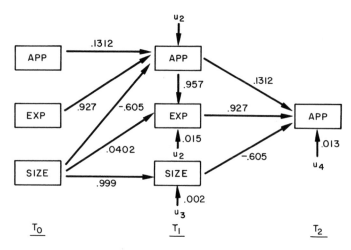

$\Delta r_{xy} \hat{r}_{xy} = -.00012$

$t = -.091$ with 8 degrees of freedom

$t_p = .923$

All values are significant at .05 level with 2-tailed test.

appropriations and expenditures no matter what time lag is employed, appropriations at t_2 cannot be viewed as a simple surrogate for expenditures at either t_1 or t_2.

C–3. SIZE affects APP negatively. That is, small agencies do relatively better than large agencies and tend to close the gap in appropriations. If, for example, there are two agencies with the same appropriations and expenditures, the smaller of the two agencies is likely to get larger appropriations in the subsequent year.

C–4. SIZE plays only a minor explanatory role for EXP. The main explanation for EXP is APP in the same year. But the fit is not, of course, perfect, since expenditures (EXP) come from a variety of sources—permanent appropriations, appropriations for open-ended amounts, a variety of fixed charges (for example, payments to retired civil servants), and appropriations for uncompleted projects whose cost of termination is greater than the cost of completion, in addition to annual appropriations for regular activities (APP) (see Weidenbaum and Larkins, 1972: Ch. 5).

C–5. SIZE of agencies in fact varies only very little from year to year. SIZE in t_0 has a path coefficient of .999 with SIZE in t_1. However, as suggested earlier, even a little bit of variance in size can produce some effect on both expenditures and appropriations. The effects run in different directions, however, and more exploration of these relationships is needed before definite conclusions can be reached.

C–6. Although three of the indicators of maturity—SG, MG, and AGE—were trimmed from the path analysis, this may indicate only that the indicators were too crude, not that the concept has no effect. More sophisticated indicators (or even the change coefficients of these simple indicators) may still have explanatory power in subsequent empirical work. MG was in fact dropped because it correlated so highly with SIZE (.96). Thus, they do seem to be tapping the same dimension—what we have called maturity. SG, on the other hand, did not have a high correlation with SIZE (.36) but did have a moderate correlation with MG (.54), which suggests it is measuring some dimension of organizational structure other than that tapped by SIZE. AGE was not highly correlated with MG (–.14), SG (.01), or SIZE (–.03) but was more highly correlated with percent of middlegrades (–.25) and percent of supergrades (.40) for an agency. Thus, while we have not yet hit on a sophisticated index for maturity, there are enough favorable portents to suggest that such an index can be developed. Such an index would provide a more sophisticated tool than any of the simple measures taken alone or any of the measures available in the literature, which tend to measure only one item (for example, span of control or morphology).

Conclusions

A number of conclusions emerge from our exploratory work:

1. A number of specific findings suggest that relatively poor (in terms of appropriations) and small (in terms of total number of employees) agencies have considerable hope for improving their position, particularly if they are also relatively young. Relatively rich and large agencies seem likely to prosper into middle age but may well face substantial decline as the years pass. In short, we find support for the notion of a cycle in the life of agencies (see Downs, 1967; Bernstein, 1955: Ch. 3). The cycle can be portrayed as in Figure 6–3.
   a. There seem to be factors, both within the structure of agencies and within the environment, that work to improve the lot of the relatively underprivileged agencies. These factors include number of supergrades, size, Democratic strength in the elec-

FIGURE 6-3: A LIFE CYCLE OF AGENCIES

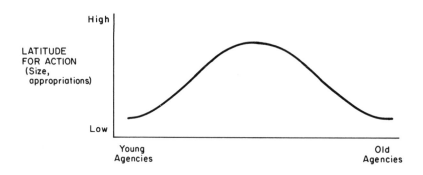

torate, and previous appropriations. (See specific findings 1, 2, 3, 6 in section B, and 3 in section C for support.)

   b. There are also factors, however, that seem to favor the already rich and large agencies at the expense of the poor and small agencies. These include middlegrades and, indirectly at least, Democratic strength and unemployment. (See specific findings 4, 7, and 8 in section B for support.)

   c. The critical differentiating element between poor, small agencies that seem to be in a position to improve and poor, small agencies that seem to be dying is age. Young, poor, small agencies are likely to have a bright future. Old, poor, small agencies are likely to have little future left. (See specific findings 2, 3, 5, 6 in section A, and 5 in section B for support.)

2. All of the major categories of independent variables have explanatory power and deserve further exploration. No one category seems omnipotent.

   a. Structural variables are important in the explanation of actions in the form of appropriations. These variables include size (see findings 1, 2, 4, 5 in section B, 3, and 4 in section C); age (see findings 1 through 6 in section A and 5 in section B); middlegrades (see 4 in section B); and supergrades (see 3 in section B).

   b. Environmental variables have limited utility in explaining raw appropriations, but there are at least enough hints based on the very tentative use made of them here that they should be explored much more fully in future work. (See findings 1 and 7 in section B on Democratic strength and 8 in section B on unemployment.)

c. Previous actions (appropriations and expenditures) do help explain appropriations, including two principal change coefficients of appropriations. But, what is particularly important is that expenditures explain more than previous appropriations and appropriations does not explain much more than size. Budgetary incrementalism has some empirical support, but our results provide substantial grounds for asserting that other factors may be just as important. (See findings 1, 3, 4, 6 in section B, 1, and 2 in section C.)

3. The hypotheses that we wished to explore in this early test of parts of our model are generally supported, although we certainly do not claim that we have made rigorous, full, and exhaustive tests of any of them.

   a. Hypothesis 1, relating immaturity to changes in policy actions, is strongly supported by all three of our techniques. (See findings 2, 5 in section A, 1, 2, 3 in section B, and 3 in section C.) Only two findings suggest some nonsupport, and therefore, the further refinement of the indicators and the hypothesis. (See findings 4 and 5 in section B.)

   b. Hypothesis 2, relating increasing Democratic strength in the electorate to changes in policy actions, seems to be generally true, although the evidence is that it is truer for small, poor agencies than for large, rich agencies. (See findings 1 and 7 in section B.) It should also be noted that the investigation of this hypothesis was very limited, but certainly nothing has convinced us that it does not deserve continued, detailed exploration.

   c. Hypothesis 3, relating rapidly changing economic conditions to changes in policy actions, was tested only indirectly. (See finding 8 in section B.) The variable, as we operationalized it (UE), did not turn out to be important when we tried it in our path model. At present, therefore, we simply have no conclusion about this hypothesis. We strongly suspect, however, that as we begin to work increasingly with change coefficients, with different measures of actions, and with more indicators for economic change, the variable will prove to be important, probably in the predicted direction.

   d. Hypothesis 4, relating previous actions to changes in actions, as explanatory but not omnipotent, is strongly supported. (See findings 1, 3 through 6 in section B, 1, and 2 in section C.)

4. Methodologically, we found all three of the techniques we chose— trend analysis based on regression; a subsample test for interactive effects; and longitudinal path analysis—to work in the sense of providing interesting findings relevant to our concerns.

Note

1. The findings of Davis et al. (1966), Fenno (1966), and Sharkansky (1969) may be more testimony to biased (inflated) estimates resulting from auto-correlation than to real relationships across time [see also Hibbs (1972) for additional evidence that this may be the case]. Alternatively, using deviates from predicted scores or partialized estimates may produce un-reliable estimates even if the predictions are done by 3 Stage Least Squares regression when the across time self-correlation is high. Variables used in policy studies often have high self-correlation across time. Thus, estimates using raw measures of change are generally suspect unless there is only low self-correlation across time for the variables being studied. Knowing that agency appropriations and size both have high self-correlations across time, raw measures of change were avoided in this study.

Appendix

This appendix first contains a discussion of the two path models that were rejected and the reasons for accepting the "best" path model over them. It also contains statistical tables relevant to the figures presented in the text and to the rejected path models that are discussed here.

Figure 6–4 shows the first of the path models (here called Model 1) that was rejected. Table 6–2 (p. 138) has a statistical summary for Model 1. Although the path coefficient from SIZE at t_0 to EXP at t_1 in Model 1 is low in absolute magnitude, it is significant at less than the .05 level. Since the absolute magnitude of a path coefficient should not be used as the principal criterion in judging the significance of a path when the coefficient is low, and since this path meets theoretical, mathematical, and substantive criteria of significance, the path should not be rejected on its face value alone. Furthermore, it is a variable that is partially manipulable by agency managers. If an agency expends $400 million a year, manipulation of size could effect expenditures by as much as $1 million. Independent of the amount of expenditures and appropriations, if an agency is successful in adding 1,000 persons to the payroll, the direct effects would be an increase in expenditures for the subsequent year of $1,550,000 —exclusive of payroll costs, since that is contained in the appropriations. In terms of developing clinical advice, the policy analyst should be reluctant to eliminate manipulable variables from his model. Thus, Model 1 is attractive.

On the other hand, Model 2, shown in Figure 6–5, has three things to recommend it. Table 6–3 (p. 139) has a statistical summary for Model 2. Model 2 is simpler than Model 1. The F value of the regression for expenditures in Model 2 is twice the size of the F value of the corresponding

FIGURE 6-4: MODEL I

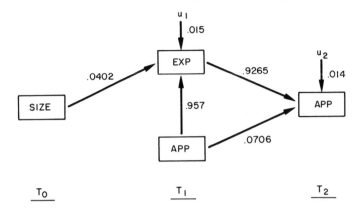

$\Delta r_{xy} \hat{r}_{xy}$ = .0105
    t = .493 with 4 degrees of freedom
    t_p = .649

All values are significant at .05 level with 2-tailed test

FIGURE 6-5: MODEL 2

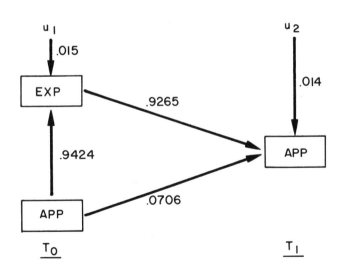

$\Delta r_{xy} \hat{r}_{xy}$ = .0261
    t = .3067 with I degree of freedom
    t_p = .809

All values are significant at .05 level with 2-tailed test.

TABLE 6-2. Summary Statistical Table for Model 1

Dependent Variable	Independent Variable	Beta	Partial b	s_b	Partial r	Simple r	F Value	Degrees of Freedom	Multiple R^2
EXP_1	$SIZE_0$	.040	1,525.92	696.32	.155	.882	4.8		
	APP_1	.957	1.006	.019	.966	.992	2,719.1	139	.985
	u_1	.015							
APP_2	EXP_1	.926	.896	.024	.938	.993	1,339.6		
	APP_1	.071	.076	.027	.201	.942	7.8	139	.986
	u_2	.014							

MODEL 1 PATH MODEL[a]

$$EXP_1 = A + b_1(SIZE_0) + b_2(APP_1) + u_1$$
$$APP_2 = A + b_1(EXP_1) + b_2(APP_1) + u_2$$

a. The fact that subscripts in the path model are identical does not imply the values are identical.

TABLE 6-3. Summary Statistical Table for Model 2

Dependent Variable	Independent Variable	Beta	Partial b	s_b	Partial r	Simple r	F Value	Degrees of Freedom	Multiple R^2
EXP_0	APP_0	.992	1.04	.009	.992	.992	12,621.1	139	.985
	u_1	.015							
APP_1	EXP_0	.926	.896	.024	.938	.993	1,339.6	139	.986
	APP_0	.071	.076	.027	.201	.942	7.8		
	u_2	.014							

MODEL 2 PATH MODEL

$$EXP_0 = A_1 + b_1(APP_0) + u_1$$
$$APP_1 = A_2 + b_1(EXP_0) + b_2(APP_0) + u_2$$

regression in Model 1 (12,661 versus 6,668, both of which are highly significant values). Third, and perhaps most telling, Model 2 is a better fit to the real world. When correlations between the variables are estimated from the path coefficients in Model 1 and subtracted from the empirical correlations, there is a .649 probability that the mean residual is truly zero. When this is done for Model 2 the probability that the mean residual is zero is .809. Since the two means have different degrees of freedom, they cannot be compared directly. However, the errors in estimating the correlations for Model 2 are both overestimations—an indication that either a positive path is included which should not be or a negative path is missing when it should be present. If the latter is true, then adding a negative path would produce a better model.

It is very likely that a negative path has been left out of Model 1. Earlier analysis of data indicated that size has a negative effect on appropriations when expenditures and previous appropriations are controlled and estimated using IV–OLS regression. This low negative path was ignored in evaluating and trimming the initial model (presented in Figure 6–1 in the text) because it was thought to be an artifact of collinearity. When this path is included in Model 1 and evaluated, a new model emerges, the "best" path model (presented in Figure 6–2 in the text). The probability that the best model is "the true model" is .923—an increase of .144 over that for Model 2.

If Model 2 is accepted over what we judge to be the best model, several difficulties are introduced. If SIZE has no direct effect on subsequent APP, what is the indirect link that accounts for this correlation? This correlation is not explained by personnel costs reflected in appropriations— since that would show up as a direct effect, which Model 2 rules out. How can the association of SIZE and APP be explained other than by the best model? Second, while one might recast the incrementalist position to say that in Model 2 appropriations is an increment over expenditures, there are questions about the empirical validity of such a strategy. Previous appropriations have been explicitly legitimized by Congress. An administrator may represent a request for similar appropriations as being based on a legitimate figure. Expenditures, however, do not have the same carry over legitimacy. They may stem from appropriations scattered over a number of preceding years. Appealing to previous expenditures as a baseline of what is needed we think is a strategy far more problematic in its success than appealing to previous appropriations. (And it is a strategy virtually never used by federal managers, at least in appearances before Congress.) As a result, the linkages used to justify (or explain) the incremental pattern are also more problematic when a shift is made to previous expenditures as a key variable. The tie between expenditures at t_1 and appropriations at t_2 is strong, but it does not rest on the kinds of perceptions the incrementalists posit.

TABLE 6-4. Estimated Trends for Linear Trend Analysis

Finding	Estimated Trend (beginning in fiscal 1952)
A-1	APP=541,010,000+38,615,033 LIN[a]+e EXP=733,330,000−1,707,307 SQUARD[b]+e
A-2	MAG.APP=1.3440−.1092 LIN+e
A-3	RATE.APP=−14.4831+1.1247 LIN+e
A-4	SIZE=21,425+5.94 SQUARD+e MG=1,029+6.099 SQUARD+e SG=525+7.373 LIN+e
A-5	MAG.SIZE=1.0453−.0001 SQUARD+e MAG.MG=1.112−.1767 SQUARD+e MAG.SG=1.247−.0007 SQUARD+e
A-6	RATE.MG=0.432−.0034 SQUARD+e RATE.SG=0.3199−.002 SQUARD+e

a. LIN = YEAR − 51
b. SQUARD = LIN^2

TABLE 6-5. Comparison of Subsample Slopes for Detection of Interaction[a]

Finding	Slope Compared		Slopes in Subsamples for Agencies Which Are:		
		Smaller	Larger	Poorer	Richer
B-1	b(APP,DV)	−11,626,000	−75,635,000	−15,502,000	−78,765,000
B-2,B-6	b(APP,MAG.APP)	−22,433,000	−5,799,850,000	−14,643,000	−601,500,000
B-2	b(APP,RATE.SIZE)	374,570	−194,080,000	159,880	−119,060,000
B-3	b(APP,SG)	6,381,800	9,722,200	21,088,000	−446,660
B-4	b(APP,MG)	870,890	237,211	77,804	342,150
B-5	b(APP,AGE)	−8,113,300	167,120,000	−3,720,700	172,030,000
B-6	b(APP,RATE.APP)	380,820	200,150,000	110,890	−25,291,000
B-7	b(SIZE,DV)	129.1	3,804.5	−285.2	3,881.1
B-7	b(SG,DV)	−6.8	−17.4	−4.8	−25.7
B-7	b(MG,DV)	−23.1	−270.0	−96.6	−55.2
B-8	b(SIZE,UE)	47.1	441.0	−202.2	4,815.1

a. t-tests were not made on the differences between slopes since hypothesis testing with such slopes should be done with partial regression coefficients from the structural equations representing one's model. At this point in the exploratory research we do not have an appropriate structural equation model for which differences in estimates may be tested. The zero order subsample slopes are to be taken as preliminary, suggestive evidence of interaction.

TABLE 6-6. Summary Statistical Table for the Best Path Model

Dependent Variable	Independent Variable	Beta	Partial b	s_b	Partial r	Simple r	F Value	Degrees of Freedom	Multiple R^2
APP_1	APP_0	.131	.141	.024	.274	.942	14.8		
	EXP_0	.927	.897	.037	.940	.993	1,384.6		
	$SIZE_0$	−.065	−2,369.6	907.7	−.189	.878	6.8	139	.987
	u_1	.013							
EXP_1	$SIZE_0$	.040	1,525.92	696.3	.155	.882	4.8		
	APP_1	.957	1.0006	.02	.966	.992	2,719.1	139	.985
	u_2	.015							
$SIZE_1$	$SIZE_0$	.999	.999	<.001	.999	.999	a	139	.998
	u_3	.002							
APP_2	Same as for APP_1 (with u_4 equal to u_1)								

THE BEST PATH MODEL

$$APP_1 = A_1 + b_1(APP_0) + b_2(EXP_0) + b_3(SIZE_0) + u_1$$
$$EXP_1 = A_1 + b_1(APP_1) + b_2(SIZE_0) + u_2$$
$$SIZE_1 = A_1 + b_1(SIZE_0) + u_3$$
$$APP_2 = A_1 + b_1(APP_1) + b_2(EXP_1) + b_3(SIZE_1) + u_4$$

a. >99,999

143

7

Explaining Changes in Budgetary Policy Actions

Randall B. Ripley, William M. Holmes,
Grace A. Franklin, and William B. Moreland

This study proceeds from the work reported in Chapter 6 and employs the same agencies, time span, and data base. This chapter presents a dynamic change model using block variable analysis. The change model is used to study the effects of change in independent variables on change in dependent variables. The independent variables are change in agency structure, change in environmental features, and change in previous policy actions, and the dependent variable is change in budgetary policy actions. The relationships among these variables are studied from two perspectives: (1) a linear, additive model is discussed; and (2) nonlinear, interactive effects resulting from different kinds of agency aging (chronological and structural) and structural change (in terms of personnel) are discussed. The linear path model shows that although change in previous policy actions does help explain change in subsequent policy actions, change in agency structure and environment are also important explanatory factors. The study concludes by presenting a general interactive model that takes into account the findings of both the linear path model and the interactive effects of aging and structural change.

As GOVERNMENTAL BUREAUCRACIES pursue their various institutional and programmatic goals, a variety of important questions present themselves to bureaucrats, to social scientists analyzing bureaucracy, and to that portion of the public interested in governmental affairs. These questions involve the size and substance of programs, the responsiveness of bureaucracy to the broad needs of society and to the narrower interests of individual clients, the relations of bureaucracy to other organs of government, and the patterns of growth and change in bureaucracy.

This latter topic of growth and change has intrigued social scientists for some time. One cluster of scholars concerned about organizational development has focused on change within governmental organizations (Kaufman, 1972, for example). A second cluster of scholars concerned with the output of bureaucracies in terms of programs, particularly as measured in dollars, has focused on explaining change in the amount of dollars received or spent by bureaus (Sharkansky, 1965, for example).

The present paper shares the concerns of the second group of scholars. We chose this focus for two reasons: first, dollars available to and spent by government agencies are good surrogate measures of all that an agency is able to do programmatically; and second, we are not convinced that the present literature on the subject has gone beyond a superficial level in explaining changes in the programmatic potential of agencies as measured by dollars. It should also be mentioned that policy-makers themselves often focus on change in budget as they proceed with their day-to-day decisions (Fenno, 1966; Wildavsky, 1964; Moreland, 1973). Thus, it makes not only good social science sense to focus on change, but it also makes sense if one is interested, as we are, in producing findings of potential interest to policy-makers themselves. In Chapter 6 we focused primarily on change in the raw values of appropriations as a dependent variable. Although we discussed two more complex measures of change, MAG and RATE, these were used only in a small part of the overall analysis. Since the empirical study reported in Chapter 6 demonstrated that the general conceptual scheme had both scientific and clinical payoff, it seemed appropriate to use portions of the scheme to begin an investigation of complex kinds of change in budgetary policy actions.

In the pages that follow, the specific test reported here will first be outlined. Following these preliminary matters the heart of the paper seeks to explain change in budgetary policy actions in two different ways. First, a linear, additive model is presented and evaluated. This discussion can be regarded as a relatively general explanation of change in agency budgets. Second, nonlinear and interactive effects are discussed. This discussion can be regarded as an exploration of some of the more complex factors explaining change in agency budgets. Nonlinear effects demonstrate that some influences are not uniform in their effect on budgetary changes. The interactive effects indicate how variations in a third variable can in some situations modify the effects of influences on budgetary changes. The two discussions are not competing explanations but rather describe impacts that occur simultaneously.

The Nature of the Empirical Test

Our general concern in the research project from which this paper stems has been to delineate the impact of external environment (defined in terms of economic and social conditions, public opinion, partisan strength, and the nature of competing coalitions) and bureaucratic structure (defined in terms of agency maturity, characteristics of agency personnel, and characteristics of agency decision-making processes) on the policy response of governmental agencies (defined as statements and actions by those agencies and results in society attributable at least in part to the statements and actions).

In pursuing our present exploration, we proceed both more deductively in the construction of the linear, additive model of agency budgetary change and more inductively in the succeeding discussion of nonlinear and interactive effects on agency budgetary change.

Table 7–1 summarizes the specific variables that were used in the research reported here. The change measures discussed in Chapter 6 (MAG and RATE) were also used in relation to most of the variables, both independent and dependent.

TABLE 7-1. Variables Used in the Analysis

Variable	Abbreviation Used in Text
Agency Structure	
Total number of employees in agency	SIZE
Number of years since creation of agency	AGE
Number of supergrade employees in agency	SG
Percent of supergrade employees in agency	% SG
Number of middlegrade employees in agency	MG
Percent of middlegrade employees in agency	% MG
Environment	
Percent of civilian labor force unemployed	UE
Standard of living (per capita income divided by consumer price index)	SOL
Percent of the two-party vote for all Democratic candidates for the House of Representatives	DV
Policy Actions	
Annual expenditures of agency minus expenditures for salaries	EMS
Annual appropriations to agency	APP

We use six different variables to measure agency structure. These include the number of people employed by the agency, the chronological age of the agency, the number and percent of supergrades (GS16's, 17's, 18's, and equivalents) in the agency and the number and percent of middlegrades (GS13's, 14's, and 15's and equivalents) in the agency. We have not yet been able to develop a single index of agency maturity, so we used these six variables to capture important aspects of agency structure that constantly appear in the literature on organizations (see, for example, Blau and Scott, 1962; Blau and Schoenherr, 1971; Weber, 1946; Downs, 1967).

We chose three variables to represent the general economic and political environment in which all agencies must work. Standard of living affects virtually all citizens directly; unemployment affects some directly and most indirectly; the relative standing of the two principal parties in the electorate provides the partisan context in Congress and the White House within which agency programs and activities are set.

Two variables were selected to represent the policy actions of the agencies. The first is annual expenditures excluding the amount for salaries. Salaries were subtracted to guard against the possibility that changes in expenditures were simply functions of changes in agency personnel size. The second is regular annual appropriations. Supplemental appropriations were excluded because they were small and also because they were sporadic and usually represented genuine "emergencies" stimulated by unexpected external events. There are also many potential nonbudgetary measures of policy actions, but we chose these two budgetary indicators in order to maintain continuity with Chapter 6 and with other previous literature.

The data used in the analysis come from a 20-year period—fiscal years 1952 through 1971. The agencies examined are the same as those examined in Chapter 6.

A Linear Additive Model of Agency Budgetary Change

The most general hypothesized relationships with which we began are presented graphically in Figure 7–1. Changes in agency policy actions are explained by changes in the external environment, bureaucratic structure, and previous policy actions of the agency. Changes in the structure of an agency are explained by changes in an agency's external political, economic, and social environment. Although previous actions by an agency undoubtedly affect agency structure at a later date, we assume that the effects of previous actions occur indirectly by changing (or failing to change) an agency's environment. Since this paper is not a study of policy

FIGURE 7-1: THE BASIC CONCEPTUAL MODEL

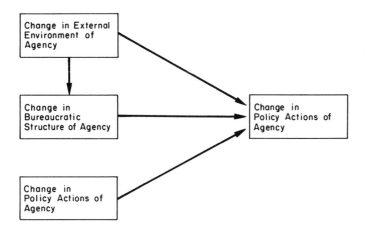

results in an agency's environment, the indirect effect of previous actions on agency structure is treated as unexplained covariation.

From the conceptual diagram, a mathematical model was developed to represent the relations being studied. This model used blocks of variables to represent the abstract and ambiguous concepts of "changes in agency environment" and "changes in agency structure." In general, the use of block variables will provide more valid estimates of abstract concepts than single indicators (Bonacich, 1972; Blalock, 1970). With this model, it was found that changes in structure and environment do affect changes in budgetary action. However, estimates of the within-block effects were not consistent because of collinearity between some variables and complete independence between others. Thus, even though the hypotheses were supported, the model had to be modified to achieve consistent estimates of the relations within each block. Technical details on this model and the reasons for its rejection are included in the chapter appendix.

A model having consistent within-block estimates resulted when the broad blocks were broken up into smaller blocks. Several alternative subgroupings were explored, but only one theoretically and empirically consistent model emerged. It is summarized in Figure 7–2. In this model, block variable effects were estimated using the procedure recently developed by Heise (1972). The numbers without parentheses are path coefficients; the numbers in parentheses are percent variance explained in the dependent variables.

In this model, change in environment was divided into a set of economic change measures (UE CHANGE, composed of MAG.UE and RATE.UE) and a group labeled Democratic Electoral Base (DEB,

FIGURE 7-2: DIAGRAM OF THE BEST PATH MODEL[a]

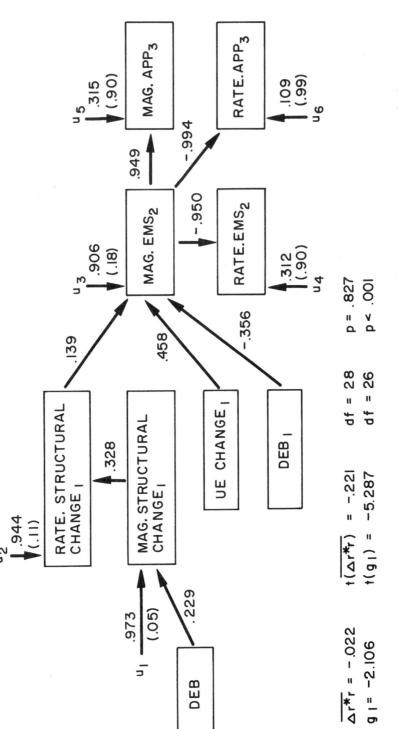

$\overline{\Delta r^{*}_{r}}$ = -.022 $t(\overline{\Delta r^{*}_{r}})$ = -.221   df = 28   p = .827

g_1 = -2.106 $t(g_1)$ = -5.287   df = 26   p < .001

a. The skewness of the distribution of the difference between estimated and observed correlations was used as a decision criterion for the "goodness of fit" when comparing alternative models. Since different models had different degrees of freedom, the comparison was made between the t-probability of the composed of raw values—not change measures—of UE, SOL, and DV). The close relationship between the state of the economy and Democratic electoral success is captured in this block. Change in structure was also broken into two categories—rate of structural change (RATE.SC, composed of RATE.–SIZE. RATE.MG, and RATE.SG, with RATE.SG, contributing more effect to this block than any other variable) and magnitude of structural change (MAG.SC, composed of MAG.SIZE, MAG.MG, and MAG.SG, all contributing to this block about equally with MAG.MG slightly more important than the others).

A summary statistical table for this model (Table 7–4) is included in the appendix to this chapter. Details are also presented on the next most mathematically plausible model, and the reasons for its rejection are explained in the chapter appendix.

The critical variable in the model presented in Figure 7–2 is the magnitude of change in expenditures at t_2. This variable explains 90% of the variance in the magnitude of change in appropriations at t_3, and 90% of the variance in the rate of change in expenditures at t_2.

The block variables at t_1—rate of structural change, magnitude of structural change, UE CHANGE, and Democratic electoral base—explain 18% of the variance in the magnitude of change in expenditures at t_2—a large figure when cast in the light of the incrementalist position that virtually nothing else explains budgetary change except previous budgetary change. Furthermore, the unexplained variance, 82%, is not accounted for by other budgetary variables. Previous appropriations and expenditures (both including and excluding salaries) at t_1 had *no* significant effect on the magnitude of change in expenditures at t_2. This is true regardless of whether previous appropriations and expenditures were operationalized in raw numbers or in terms of change measures.

The unexplained variance in magnitude of expenditures is not accounted for by any of the individual components of the block variables. Agency size, number of middlegrades, number of supergrades, percentage of middlegrades, percentage of supergrades, age of agency in years since its founding, and the size of the Democratic majority in Congress were found to have no explanatory power for magnitude of expenditures at t_2. Our guess is that additional environmental and structural variables are likely to add to the explanatory power of our model. [See Moreland (1973) for a discussion of some alternatives.]

Other findings emerge from inspection of Figure 7-2. First, agency structure changes in response to factors favorable to Democratic electoral strength and in response to changes in differing parts of agency structure. For example, a 1% increase in Democratic electoral base results in a 3% increase in magnitude change of agency structure. A 10% increase in magnitude change of agency structure results in a 52% increase in rate of change in agency structure in the same year.

Second, agency expenditures change in response to change in environment and structure (employment changes and structural changes) and to the state of the environment (the Democratic electoral base). The direct effect of both UE change and rate of change in structure is positive, while the direct effect of Democratic electoral base is negative. For example, a 10% increase in UE CHANGE results in a 31.4% increase in the magnitude of change in expenditures. A 100% increase in the rate of change in agency structure results in a 16.8% increase in magnitude of change in expenditures. A 1% increase in Democratic electoral base results in an 8.9% decrease in the magnitude of change of expenditures.

Third, Democratic electoral base has indirect positive effects on magnitude change in expenditures (operating through change in agency structure). The initial effect of an increase in the Democratic electoral base is to stabilize agency expenditures for the following year (that is, the magnitude of change is reduced), but the indirect effect in the second year will be to produce a slight increase in the magnitude of change in agency expenditures. The increase in the second year is not sufficient to offset the decrease of the previous year, however. For example, the first year effect of a 1% increase in the Democratic electoral base is an 8.9% decrease in the magnitude change of an agency's expenditures. The second year indirect effect of a 1% increase in Democratic electoral strength is a 2.5% increase in the magnitude increase of an agency's expenditures. This means that the net effects of a 1% increase in the Democratic electoral base is a 6.4% decrease in the magnitude increase of an agency's expenditures after two years—rather than an 8.9% decrease.

Another way of considering Figure 7–2 is to work backwards. For example, if increases in the magnitude of change in appropriations are observed in a given year (t_3), they can be explained by increases in the magnitude of change in expenditures for the previous year (t_2). These increases can in turn be explained by increasing rate and magnitude of structural changes and increasing change in unemployment and decreasing Democratic electoral base in the preceding year (t_1). Decreasing magnitude of change in appropriations can be explained by opposite conditions.

What more general statements are supported by this model? It strongly suggests that governmental spending is, in fact, significantly related to changes in society, including changes in the voting habits of the electorate. Governmental spending is also related to changes in bureaucratic structure (which is also affected by Democratic electoral base). A changing partisan voting pattern acts as a stabilizing factor because it indirectly produces increasing magnitude of change (acting through structural changes), but its direct effect is to reduce the magnitude of change in expenditures. (It should be noted, of course, that change can move in either direction—an increasing magnitude of change in expenditures may reflect either large budget cuts or large increases.) Thus, a period of great magnitude of change in expenditures and appropriations could be explained by a situation in which the Democratic electoral base was high in a given year and had shrunk in the succeeding year. A period of small magnitude of change in expenditures and appropriations could be explained by a situation in which the Democratic electoral base had been relatively poor to start with and had improved.

The relationship between partisan strength and governmental spending is complicated—and not at all the simple relationship the parties themselves try to portray at least in referring to the other party ("irresponsible Democratic spending" and "the Republican meat-axe," for example). These findings do not suggest that partisan preferences in elections are immediately translated into specific programs, but they do suggest that partisan voting makes a difference at least at the level of aggregate policy.

But partisanship certainly does not explain all changes in spending and appropriations. Economic environmental factors—symbolized here by change in unemployment—and structural factors also have an impact. Indeed, the conservatizing effect of an increase in the Democratic electoral base is not simply a bad economy helping the Democrats and preventing budget increases. Both factors have separate influences on the budget.

Nonlinear and Interactive Effects on Agency Budgetary Change

In addition to the linear and additive effects on budgetary change just discussed, some nonlinear and interactive effects were explored in an inductive fashion. The exploration focused on the effects of agency aging and the effects of structural change because a number of studies have suggested that nonlinear and interactive effects occur in response to organizational maturation (Blau, 1970; Blau and Schoenherr, 1971; Childers et al., 1971; Haas and Collen, 1963; Hendershot and James, 1972; Hummon, 1971; Mayhew et al., 1972a, 1972b; Scott, 1964). The focus on aging and structural change has clinical as well as theoretical importance. The structural maturity of an agency is manipulable by agency administrators. In addition, deliberate change (or reorganization) in executive branch agencies is frequently an attempt to rejuvenate the agency and its program performance. Our findings have direct bearing on the consequences of several types of reorganization—rapid versus slow change, reversing the direction of change, and high versus low magnitude changes. How an agency responds to its environment varies with the degree of agency maturity.

THE EFFECTS OF AGENCY AGING

Aging is a multidimensional concept. It can mean simply the length of time an agency has been in existence. It can mean vertical and horizontal differentiation of organizational parts. Or it can mean decreasing responsiveness of an agency to its environment, or slow rates of promotion for its employees. Our exploratory analysis suggests there are two principal dimensions of agency aging: chronological and structural.

Chronological aging is simply the passing of time—the longer an agency has been in existence, the older it is chronologically. For this study we used the number of years since the creation of the agency as the measure of chronological agency age. Structural aging is a bit more complex. It has at least three subdimensions—organizational change, agency size, and degree of differentiation. Blau (1970), Childers et al. (1971), Hummon (1971), and Mayhew et al. (1972b) focus on these characteristics. These studies assert there is a positive relationship between organizational size and degree of differentiation, but the exact nature of this positive relation has not been determined. A negative relation is believed to exist between size and rate of change in organizations.

Structurally old agencies are large, highly differentiated, and slowly changing. Since good data were not available on structural differentiation of the agencies, only the effects of organizational change and size are examined in the section on structural aging.

The dichotomization of aging into chronological and structural components corresponds to dynamic and static conceptions of aging. The structural age of an agency is almost time-independent. Its defining properties are mainly characteristics and relations internal to agencies, (which does not mean it is caused just by internal processes, only that it is defined in terms of internal characteristics and relations). The defining properties of an agency's chronological age, however, are essentially external to the agency (usually authorizing legislation) but this does not preclude internal influences. Inefficiency of agency actions or political considerations could bring about dissolution of the agency or its incorporation into another agency. The dynamic aspect of chronological aging is evident in its temporally dependent nature. Although these two dimensions of aging have a low statistical relationship, they both produce similar consequences. The implication for research is that different kinds of aging may be functionally interchangeable because they produce similar effects. The clinical message is that even though aging may be a multidimensional phenomenon, the policy consequences of aging in any dimension may be similar.

THE EFFECTS OF CHRONOLOGICAL AGING

Using a cutoff point of 25 years or more to define older agencies, it was found that chronologically older agencies tend to be richer and larger and to have smaller and slower changes than younger agencies. Table 7–6 in the chapter appendix contains the comparison of means for the subsamples of older and younger agencies that supports the discussion that follows. A summary of the different change patterns for young and old agencies is presented in Table 7–2.

TABLE 7–2. Patterns of Change for Young and Old Agencies (average annual change)

	Young Agencies	Old Agencies	Significant[b] Difference
MAG.APP	26%	6%	yes
RATE.APP	803%[a]	3%	yes
MAG.SIZE	5%	0%	no
RATE.SIZE	90%[a]	25%	yes
MAG.MG	12%	4%	no
RATE.MG	−48%	−45%	no
MAG.SG	20%	11%	yes
RATE.SG	−60%	−37%	yes

a. Designates reversal in direction of change.
b. The difference between the means is significant at the .01 level using a two-tailed test.

Overall, older agencies receive more appropriations than younger agencies. However, when age is plotted against appropriations, two distinct subgroups emerge. One group clearly follows the general relationship just stated: as age increases, appropriations increase. The other group does not follow this pattern, and in fact, shows no significant relationship between aging and appropriations. The explanatory factor may be the interactive effect of agency type (regulatory versus nonregulatory) on age, appropriations, and size. Nonregulatory agencies (for example, REA, NCI) fell into the first category, while regulatory agencies (for example, FTC, ICC) fell into the second group. It should be noted that only agencies less than 42 years old fell into the first group. Beyond 42 years, all agencies seemed unresponsive to the effects of chronological aging, probably because such effects would have already been felt.

As agencies become older, the rate of change in appropriations decreases. Older agencies average only a 6% annual growth in their appropriations, compared to 26% for younger agencies. And a plot of age and magnitude of appropriations change shows that as agencies get older there is an exponential decrease in magnitude of change of appropriations. Thus, older agencies get smaller increases in funds at a slower rate than younger agencies (although overall they still have more absolute dollars than the younger agencies).

Younger agencies tend to be smaller and to have larger and more rapid changes in total personnel than older agencies. They have larger magnitude changes in middlegrades and supergrades as well. Two interesting effects that contradict common sense expectations about younger agencies are evident, however. First, younger agencies tend to have more supergrades than older agencies—even though the number of supergrades increases across time for both older and younger agencies. This may be the result of the work requirements of the agency—for example, newer agencies that are more science and research oriented may require more supergrades. The younger agencies in our sample (NCI, AID, USIA, and some of the AEC agency years) do tend to be science and/or research oriented. Second, younger agencies change more slowly in their middle-grade and supergrade personnel (−48% change in the rate of change of middlegrades for younger agencies versus −260% for older ones, and −140% change in the rate of change of supergrades for younger agencies versus −144% for older ones). This may be because as agencies age they are given responsibility (usually by statute) for an increasing number of programs that require an increasing number of managerial personnel.

Younger agencies tend to be more responsive financially to environmental influences than older agencies. (See Table 7–7 in the chapter appendix for the comparison of slopes on which the following conclusions are based.) The influence of UE, SOL, and %DV on APP, RATE.APP, and MAG.APP, using a one-year lag, is almost uniformly greater for younger agencies than for older ones. Younger agencies are also less responsive structurally to environmental influences than older agencies. For example, a 1% increase in UE results in an average 4,200-person gain in total personnel for older agencies, but a 1,400-person drop in total personnel for younger agencies. A 1% increase in DV results in an average 566-person decrease for younger agencies, but a 1,500-person gain for older agencies.

As younger agencies get older they become more stable, shifting from a pattern of fluctuating increase and decrease in appropriations, size, and supergrades to a pattern of steady growth in appropriations and supergrades (6% and 11% annual rates respectively) and no growth in size.

The effect of chronological age itself seems to vary as an agency gets older. AGE will generally increase the appropriations of young agencies, but have little effect on appropriations for older agencies. Increasing AGE will also tend to result in fluctuating appropriations becoming more steady, either in an increasing or decreasing direction. AGE brought decreases to NASA and AID, but also brought increases to NCI and REA. The effect of AGE on size is negative both for older and younger agencies, but much more for older agencies (−1000 persons per year) than for younger agencies (−520 persons per year). The fact that older agencies are larger despite the negative effect of age probably results from their being created with a much larger initial personnel base.

THE EFFECTS OF STRUCTURAL AGING

For this part of the study, the effect of structural aging, using the dimension of size, is examined. The number of middlegrades was used as the criterion variable for structural age since it had the highest correlations with other measures of this dimension. A cutting point of 1,800 middlegrades was used to establish subsamples of structurally old agencies (more than 1,800 middlegrades) and structurally young agencies (less than 1,800 middlegrades).

The effects of structural aging thus defined were similar to the effects of chronological aging. Structurally old agencies on the average are larger and richer than structurally young agencies. Their magnitudes of change are generally smaller. Their rates of change tend to go from fluctuation for structurally young agencies to acceleration for structurally older agencies; this acceleration tends to become smaller over time. Plotting appropriations against size reveals two subgroups of agencies similar to the subgroups found when plotting appropriations and age. One subgroup of agencies increases its appropriations as it gets larger, the other does not. Remarks concerning the interactive effect from the discussion of chronological aging apply here too.

One major difference between chronological and structural aging appears. Larger agencies (structurally older agencies) are more budgetarily responsive than smaller agencies. Yet, chronologically older agencies are less budgetarily responsive than younger agencies. It is hard to tell why these differences occur. Looking at Table 6–5 from the previous chapter, it would seem that larger and richer agencies may be more responsive to environmental influences than smaller or poorer agencies. On the one hand, this seems reasonable because larger and richer agencies by definition have more power and resources with which to respond. On the other hand, if high numbers of middlegrades (or total personnel or supergrades or whatever other measure seems appropriate), constitute structurally old agencies, then the two major dimensions of aging do not have similar consequences. However, Chapter 6 shows that old agencies eventually decline. If this is the case, the contradictory findings are a result of the confounding influence of chronological age on structural age. Large agencies then would be middle-aged agencies, not structurally old ones. Obviously, this question needs additional exploration.

THE EFFECTS OF STRUCTURAL CHANGE

Despite the frequency with which some organizations undergo change —often in an attempt to rejuvenate themselves—not much is really known about the effects of such change. In this section three kinds of organizational change are examined: rapid change in agency size, reversal of the direction of change, and high magnitude change.

RAPID CHANGE IN AGENCY SIZE

Rapid change in agency size means that the number of personnel added to or subtracted from the agency in a given year is substantially greater than in the previous year. In this study, the cutoff of twice the amount of change in the previous year was used. The choice is admittedly arbitrary but it seems intuitively reasonable, and significant differences between agencies do turn up in the analysis when using this cutting point. Instances of rapid change are less numerous than instances of slow change (26.1% of the agency years—46 cases—were rapidly changing).

Agencies undergoing rapid change in personnel size tend to differ from slowly changing agencies in a number of characteristics. The most general differences can be stated simply: rapidly changing agencies tend to have more money, more total personnel, and more supergrades than nonrapidly changing agencies. (See Table 7–6 in the chapter appendix for a number of comparisons of rapidly changing and slowly changing agencies.)

The most important differences between rapidly changing agencies and slowly changing agencies are summarized in Table 7–3. The tendency is for slowly changing agencies to change in smaller magnitudes, with smaller reversals in direction of change, and not to have larger changes.

TABLE 7–3. **Patterns of Change for Rapidly and Slowly Changing Agencies (average annual change)**

	Rapidly Changing Agencies	Slowly Changing Agencies	Significant[b] Difference
MAG.APP	30%	12%	yes
RATE.APP	170%[a]	−17%	yes
MAG.SIZE	2%	4%	no
RATE.SIZE	−75%	−23%	yes
MAG.MG	6%	10%	no
RATE.MG	−87%	−77%	yes
MAG.SG	17%	17%	no
RATE.SG	−87%[a]	−80%	no

a. Designates reversal in the direction of change.
b. The difference between the means is significant at the .01 level using a two-tailed test.

The effect of the reductions in magnitude and reversals in direction of change is to push both types of agencies toward a quasi-equilibrium. That is, magnitudes and rates decrease but never approach zero—except for limited periods. The state of and changes in an agency's environment continuously act as shocks disrupting this tendency towards equilibrium. Rapidly changing agencies have less of a tendency towards equilibrium than slowly changing agencies.

Profiles of agencies, however, do not tell whether rapidly changing agencies are more responsive to environmental and structural influences. This can be examined by comparing regression slopes between variables for the rapid and slow agency year subsamples. (See Table 7–8 in the chapter appendix.) By and large, these slopes indicate that rapidly changing agencies are more responsive *financially* to environmental and structural influences, but less responsive *structurally*. An agency with rapid changes in personnel has greater reversals in its appropriations as a result of increases in DV, UE, MAG.SIZE, and RATE.SIZE and greater increases in appropriations resulting from SOL, AGE, and trend across time than occurs in more slowly changing agencies. On the other hand, an agency's structure and changes therein are more responsive to these variables when an agency is changing more slowly. The net result seems to be that rapid personnel change tends to cause agencies to get more money and personnel in response to environmental and structural conditions than they would have if they were more slowly changing.

DIRECTION OF PERSONNEL CHANGES

Reversing the direction of personnel changes is another way of "shaking up" an agency. Cutbacks in a growing agency or increases in an agency that had been declining in size can both disrupt agency activities. Reversals in personnel changes are more common than very rapid changes in personnel (31.9% of the agency years had reversals in direction of change in total personnel). Reversals tended to occur more in older, larger, and richer agencies than in younger, smaller, or poorer ones. Reversals also tended to occur with smaller changes in appropriations, but larger changes in structure. Thus, shaking up agencies by reversing their direction of change in personnel actually tends to occur with no reversal in the direction of change in appropriations. Since budgetary reversals do tend to affect personnel reversals, the asymmetry is remarkable, but explainable. A frequent intent of such reversals may be to shift agency emphasis from service to clients (which requires large numbers of employees) to spending on programs. If a source of shakeups is that agencies have overly large overhead relative to the benefits produced, then this explanation of the asymmetrical relation between personnel and budgetary reversals is plausible. In addition, a shifting policy emphasis would not necessarily affect the total budget or changes therein, since the shift in emphasis could occur by changes between line items of a budget such as from personnel to "direct benefits." Although changing direction of appropriations growth or decline could also indicate shakeups, those reversals are likely also to affect personnel changes. Thus, the same or similar results of budgetary reversals could be expected to occur.

HIGH MAGNITUDE CHANGES

Yet another way of shaking up an agency results from high magnitude changes—for example, large percentage increases or decreases in total personnel or appropriations. However, examination of differences between agencies with high magnitude changes (defined by greater than 10% change in total personnel) indicates that the high magnitude changes are artifacts of small agencies (mean total personnel of 7,000, as contrasted with a mean total personnel of 22,000 for all agency years). If this is the case, differences between these subsamples will be mainly effects of agency size. On the other hand, if small agencies are especially prone to shakeups, these differences would bear further investigation. Since shakeups, as measured by rates of change and reversals of change, occur more frequently with larger agencies, it seems probable that effects resulting from high magnitude change are spurious and are actually effects of agency size, except perhaps in the cases of large agencies that are gaining or losing programs based on changing patterns of grants of statutory authority.

Conclusion

It now seems clear that the model presented in Figure 7–2 must be revised to take into account the interactive effects stemming from organizational change (in terms of personnel) and the aging of agencies, both chronologically and structurally. In addition, some of our findings have hinted at the impact of the type of agency in terms of substantive mission. Other inquiries, not reported here, indicate that agency growth and historical events of an external character also have such interactive effects. These effects must also be incorporated into the model.

Including these interactive effects in our model of agency change will increase its predictive and explanatory power. A diagram of the amended model is presented in Figure 7–3. From the diagram and the previous analysis, it is obvious that these interactive variables have an influence on budgetary change not only through their influence on block variables (change in unemployment, Democratic electoral base, and rate

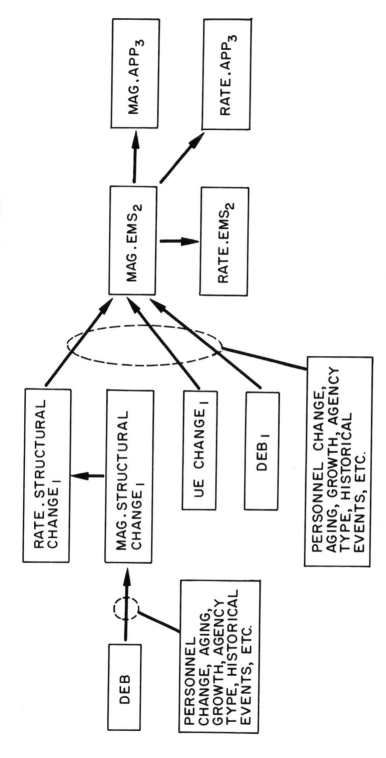

FIGURE 7-3: INTERACTIVE MODEL OF AGENCY CHANGE[a]

a. Dotted lines indicate presence of interactive effects. Their nature is not yet sufficiently understood to allow causal modeling with empirical data.

161

of structural change) but also through their independent influence on
change in policy actions. This would explain some of the skewness of
residuals for estimates in Figure 7–2. However, because these interactive
effects are complex, evaluating the fit of the model, including interactive
variables, is a very problematic venture and one beyond the scope of this
paper. This conclusion, however, is a classic instance of how one set of
findings and explorations point—in this case quite clearly—to the next
important research enterprise that should be undertaken.

Appendix

The text indicates that the initial path model that was developed had
to be rejected because of problems with validity and consistency. Likewise, the most plausible alternative to the "best" path model was also
rejected. This appendix discusses these rejected models (called Model A
and Model B) as well as technical aspects of the accepted model (presented in the text in Figure 7–2). The appendix also presents statistical
tables relevant to the text discussion of nonlinear and interactive effects
(Tables 7–6, 7–7, and 7–8).

THE INITIAL MODEL

The initial model is presented in Figure 7–4. The same dependent
variables—change in expenditures and change in appropriations—were
used in both Model A and the best path model. The arrangement of the
remaining blocks of variables was suggested by previous empirical research, some of which is reported in Chapter 6. In Model A both change
measures, MAG and RATE, were treated together.

During testing, evidence indicated that this model produced inconsistent estimates—for example, partial Betas were greater than 1.0. In
addition, several variables within the blocks had very low validity coefficients (two were less than .20). Because of the doubts about consistency and validity, this model was not evaluated for its fit with empirical predictions.

THE BEST PATH MODEL

Table 7–4 presents the summary statistics on the "best" path model
that is used in the text as the basis for the substantive discussion. When
zero order correlations are estimated for this model and the observed

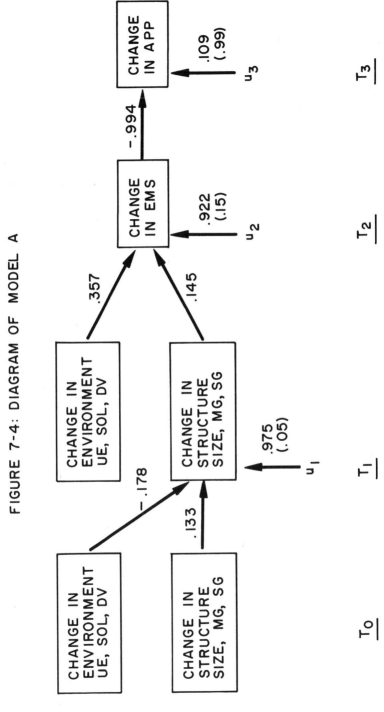

FIGURE 7-4: DIAGRAM OF MODEL A

TABLE 7-4. Summary Table for the Best Path Model

Dependent Variable	Independent Variable	Path Coefficient	Direct Effects Raw Coefficient	Partial r Squared	F	Net Effects Simple r Squared	Multiple r Squared
Mag. SC_1	DEB U1	.229 .973	0.030	.052	2.68	.052	.052
Rate. SC_1	Mag. SC_1 U2	.328 .944	5.223	.108	4.6	.108	.108
Mag. EMS_2	DEB UE Change$_1$ Rate. SC_1 U3	−.356 .458 .139 .906	−.894 3.137 0.168	.020 .129 .033	3.7 24.6 2.4	.011 .070 .018	.183
Rate. EMS_2	Mag. EMS_2 U4	−.950 .312	−8.048	.902	1,734.5	.902	.902
Mag. APP_3	Mag. EMS_2 U5	.949 .315	0.111	.901	1,513.3	.901	.901
Rate. APP_3	Mag. EMS_2 U6	−.994 .109	−8.049	.988	14,926.9	.988	.988

$$MAG.SC_1 = a_1 + b_1 DEB + U1$$
$$RATE.SC_1 = a_2 + b_1 MAG.SC_1 + U2$$
$$MAG.EMS_2 = a_3 + b_1 DEB_1 + b_2 \, UE \, CHANGE_1 + b_3 \, RATE.SC_1 + U3$$
$$RATE.EMS_2 = a_4 + b_1 MAG.EMS_2 + U4$$
$$MAG.APP_3 = a_5 + b_1 MAG.EMS_2 + U5$$
$$RATE.APP_3 = a_6 + b_1 MAG.EMS_2 + U6$$

correlations are subtracted from the estimates, the mean residual correlation is −.022. This value has a probability of .827 of coming from a universe whose mean is zero (as estimated by use of a t–test)—which is relatively good support for believing the model fits the data. Unfortunately, this distribution of residual correlations appears to be skewed. Fisher's g_1 measure of skewness is −2.106 (in the direction of underestimating the observed correlations). The probability that such a skewed value would occur by chance is less than .001. The most extreme underestimation occurs for the estimated correlations between UE CHANGE with RATE.EMS and RATE.APP. Given the high collinearity between change measures of appropriations and expenditures, the standard errors of estimates using these variables is quite high. One would normally expect those estimated correlations to be more subject to error than the others.

The effect of these errors on the results is quite marked. If one looks at all residuals other than those two, the mean is .0089, with a .994 probability of being zero. The skewness would then be −.0123 with a .976 probability of being zero (having no skewness). Thus, not only are the errors of prediction greatest for those estimates known to have the largest standard errors, but if those errors are attributed to the sampling variability resulting from the large standard errors, then the residual correlations have a nearly zero mean and virtually no skewness at all.

THE REJECTION OF THE MOST PLAUSIBLE ALTERNATIVE TO THE BEST PATH MODEL

Since the errors of prediction may or may not be the result of the standard errors for the collinear variables, the next most mathematically plausible model was also evaluated. This model, called Model B, is presented in Figure 7–5. Summary statistics for Model B are presented in Table 7–5. The deleted path had the lowest F value of all other paths, and dropping it eliminates the underestimation of the correlations. However, Model B has a higher mean residual (.07 with a .509 probability of being zero) than the model used in the text and its results in a far more skewed distribution of residuals ($g_1 = 282.23$ with a t-score of 472.0— having a probability of much less than .001 of equaling zero). This poorer fit results from considerable overestimation of the correlation values. Since this next most plausible model clearly has a worse fit with the observed relations than the model used in the text, and no alternative confounding variables were noticed in the correlation matrix, the skewness of that model (the best path model) can be reasonably attributed to random variability. The model presented in the text is the model that best represents the relations between the variables studied.

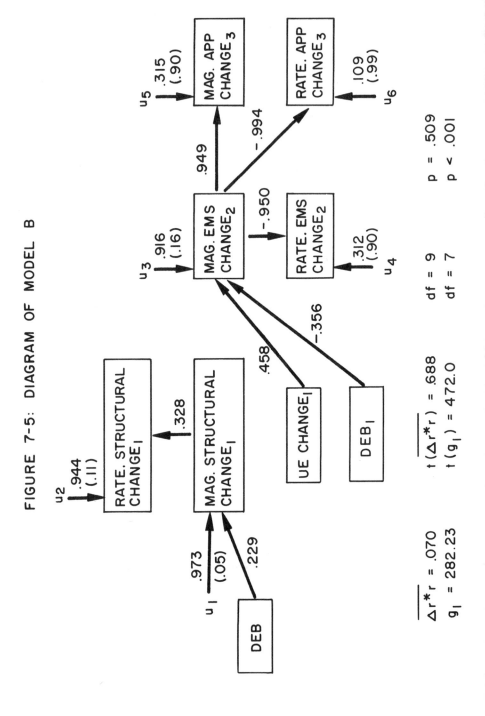

FIGURE 7-5: DIAGRAM OF MODEL B

$\overline{\Delta r^* r} = .070$ $t(\overline{\Delta r^* r}) = .688$ $df = 9$ $p = .509$

$g_1 = 282.23$ $t(g_1) = 472.0$ $df = 7$ $p < .001$

TABLE 7-5. Summary Table for Model B

Dependent Variable	Independent Variable	Direct Effects			F	Net Effects	
		Path Coefficient	Raw Coefficient	Partial r Squared		Simple r Squared	Multiple r Squared
Mag. SC_1	DEB U1	.229 .973	0.030	.052	2.68	.052	.052
Rate. SC_1	Mag. SC_1 U2	.328 .944	5.223	.108	4.6	.108	.108
Mag. EMS_2	UE Change$_1$ DEB_1 U3	.458 -.356 .916	3.137 -0.894	.070 .011	24.6 13.7	.070 .011	.163
Rate. EMS_2	Mag. EMS_2 U4	-.950 .312	-8.048	.902	1,734.5	.902	.902
Mag. APP_3	Mag. EMS_2 U5	.949 .315	0.111	.901	1,513.3	.901	.901
Rate. APP_3	Mag. EMS_2 U6	-.994 .109	-8.049	.988	14,926.9	.988	.988

$$MAG.SC_1 = a_1 + b_1 DEB + U1$$
$$RATE.SC_1 = a_2 + b_1 MAG.SC_1 + U2$$
$$MAG.EMS_2 = a_3 + b_1 DEB_1 + b_2 UE\ CHANGE_1 + U3$$
$$RATE.EMS_2 = a_4 + b_1 MAG.EMS_2 + U4$$
$$MAG.APP_3 = a_5 + b_1 MAG.EMS_2 + U5$$
$$RATE.APP_3 = a_6 + b_1 MAG.EMS_2 + U6$$

TABLE 7-6. Comparison of Mean Values of Variables for 187 Agency Years and Subsamples Thereof[a]

Agency Years	Variables													
	App	Mag. App	Rate. App	Sz	Mag. Sz	Rate. Sz	Mg	Mag. Mg	Rate. Mg	Sg	Mag. Sg	Rate. Sg	Age	N
All	.907 E9	1.16	-3.8	.22 E5	1.03	-.43	.18 E4	1.08	.02	78	1.16	.08	27.3	187
Young	.637 E9	1.26	-9.03	.14 E5	1.05	-1.9	.18 E4	1.12	.52	83	1.20	-.40	13.2	100
Old	.116 E10	1.06	1.03	.31 E5	1.00	1.25	.19 E4	1.04	-.54	72	1.11	.63	44	87
Rapid Change	.111 E10	1.30	-17.96	.26 E5	1.02	0.25	.18 E4	1.06	.13	80	1.17	-.13	27	46
Slow Change	.840 E9	1.12	.83	.22 E5	1.04	-.77	.18 E4	1.10	.33	71	1.17	.20	27	126
Reversing	.134 E10	1.06	.13	.36 E5	1.00	-9.3	.23 E4	1.07	-.40	78	1.12	.17	30	55
Nonreversing	.712 E9	1.22	-6.19	.17 E5	1.04	3.75	.17 E4	1.09	.21	80	1.19	.28	27	117
High Mag. Mg	.237 E9	1.24	3.0	.70 E4	1.15	1.31	.62 E3	1.20	1.30	34	1.26	-.68	20	32
Low Mag. Mg	.107 E10	1.15	-5.2	.25 E5	1.00	-1.70	.20 E4	1.06	-.26	87	1.14	.24	29	155
Small	.366 E9	1.18	-4.87	.36 E4	1.03	-.63	.60 E3	1.08	.16	61	1.14	-.23	29	154
Large	.329 E10	1.09	-.56	.11 E5	1.03	.44	.78 E4	1.12	-.63	156	1.25	1.14	21	33
Poor	.170 E9	1.18	-5.02	.70 E4	1.04	-.53	.90 E3	1.09	.44	43	1.16	.26	29	146
Rich	.371 E10	1.10	.79	.84 E5	1.00	-.08	.53 E4	1.05	-1.61	218	1.14	-.44	24	41
Low Mg	.213 E9	1.20	-5.21	.34 E4	1.03	-.79	.40 E3	1.08	.17	39	1.16	-.03	30	143
High Mg	.305 E10	1.06	-.68	.83 E5	1.01	.68	.64 E4	1.08	-.46	206	1.15	.32	21	44

a. Averaging the subsample means may not equal the grand mean due to rounding error. Some subsamples had fewer cases because of the absence of data for a criterion variable.

TABLE 7-7. Comparison of Slopes Between Variables for Old and Young Agencies

Dependent Variables	Independent Variables						
	%DV	%UE	SOL	SZ	MAG.SZ	RATE.SZ	AGE
App							
Young	−.43E8	−.10E9	.57E8	.17E5	−.16E10	.12E7	.30E8
Old	.96E7	.93E8	.18E8	.36E5	−.23E10	−.14E8	−.40E4
Rate.App							
Young	−.15E-1	.69E1	.20E1	.10E-3	.62E2	−.20E-1	−.54E0
Old	−.18E0	.59E0	.67E-1	−.70E-5	−.71E1	.43E-3	.28E-1
Mag.App							
Young	.38E-1	−.56E-1	−.50E-1	.35E-5	.30E-1	−.25E-3	.23E-2
Old	.30E-2	.33E-1	−.45E-2	0	.47E0	.32E-4	.52E-3
Sz							
Young	−.56E3	−.14E4	.33E3	1	−.15E5	.47E1	−.52E3
Old	.15E4	.42E4	−.16E4	1	−.57E5	−.31E3	−.10E4
Rate.Sz							
Young	−.42E1	−.23E1	.44E0	−.75E-5	.90E1	−.75E-2	.65E0
Old	.28E0	−.18E1	.22E0	−.17E-4	.62E0	−.16E-1	.23E0
Mag.Sz							
Young	.37E-2	−.23E1	.44E0	.50E-6	.30E0	−.75E-2	.65E0
Old	.55E-3	.70E-2	−.26E-2	0	.22E0	.46E-5	.12E-3

TABLE 7-8. Comparison of Slopes between Variables for Rapidly and Slowly Changing Agencies

Dependent Variables	Independent Variables							
	%DV	%UE	SOL	SZ	MAG.SZ	RATE.SZ	AGE	YEAR
App								
Rapid	-.20E9	-.43E8	.16E9	.33E5	-.77E10	-.10E8	.47E7	.11E9
Slow	.67E8	.11E8	.19E8	.30E5	-.19E10	-.14E6	-.36E7	.13E8
Rate.App								
Rapid	.42E10	.79E1	.62E1	.18E-3	.20E3	.19E-1	.57E0	.52E1
Slow	.20E10	.61E0	-.15E0	-.15E-4	.33E1	-.13E-2	.12E-1	-.10E0
Mag.App								
Rapid	-.32E-3	-.27E-1	-.68E-1	-.20E-5	.42E0	-.10E-1	-.80E-2	-.51E-1
Slow	.21E-1	.44E-1	-.18E-1	-.73E-6	.48E0	.30E-3	-.16E-2	-.11E-1
Sz								
Rapid	.22E4	.93E3	.16E4	1	-.15E6	-.14E4	.69E2	.11E4
Slow	.11E4	-.35E3	-.90E2	1	-.39E5	-.17E2	-.98E2	-.51E2
Rate.Sz								
Rapid	.43E-1	.10E0	.69E-1	-.70E-5	.21E2	1	.73E0	.61E-1
Slow	-.17E1	-.33E1	.66E0	-.99E-5	.94E1	1	.29E0	.35E0
Mag.Sz								
Rapid	.53E-2	.13E-1	-.31E-2	-.11E-6	1	.29E-2	-.44E-3	-.17E-2
Slow	-.15E-2	.46E-2	-.35E-2	-.31E-6	1	.13E-3	-.11E-2	-.22E-2
% Mg								
Rapid	-.51E-2	.29E-2	.74E-2	-.86E-6	-.23E0	.16E-2	.35E-3	.52E-2
Slow	-.65E-2	-.66E-2	.92E-2	-.89E-6	-.73E-1	.26E-3	.93E-3	.62E-2

8

The Empirical Analysis of Federal Policy-Making

Randall B. Ripley and Grace A. Franklin

This chapter opens by suggesting the most fruitful general questions for future research in the same general area addressed by the book. Next, a summary of the central empirical findings from chapters 2 through 7 is presented along with a number of additional specific suggestions for future research. The most general findings are:

1. The incrementalist perspective on budgetary policy-making is incomplete and sometimes inaccurate. Any explanation of budgetary policy actions that relies wholly or almost wholly on previous budgets presents a misleading view of reality.

2. A single phenomenon called agency maturity that both adequately captures the various meanings of maturity and is at the same time empirically usable was not defined. There seem to be at least four separate dimensions to the maturing process in an agency: chronological maturation, structural maturation, organizational maturation, and administrative maturation.

3. There seem to be agencies that are particularly favored by Democrats and other agencies that are particularly favored by Republicans.

4. Functional policy actions are at least partially independent of budgetary actions.

5. The concept of policy statements seems to have some limited empirical utility.

Finally, the "clinical" utility of this kind of research is discussed.

IN THIS VOLUME we have set forth a comprehensive conceptual framework for analyzing policy-making in the federal executive branch, and we have tested parts of that framework in a variety of ways. In general, we have tested a number of propositions about the determinants of federal agency budgets measured in terms of appropriations and expenditures and changes in appropriations and expenditures. In Chapter 5 we also dealt with non-budgetary policy actions. Elements of what we have called agency maturity, party strength, coalitions, and economic and social conditions all proved to be explanatory of many of the budgetary patterns we found. Nine very general research hypotheses presented in Chapter 1 stimulated the specific research undertaken, but were not themselves directly tested. Rather, the tests in Chapters 2 through 7 were of more limited hypotheses derived from four of the broader research hypotheses.

At the very least we hope that this first extensive empirical use of the conceptual framework will lead in three broad directions in future research on bureaucratic policy-making, not just at the federal level in the United States but at other governmental levels in the United States and in foreign bureaucracies as well (with appropriate changes in the details of operational definitions of variables to fit different settings).

First, the research on the four relationships investigated in this volume can be replicated and extended. The design and execution of any of the empirical chapters can be reproduced simply to verify the results reported here. More interesting and probably more fruitful would be the use of more and/or different agencies and different time periods to discover whether the results reported are generalizable to a larger set of agencies and to periods other than the 1950s and 1960s. Or, a variety of different operationalizations could be used for the variables. For example, we barely scratched the surface of dealing with economic and social conditions. Many different measures of these phenomena should be tried, especially as increasingly refined theorizing points the way to critical phenomena.

Second, five out of the nine broad research hypotheses received no treatment—even derivatively—in this volume. The relationship between internal agency characteristics (personnel features, decision-making characteristics) and agency policy actions, and the factors affecting policy results (economic and social conditions, public opinion, and previous policy actions)—all await exploration.

Third, the application of new "methodologies" (for want of a better word) or perspectives to any or all of the general hypotheses constitutes a third endeavor worth undertaking. A particularly fruitful new perspective involves experimentation with different conceptions of policy actions. For example, are program level or line item level actions susceptible to the same influences as aggregate budget actions? Nonbudgetary policy actions likewise need a great deal of attention. Political scientists and other social scientists run the risk of focusing exclusively on budgets seemingly forever because of the relative availability of data. This may produce very sophisticated knowledge about budget-making, but it also leaves large areas of policy-making still uncharted. The analogy to American election studies is instructive: we know a lot about the voting choice in presidential elections, but our knowledge of that choice in other elections is rough at best. We now know a great deal about budget-making (and, hopefully, this volume has contributed some new thoughts), but systematic exploration of other aspects of policy-making is in its infancy.

The above thoughts about the future are more than pious hopes. Although we expect to undertake some of the suggested enterprises ourselves, we both hope and expect to be joined by a number of other scholars. But the future is not now, and so we wish to use the rest of this concluding chapter to highlight what we consider the most interesting and important findings of the research reported in the foregoing chapters.

Empirical Findings

INCREMENTALISM

Five of the preceding empirical chapters (all but Chapter 5) dealt directly with the incrementalist analysis of budget-making in one way or another. Even Chapter 5 presents data relevant to an assessment of the incrementalist argument. The single finding that emerges most clearly from all of these chapters is that the incrementalist perspective is an incomplete and sometimes inaccurate way of explaining budgetary policy actions.

At a simple descriptive level, using a cutting point of $\pm 10\%$, budgetary policy actions were found to be nonincremental a significant portion of the time. This was true for year to year differences in both raw appropriations and raw expenditures, and also for differences in change measures of appropriations and expenditures. (See Figures 3-3, 4-2, 5-1, and 5-2 and Tables 4-1, 4-2, and 5-1.)

Furthermore, previous budgetary actions were not the most explanatory variables. Elements relating to agency maturity, coalitions supportive of the agency, party strength, and economic and social conditions are more explanatory than previous budgetary actions and can also be used to explain budgetary policy actions in previous years. Thus, the inclusion of explanatory variables in addition to previous budgetary actions not only suggests the relatively weaker influence of those actions but also suggests the reasons for the observed relationships over time between budgetary actions: budgetary actions at both t_1 and t_2 can be explained by elements of maturity, coalitions, party strength, and economic and social conditions; budget actions at t_1 do not explain budget actions at t_2 in any sense but a statistical one and even that relationship is often weaker than other statistical relationships.

We are confident of the critical position we have taken on the incremental description of budget-making because numerous and varied tests have always yielded the same general results. The chapters dealing directly with incrementalism use four different groupings of agencies (12 are used in Chapter 2 and are chosen to represent seven different issue areas; 40—all in the same department—are used in Chapter 3; eight—chosen because they are "politically salient"—are used in Chapter 4; and ten—chosen to represent a mixture of size of work force and budget and substantive mission—were used in Chapters 6 and 7). Different independent variables are used to "compete" with previous budgetary actions. And different methodologies are used in performing the analysis. In Chapter 7 salaries are subtracted from expenditures to make sure that those figures did not somehow distort the findings (they did not). In Chapter 3 controls were used to compensate for inflation to make sure that that factor did not inject some systematic bias into the findings (it didn't). But with all of these internal differences, the same conclusion repeatedly emerges: any explanation of budgetary policy actions that relies wholly or almost wholly on previous budgets presents a misleading view of reality.

Changes in budgetary decisions are not necessarily small, nor are they necessarily predictable as a function of a previous budgetary base. Many changes are large, and there are many explanations of both base year figures and the changes from those figures that involve a much richer understanding of political reality than just the insight that policy-makers may focus on what base exists and the margin of change from that base. In addition, some technical quirks of methodology have led some of the incrementalists to overstate their case about the relation of changes to a base figure. (See AUTOCORRELATION and OLS REGRESSION in the Methodological Glossary.)

Other recent literature also attacks the incrementalist perspective from other angles. Natchez and Bupp (1973) add the finding that program level data do not present an incremental picture. Gist (1974) argues that given a high proportion of budget items that are "uncontrollable" in the short run because they are legislatively mandated outside of the regular appropriations process even "incremental thinking" on the part of policy-makers about bases and margins cannot meaningfully take place about much of the budget. The data problems in sorting out which parts of a budget are controllable are enormous (see Weidenbaum and Larkins, 1972) and was a process we did not attempt. If Gist is correct, then sorting out the controllable items alone and performing analyses similar to what we have done on them should make the empirical weakness of the incrementalist position even more evident.

In fairness, although we in no way want to mute our basic empirical disagreement with the incrementalists, it should be added that incrementalism has many different meanings. By making the empirical claim that budgets are explained not by previous budgets but by other factors and that changes are not always small, we are not disputing the claims that the rationality of persons dealing with complex phenomena is limited, and they therefore deal with "successive limited comparisons" in thinking about and acting on reality. Nor, despite Gist's caveat, are we disputing the claims that budget-makers in particular think in terms of a base situation and the increments of change in it. Our data do not permit us to comment empirically on these claims and, at the level of hunch, we think they are probably in good measure true. They are certainly sensible claims, which explains in part the pervasiveness of those parts of the incrementalist perspective.

The pervasiveness of the parts of the incrementalist perspective that we are challenging is also understandable: it makes reality look relatively simple and ordered and predictable. Social scientists yearning for the respectability of being able to predict accurately are naturally attracted to a scheme that seems so plausible and so well buttressed empirically. Unfortunately, our findings lead us to the conclusion that it is inaccurate enough to require replacement. We do not yet claim that the conceptual framework presented in Chapter 1 represents that replacement in fullblown form. Indeed, part of that framework is as yet in the both enviable (because it is hard to attack) and damnable (because it has no empirical backing) position of not having received even preliminary testing. But our findings give us confidence that we are, in fact, working toward an adequate—although not nearly as simple—replacement.

AGENCY MATURITY

At the outset of developing the theoretical framework, we constructed a concept called agency maturity based on a wide reading of a diverse literature on organizations. This literature hinted, obliquely, at a concept called maturity and suggested various aspects of it, such as size, age, and complexity. We assumed a valid, single concept existed and could be measured. But the resounding judgment of the empirical explorations with the indicators used to date must be that agency maturity is an elusive, if not illusive, concept.

Because it encompasses a variety of aspects—physical, structural, organizational, experiential—the concept generates confusion. This confusion is evident in the different ways the empirical chapters approached the concept. Chapters 2 and 6 treat it as a single unified concept. Chapter 3 differentiates between aspects of maturity and addresses a component labelled administrative maturity. Chapters 4 and 7 make no assertion about agency maturity, and instead deal only with indicators of the block labelled agency structure in the theoretical framework presented in Figure 1–1.

In only one of the five chapters dealing with agency maturity in some way did the author state that the indicators of maturity moved together and that their relationship to policy actions was in the predicted direction (Chapter 2). In the other chapters (Chapters 3, 4, 6, and 7), the indicators either failed to move together in the expected direction, or their relationship to policy actions was not in the predicted direction, or the same indicator used in different chapters yielded different results.

For example, of the indicators selected in Chapter 3 for the component of administrative maturity, two (size and cumulative staff experience) were related to policy actions as predicted, one (cumulative experience of agency head) was unrelated, and one (ratio of supergrades to size) was related but in the opposite of the predicted direction. As another example, agency size was used in several of the chapters with differing results. In Chapter 2, size was positively related to change in policy actions. In Chapter 3, size was positively related to increasing policy actions, and in Chapter 4, percent change in size was positively related to percent change in policy actions. But the path model presented in Chapter 6 showed size to have an inverse relationship to policy actions.

An additional problem regarding indicators for agency maturity exists: the hierarchy measures, much touted in Chapter 1, yielded a very mixed bag of results, and as yet don't appear to contribute much to the maturity concept. In Chapter 6, number of supergrades and number of middlegrades had to be dropped from the path model because of their weak relationship to policy actions. In Chapter 3, the supergrade to size ratio showed no relationship to policy actions. Similarly, in Chapter 4, percent change in the ratios of supergrades to size and middlegrades to size showed no relationship to policy actions. On the other hand, in Chapter 2, the magnitude of change in supergrade personnel was related to change in policy actions in the predicted direction. And in Chapter 6, number of supergrades was inversely related to policy actions for a subsample of rich agencies.

The foregoing paragraphs confirm what is no doubt obvious—the indicators tested so far do not support a single concept of agency maturity.

At this point we would take the following positions on maturity: first, there does not seem to be a single phenomenon called agency maturity; second, there are at least four separate dimensions to the maturing process in an agency; and third, each of these separate dimensions deserves exploration in relation to policy actions and, ultimately, policy results.

The first two dimensions of maturity relate to the types of aging discussed in Chapter 7. Chronological aging is completely time-dependent—it is simply the length of time the agency has been in existence. We would expect that, all other things being equal, chronologically more mature agencies would have decreasing change in policy actions (slower rate and lower magnitude, although the absolute size of appropriations would probably continue to increase over time). Agencies that are less chronologically mature would have greater rate and magnitude changes in policy actions.

Structural aging or maturity can be independent of time. It is characterized by internal properties of the agency such as size, hierarchical organization, functional differentiation, and complexity. The interaction of these components of structural maturity is complex and more experimentation is needed to derive an index of structural maturity indicators. In general, we would expect that larger, more structurally complex agencies would be more mature and would have smaller changes and slower growth in policy actions (less rate and lower magnitudes) than smaller, less structurally complex agencies. The findings in Chapter 7 dealing with structural aging support these expectations, but more work with additional indicators of structural aging (only one was used in Chapter 7) needs to be done to confirm them.

Yet a third type of maturity can be identified. Organizational maturity refers to the frequency of changes experienced in an agency's organization —functions transferred in or out, additions or losses of statutory authority, personnel moving in or out, or up or down, consolidations or mergers with all or part of another agency. An agency undergoing periodic reorganizations may retain a more "youthful" (less mature) perspective than an agency that rarely or never experiences these changes. We expect that less organizationally mature agencies would have greater changes and growth in policy actions than more organizationally mature agencies.[1]

Yet another kind of maturity involves the administrative maturity concept discussed in Chapter 3. Administrative maturity focuses on the experience and presumed expertise of personnel within the agency rather than on features of the agency or its structure. The expectation is that agencies that are more administratively mature will have increasing changes and greater growth in policy actions than agencies that are less administratively mature. Of the indicators used in Chapter 3, only administrative experience (measured by appearances at appropriations hearings) was highly explanatory for budgetary policy actions. Two additional (and interrelated) measures of administrative experience that await testing are tenure of the agency head (length of time in office) and turnover of agency head (number of times agency head changed in a time period). Both of these measures should have a curvilinear relationship with policy actions. Too little turnover or very short tenure (characteristics of an administratively immature agency) would result in stagnant or decreasing policy actions. A high degree of turnover or excessive tenure (characteristics of an administratively overmature agency) would also result in decreasing policy actions. Increasing policy actions would be most likely when tenure and turnover were both moderate.

Obviously there is a good deal yet to be done in order to clarify these dimensions of agency maturity, the interrelationships among them, their relationship to policy actions, and their relationship to external environmental factors.[2] These relationships are far more complex—and interesting—than the organizational theory literature had initially suggested to us.

PARTISAN AGENCIES

Chapters 6 and 7 suggest that agencies' policy actions may vary depending on different conditions of party strength in the electorate and in government (strength of numbers and of attitude). The possibility that there may be "Democratic agencies" and "Republican agencies" is a complex one, however. Some of the findings of Chapter 6 suggest that Democrats might be particularly favorable to agencies that concentrate on spending (that is, that have a high ratio of dollars to personnel) and to agencies that are relatively small and poor during periods when Republican strength is at its greatest. Thus, Democrats seem to concentrate more on increasing the dollars available to agencies they particularly favor and less on expanding the size of the work force of those agencies.

It seems reasonable to assert that differentiated partisan support for various agencies is based on what those agencies do and the clientele they serve. The tests conducted did not address this question, but additional hypotheses come to mind that deserve testing. For example, it might be hypothesized that agencies whose major programs fall into the redistributive arena (Lowi, 1964) will be more strongly supported under conditions of greater Democratic strength than under conditions of lesser Democratic strength. It might also be hypothesized that agencies focusing on providing services to the poorer classes in society will also fare better under conditions of greater Democratic strength. These hypotheses and ones similar to them deserve systematic testing. Likewise, partisan strength inside the government as well as that in the electorate needs to be explored in relation to the relative budgetary patterns pertaining to different agencies.

Still another possibility that requires exploration is that administrations of different presidents (or even different periods of the administration of a single president) evolve broad strategies for dealing with domestic problems that naturally favor some agencies budgetarily at the relative expense of other agencies. Thus, for example, Rivlin (1974) suggests that much domestic policy for the 40 years beginning in the early 1930s can be viewed as relying either on a social insurance strategy or on a federal grant for human services strategy. In the last few years four new strategies have evolved and have been used experimentally, although none of them has become as compelling as either social insurance or federal grants. Rivlin calls these strategies (1) reducing disparities in individual cash income (for example, through tax credits or a negative income tax), (2) financing individual services (for example, through various voucher systems), (3) revenue sharing (both general and special as currently being tried in the manpower and housing and community development fields), and (4) institution changing (a mixture of the previous three with stress on "incentives" or "bribes" to induce desired institutional behavior).

The relative reliance of a presidential administration on various strategies should be injected as a variable that might explain both budgetary patterns and other kinds of policy patterns. There may be "social insurance" agencies and "revenue sharing" agencies and "federal grant" agencies instead of "Democratic" agencies and "Republican" agencies, although, of course, each party may have strategy preferences that persist over long periods of time. Obviously, data problems are severe in giving this possibility a rigorous test. Particularly tricky are the necessity of a long time period to separate strategy differences from partisan differences and the question of how to operationalize strategies.

THE RELATIONSHIP BETWEEN BUDGETARY AND FUNCTIONAL POLICY ACTIONS

Chapter 5 offers the intriguing hint that "functional" actions (that is, actions measured in ways other than dollars of appropriations or expenditures) are at least partially independent of budgetary actions.

In a common sense way, of course, the totality of agency actions will always be related strongly to the limits set by available dollars. In some cosmic sense dollar output has to equal dollar input. Thus, the language in several chapters about budgets forming limits on actions is generally true and an intuitively useful notion. However, Chapter 5 also makes clear that this general notion should not be pushed too far. That is, agency and program administrators have considerable latitude in choosing the purposes for which they will use their dollars. And they can alter the mixture of purposes quite dramatically independent of short term changes in dollars. Even if total dollars available to an agency in a given year increases by 5% compared to the previous year, it is still quite possible for action A to increase by 100%, action B to increase 50% and action C to decrease 50%, and so on. The outer boundaries of actions are set by total available resources, but the possibilities for quite different internal options are numerous.

The findings of Chapter 5 also offer a supplement to the program level analysis of Natchez and Bupp (1973) and Kanter (1972). Those researchers claim that treating total agency budgets masks important program level changes. Chapter 5 suggests a further disaggregation—to the level of specific actions within agencies and programs. It may be that treating a given program as a single entity masks important differences in the actions within that program. And, of course, changing mixtures of nonbudgetary actions may reveal changing patterns of substantive emphasis within a program or within a set of agency programs.

POLICY STATEMENTS

Although the concept of policy statements was not included in the theoretical framework presented in Chapter 1, Chapter 2 uses this concept in a limited, but useful way. The principal reason for the exclusion of the concept in Chapter 1 was the massive commitment of time required to collect and analyze statements for the very large number of participants from a variety of often fugitive sources. This problem was overcome in Chapter 2 because of ready access to a precoded data set of statements for one actor (the President) from one set of his messages (State of the Union addresses). Unless similar data sets for the statements of other actors become available, however, we believe that the exclusion of policy statements from the theoretical framework is wise.

From a theoretical rather than practical point of view, the findings of Chapter 2 suggest the utility of using policy statements in an *ad hoc* and limited way—with full recognition that the President is only one of numerous policy actors, that although he is important in the broad sweep of policy he cannot be involved in the detailed decisions of all agencies and programs, and that all of the policy statements of even this one actor are not available (especially since the taping of presidential conversations has presumably ceased!). Specifically, the most intriguing finding to emerge from Chapter 2 was that changes in policy statements were more explanatory of changes in budgetary policy actions than changes in general social conditions or changes in agency maturity (although less explanatory than changes in issue-related social conditions). Thus, we think that, when available and when used with caution and discretion, policy statements may have limited utility in specific studies.

Empirical Findings and the Real World: Clinical Utility

Basic social science research (such as that reported in this book) is often divorced from the concerns of the federal agency and program manager. Research designs are constructed with little thought for the subjects that could be of interest to managers, and research results are secreted away in obfuscating professional journals and conferences, with no effort to extract and disseminate findings that may have relevance to the manager. We feel this "isolationist" attitude on the part of social scientists, whether conscious or unconscious, is wrong-headed, because it renders the various disciplines at least partially sterile and impotent. It is, of course, difficult to bridge the gap between the interests of the social scientist concerned with mapping and explaining the world of policy and politics and the interests of the bureaucrat concerned with surviving in and, hopefully, improving his position in the world of policy and politics. But difficulty does not imply impossibility, and we heartily endorse the position that social science should be concerned with and responsive to the needs of policy-makers at least part of the time.

This recommendation does not mean that all research should be directed at policy-makers, or that only research requested by policy-makers should be undertaken. Such an approach—a series of unrelated *ad hoc* efforts addressing numerous "interesting" questions—would quickly render the discipline sterile and impotent in another sense, in that a cumulative knowledge of basic processes would not be developed.

But those who stress the difference between the idiosyncratic concerns of a specific manager and the basic knowledge and patterns concerns of a specific social scientist often push the distinction too far and claim too much for it. Inevitably, much of what the good social scientist does will at most be of only tangential interest to the manager. And many of the manager's needs will be of little concern to the social scientist. However, just because the sets of managerial concerns and social science concerns are not congruent does not mean that there is no significant intersection between them. And it is the task of the social scientist who wants to be heard by the manager to identify those intersections and put his or her message in language meaningful and comprehensible to the manager.

In the research reported in this book we have dealt with the impact of a number of environmental and structural variables on the policy actions of agencies over time. In a broad sense agency managers need to be interested in the impact of environmental factors on their programs not because these are conditions they can manipulate but because they need to know what to expect when certain external changes occur, and because they need to know what features of the environment to monitor systematically in order to enhance their predictive capability. In a very important sense one of the secrets of good management is the ability to predict, just as that is the goal of good social science.

In an equally broad sense, agency managers need to be interested in the impact of structural factors on their programs because it is in the area of structure that they have some ability to manipulate arrangements to produce desired changes or at least prevent undesired changes. Not everything about an agency's structure can be manipulated, no matter how skillful a manager is. But even small latitude for maneuver may have large scale ramifications for the shape of policy actions emerging from the agency. And we would also speculate that even modest room for manipulation might well have important consequences for policy results.

Each of the six empirical chapters in this volume contributes some explicit messages for agency and program managers. A summary of those messages will both underscore the specific potential utility of the kind of research reported here and will also allow us to comment further on the general utility of social scientists to federal bureaucrats and on the limits to that utility.

The clinical messages contained in the empirical chapters are presented here in a conditional form: If an administrator wants to accomplish X, he should do more (or less) of Y. In utilizing this conditional form, we are not presuming to dictate the goals that agencies should pursue. Rather, we wish to demonstrate the links between the research we have undertaken and the world of the agency or program administrator seeking to achieve specific kinds of goals. The foregoing chapters, then, support the following advice to agency administrators:

1. If an administrator wants to maximize the responsiveness of his agency to social conditions, he should self-consciously identify the issue areas in which the agency's programs have impact because the constraints in different issue areas are different and the administrators can package programs to increase their relevance to different issue areas.

2. If an administrator wants to maximize the number of dollars available to his agency through congressional appropriations, he should be aggressive in increasing requests for appropriations over previous requests and over previous appropriations figures.

3. If an administrator wants to maximize the number of dollars available to his agency, he should concentrate more heavily on building support within the executive branch (especially the Office of Management and Budget) than on building support within Congress.

4. If an administrator wants to maximize the number of dollars available to his agency, he should actively seek public attention and support for the agency from the President.

5. If an administrator wants to maximize the number of dollars available to his agency, he should attempt to increase the size of his agency simply in terms of total number of employees.

6. If an administrator wants to maximize the number of dollars available to his agency, he should attempt to minimize congressional controversy over the agency's programs.

7. If an administrator in a relatively poor agency wants to improve the budget of his agency, he should work particularly hard to get authorization to hire additional supergrades, and he should make sure that all such slots are filled.

8. If an administrator wants to maximize the number of dollars available to his agency through congressional appropriations, he should spend all of the money available to his agency for a fiscal year before the end of that fiscal year.

A scheme for categorizing clinical messages to managers begins to emerge from just these few messages. First, there are messages that confirm conventional wisdom that is found in the literature (usually based on interviews with participants). Statements 6 and 8 fall in this category. Administrators have been telling each other (and social scientists) that controversy in Congress should be avoided and that all money should be committed by June 30 of each year in order to increase the chances of favorable budget action for the future. Our findings confirm the wisdom of this behavior in concrete terms.

Second, there are messages that disconfirm conventional wisdom. Statement 3 falls in this category, as much of the literature suggests Congress is the most potent determinant of final budget figures (see, for example, Freeman, 1965: 54–55).

Third, there are messages on which there had previously been mixed evidence both in the social science literature and in the conventional wisdom passed orally from administrator to administrator. Statements 2 and 4 fall into this category. Both scholars and administrators have debated the consequences of an aggressive budgetary request strategy. Our evidence suggests it is a wise strategy if the goal is to maximize the budget coming from appropriations. Both scholars and administrators also have debated the wisdom of trying to involve the President personally. Some have taken such involvement as a sign of desperation indicating an agency to be in deep trouble (the foreign aid agency is often used as an example to support this point of view). Others have taken it as a positive sign—an agency has presidential attention and support and therefore can expect a period of vigorous growth (NASA is often cited as an example). Our evidence suggests that, on balance, personal presidential involvement of a supportive nature helps an agency achieve an expanded budget.

Fourth, there are messages on topics little treated either in the social science literature or in the oral tradition of the administrators. That is, this style of research promotes clinical messages in genuinely unexpected areas. Statements 1, 5, and 7 fall into this category.

In short, we argue that this style of research on policy-making—despite the occasionally "fancy" methodology—can, in fact, produce findings that can be rendered into straightforward English and transmitted to program operators. Furthermore, these findings have practical implications that are not always along expected lines. Much more than conventional wisdom gets discovered by careful and rigorous research.

Notes

1. Economist W. A. Niskanen's behavioral hypotheses offer some support for these expectations (1971: 77). He states that budgets and services of bureaus will increase in response to reduced elasticity of demand. If one assumes that an effect of mergers and consolidations of bureaus is to reduce elasticity of demand (by reducing the number of competitors), then consolidations should have a positive relationship with growth in policy actions. Whether internal agency reorganizations have the same effect on elasticity of demand needs to be explored. An initial empirical test of this part of Niskanen's theory is found in Hobbie (1975).

2. An additional possibility, developed only occasionally in the literature on organizations or bureaucracy (see, for example, Bernstein, 1955: Ch. 3), is that the dimensions of maturity outlined above are related to the degree of political support for an agency and its programs. In terms of our conceptual framework, the nature of the supportive coalition may be related to several levels of maturity. Bernstein suggests that there is a natural progression in the level and source of support or hostility for independent regulatory commissions and that this support or hostility is the central factor in determining the general policy stance of a commission. Such a notion is intriguing and deserves rigorous testing not only on independent regulatory commissions but on a wide variety of agencies. Naturally, there are practical problems: getting reliable data for a time span long enough to cover the hypothesized "life cycle" of a wide variety of agencies, dealing

with agencies created far apart in time so that the "life cycle" is not simply the product of a broader political trend affecting all agencies, and operationalizing the concepts of both maturity and coalition support in convincing and theoretically justifiable ways. It may be that there is a natural curve of maturity (such as that suggested in Figure 6–3) and a natural curve of support that work together to produce at least gross programmatic predispositions on the part of agencies and the degree of latitude afforded those predispositions on the part of agencies by influential actors.

Methodological Glossary

THE FOLLOWING ENTRIES provide the reader with a better understanding of the more technical aspects of the methodologies that were employed in the preceding empirical chapters. Entries are in alphabetical order.

Autocorrelation

Autocorrelation is a statistical term used to denote a condition where successive observations of the same variable through time are so highly interrelated that independent effects of other variables are "washed out" when they are included in a regression (or multivariate) equation. A simple example will, perhaps, aid an understanding of this problem.

Suppose an observer recorded the height of a child over a period of time—say, at daily intervals. If the observer wished to explain any changes, then variables such as chronological age, weight, or protein intake might form a partial explanation. But suppose that among the independent criteria variables was the original height measurement lagged by one observation period. It is quite likely that a statistical analysis that included this "lagged endogenous" variable would be severely biased. And the principal finding of such an analysis would probably assert that the foremost determinant of a child's height is the previously observed height of the same child. An incorrect inference could be made as a result of a statistical artifact. No doubt a child cannot grow to a height of five feet without reaching four feet at some point in his development. But it is a very different thing for an analyst to attribute the cause of the growth to previous growth. This statistical phenomena is referred to as autocorrelation, and occurs frequently among time-series data that are derived from successive observations of the same unit(s) of analysis. For a statistical discussion, see Malinvaud (1970) or Wonnacott and Wonnacott (1970).

Block Variable Analysis

Block variable analysis estimates the combined influence of a group of variables or indicators using multiple indicators, rather than examining the influence of single variables. This is done when several variables can be seen as expressions of the same general concept. It is similar to factor analysis, but uses a regression model to estimate the relation between the indicators, the combined effect, and the dependent variable (Hauser and Goldberger, 1971; Heise, 1972).

Consistent Estimates

An estimate is consistent if it is both unbiased and the standard error of the estimate approaches zero as the sample size approaches infinity. Time-series data frequently fail on both counts because estimates of the correlations and covariances for variables having time-series trends may be biased (usually inflated) and unstable (as when new federal regulations change the way an agency responds to its environment). IV regression can solve the problem of bias from time-series trends. If the trends are stable, IV regression allows getting consistent estimates when the predicted values are substituted for observed values (see IV regression). Typically, one assumes a process is stable for the time period studied. However, some of the findings we report regarding changes over time suggest this is not the case for federal agencies. Major events (such as war or agency reorganization) may change the way an agency responds to its environment. Subsample comparisons aid in the detection of unstable trends. Solving the problem of unstable trends may involve breaking the time-series into stable subperiods or controlling the factors that make the relations unstable over time. This is necessary if estimates are to be consistent.

Correlogram Analysis

Correlogram analysis is a method for determining the pattern of the correlations of the errors in predicting a variable with those errors at a different point in time. The self-correlations for the errors are plotted against different time lags for these correlations. If the self-correlations of the errors continually decrease for greater time lags, the process generating the correlations is said to be autoregressive. If the self-correlations suddenly drop to zero, the process generating the correlations is said to be a moving average. Knowing which process is present aids in removing bias resulting from the correlated errors (see Hibbs, 1972; Malinvaud, 1970; see also, 3 Stage Least Squares).

Evaluating the Fit of a Path Model

Although what follows was written specifically for the path model analysis performed in Chapter 6, the principles apply to all path models.

The fit of a path model should rarely be based on the absolute values of the path coefficients. If one's theory that generates the path model does not predict what the absolute values will be, it makes no difference whether the value is .10 or .80. The hypothesis corresponding to a link in the path diagram will be supported so long as the value is not insignificant. The real test of a path model is its overall fit with the data. Thus, the two central questions for evaluating the fit are: How does one tell when the value of a path coefficient is not insignificant and how does one evaluate the overall fit of the model?

One must use theoretical, mathematical, and substantive criteria in deciding whether a value is insignificant. All of these get at the credibility of a path value in one way or another.

Theoretical criteria come into play because there is always the possibility of nonsense correlations in the data. The analyst must be able to make sense of his findings. If it is not possible to explain why a path is present, any theorizing or conclusions made from the model are questionable (more specifically, any inferences made from findings that directly or indirectly include the unexplained path are of doubtful validity). This does not mean the analyst can drop paths simply because they are unaccounted for in his or her theory. It means that a path that agrees with no other theory at all is a questionable path. If, in addition, there exists an explanation how the nonsense correlation was generated, the analyst should then consider dropping the path. If a wrong decision is made at this point, it should show up in the evaluation of the overall fit—which means it can be added or dropped from a subsequent trimmed model.

Mathematical criteria are also used in deciding the significance of a path coefficient. While there are grave problems with doing significance tests on nonrandom samples and debate about the applicability of such tests to 100% samples of a universe, we feel two arguments justify its use. First, every sample is representative of some universe. One can talk about the significance of the estimates in the universe represented by the sample. Convincing the reader that one's sample does represent the universe it is alleged to represent is an issue separate from evaluating the significance of a path value in the universe represented by the sample. Second, most universes are subunits of larger universes. What is a universe from one perspective is a sample from another. For a 100% sample of a universe there is some other universe of which this sample is only a part. One can meaningfully talk about the extended universe of which the sample is a part. Since subuniverses represent some other extended universe, inferences can be made about the extended universe. However, the researcher should specify the extended universes he feels are not represented by his subuniverse.

He have used an F-test as a mathematical criteria to test the significance of the path coefficients. The F-test is a fairly straightforward test using the number of degrees of freedom for the regression.

The substantive significance of a path coefficient can be seen from its unstandardized regression coefficient (the b's). Even though a path coefficient may be small, the corresponding raw coefficient may be large enough to have substantive significance. For example, the path coefficient in Figure 6–2 from $SIZE_0$ to EXP_1 was small (.04), but the raw regression coefficient was equal to $1,525 per employee. For an agency with 5,000 employees that is an effect of over $7.6 million. The combined theoretical, statistical, and substantive significance of this path justified its inclusion—even though an "eyeball" test of the path coefficient might lead (or mislead) one into thinking the path should not be in the model. Again, it is not the absolute magnitude of a path coefficient that matters when evaluating its significance. What matters is the theoretical, mathematical, and substantive significance of the path. If a path fails these criteria, then clearly it should not be included. If it meets them, then the path coefficient value is not insignificant. However, because of the human phenomenon of tending to disbelieve small numbers, the smaller the absolute value of a path coefficient, the more we tried to see that the paths met the above three criteria.

Once satisfied that all the paths in a model are not insignificant, a difference of means test can be used to evaluate the overall fit of the model. This test is based on estimating the nonpredetermined correlations and comparing those estimates with the empirical correlations. (For examples of how the estimations are done, see Duncan, 1969; Heise, 1969; Land, 1969.) Unless one computes these estimated values, no test of the overall fit of the model is possible. The consistency of the model with the data is gauged by how close the estimated values agree with empirical parameter estimates. If there is not a close overall fit, the model must be modified and reevaluated. Deciding if a fit is good enough is facilitated by working with alternative models simultaneously to see if one's favorite model has a better fit than competing models.

One should note that these comparisons were made between only the correlations that were not mathematically predetermined. Predetermined correlations are of three sorts: correlations between exogenous variables, correlations between a dependent variable and its independent variable when it has only one independent variable, and correlations duplicated by repeating one part of a model in another part of the model. In the first two cases, the estimated correlation will always equal the empirical correlation. They should not be considered in testing the fit of the model since they will always have a perfect fit with the data no matter how badly specified the model might be. The third kind of correlations that are predetermined are those that duplicate other correlations by repeating parts of one's model. The values of the correlations estimated from the repeated part to the model are mathematically predetermined by the values estimated from the original part. They add no degrees of freedom to the residuals between estimated and real correlations. They frequently confuse the analyst when trying to do his estimation procedure and can result in inconsistent estimates if a duplicated path is counted as more than one path. For diagrammatic purposes we have repeated parts of the path diagram; but the evaluation was done with one of the repeated dependent variables treated as a predetermined ("exogenous") variable to prevent inconsistent estimation. The degrees of freedom for the residual correlation matrix when one of the repeated dependent variables is made an exogenous variable is simple to compute. One begins with the number of correlations in the matrix and subtracts the number of correlations between exogenous variables (excluding self-correlations). One then subtracts twice the number of variables with only one independent variable and also subtracts the total number of variables. The remaining figure is divided by 2. This equals the number of nonpredetermined correlations. Subtracting 2 gives the degrees of freedom for the residuals. Algebraically:

$$n = \frac{c - e - 2s - t}{2} - 1$$

where $c =$ total number of correlations, $e =$ number of correlations between exogenous variables excluding self-correlations, $s =$ the number of variables with only one independent variable, and $t =$ the total number of variables.

The easiest way of computing the mean residual is to use the following formula which takes into consideration the degrees of freedom:

$$\triangle \hat{r}_{xy} r_{xy} = \frac{\displaystyle\sum_{x,y=1}^{t} r_{xy} - \hat{r}_{xy}}{2_n + 2}$$

This difference of means test can be used for evaluating the overall fit of the model. A difference of means test is both simpler and more reliable than most of the other available tests when there are only a few nonpredetermined correlations (for more sophisticated methods, see Jennrich, 1970; Kullback, 1970). With this test one computes the mean residual for the difference between estimated and real correlations for the degrees of freedom involved along with the standard deviation of the residuals. One can then do a t-test with the null hypothesis that the mean is zero. This allows one to compute the probability that the residuals come from a universe whose mean is truly zero. If the model is consistent with the data, the mean residual should be zero. One cannot tenably say a model has a good fit with the data if there is a low probability that the mean residual is zero. If a researcher is uncertain whether he should include a path in his model, it may help to evaluate the fit of the model with and without the path. If including a borderline path results in a substantial improvement in the probability of the mean residual equaling zero, the path should be included. This test gives results identical to a test for a difference of means for related samples, where the related samples are the estimated and observed correlations. In the figures of the models in Chapters 6 and 7, the notation t_p is the probability that the mean residual is truly zero. The higher the probability, the better the overall fit of the model.

GLS Regression

Generalized Least Squares regression is a regression that minimizes the variance of the estimates of the regression slopes (the standard error of the regression slopes). The procedure solves simultaneous equations for estimates of the regression slopes, rather than solving for the slopes in each equation separately (as in OLS regression). Unlike Ordinary Least Squares regression, the error terms in the equations may be correlated without biasing the estimates of the regression slopes (Wonnacott and Wonnacott, 1970).

IV Regression

Instrumental Variable regression is a regression using only variables not correlated with any error terms in a model. The predicted value of the dependent variable is substituted for an observed value when the error term for the observed value is correlated with an independent variable in one's model to allow getting unbiased estimates of the regression coefficients where that variable occurs in the equations of one's model. Correlated errors frequently occur with time-series data. If the process generating the correlated errors is stable over time, the standard error of estimates using values predicted by IV regression will approach zero as the sample size increases (Wonnacott and Wonnacott, 1970; see also, consistent estimates and 2 Stage Least Squares).

IV-OLS Regression

See 2 Stage Least Squares.

Longitudinal Trend Analysis

Tintner (1968: 48) has noted that the traditional method of analyzing time-series data has primarily been isolating the trends, cycles, and random components of the data. Trend analysis is the method most relevant for our analysis of the effects of maturity on agency characteristics and policy actions. By studying the trends of the characteristics and actions over time, one can see what happens as the agency gets older. One may do this by plotting the data and eyeballing any trend that appears, by fitting equations to the time-series data, or by spectral analysis using Fourier transforms of the time-series (Tintner, 1968; Hannan, 1960). Eyeballing is most efficient for discerning unusual and irregular patterns in the data. Equation fitting is most efficient for discerning the simpler, more general trends in the data and allows more precise comparisons between trends than eyeballing. Spectral analysis is best for determining cycles, fluctuations, and complex trends. Since this is an exploratory study, we chose equation fitting to get at the more general effects of maturation in a manner that allows us to do quantitative comparisons between trends. As the simpler trends become more established, we intend to add spectral analysis to study processes that generate deviations from these trends.

Two equations were chosen for this initial trend fitting: one linear and one quadratic. The quadratic equation was included to get preliminary evidence on possible curvilinear or nonmonotonic trends. Equations which combine a linear and a quadratic term allow for representing a large number of possible trends while keeping the mathematics as simple as possible. The basic form for this equation is:

$$Y = a + b_1 \text{ (year–51)} + b_2 \text{ (year–51)}^2 + e$$

Since these are preliminary approximations, no significance is imputed to the specific value of the parameter estimates. Only their direction and general form is significant, and only that is discussed.

Markov Equations

Markov Equations, or difference equations as they are sometimes called, are formed by assuming that a variable at one point affects itself at some later point. Other variables may be included in an explanation, but time lag dependence between a variable and some later value of the same variable is the defining characteristic of Markov equations.

Multicollinearity

Problems of multicollinearity may occur when using multiple regression. The difficulty occurs when independent variables are correlated. This results in an inability to tell how much variance in the dependent variable is due to any one independent variable. The problem is exacerbated as the independent variables are more highly correlated.

OLS Regression

This is the conventional method for obtaining estimates of a regression model. In the presence of autocorrelated disturbances OLS will produce biased estimates (usually in a negative direction) of the coefficient variances. ". . . The estimated variances and standard errors will understate, perhaps seriously, the true variances and standard errors. This produces inflated t ratios, parameter estimates, and often leads to spurious attributions of 'significance' to the independent variable" (Hibbs, 1972:9).

Skewness in Residuals

Skewness in the distribution of residuals means that values of the residuals bunch above or below the mean residual and that extreme values of the residuals tend to bunch on the opposite side of the mean residual as the majority of the residuals. It generally indicates that estimates of the residuals are systematically biased.

Subsample Test for Temporal Interaction

A subsample test for interaction determines whether a particular relation holds for different situations. This method splits a sample for major variables presumed to be changing over time (older versus younger, larger versus smaller, richer versus poorer, having more supergrades versus having less supergrades, etc.). Comparisons are made between the unstandardized regression slopes for pairs of variables in each dyad of subsamples. If the relationship between a pair of variables is changing over time, then the raw regression slope between these variables in the two subsamples will differ. The results suggest what kinds of changes are happening between variables over time. Although comparisons can be made between higher order partial regression coefficients to examine complex changes in relations over time, our use of this procedure was confined to comparing zero-order regression slopes because of the exploratory nature of the study.

2 Stage Least Squares

2 Stage Least Squares is a two-step regression procedure. Values of a dependent variable in a model are estimated using instrumental variables. The estimated values are substituted for the observed values for those variables where the residual from predicting the variable is correlated with predictors of the dependent variable. An Ordinary Least Squares regression is then run for the equation using the estimated data. This procedure is necessary for obtaining consistent estimates of the regression slopes when an error term is correlated with an independent variable in an equation.

3 Stage Least Squares

3 Stage Least Squares is a regression procedure that combines 2 Stage Least Squares regression with Generalized Least Squares regression. One first does 2 SLS regression to estimate the residuals for each dependent variable. These residuals are correlated to estimate the correlation of the

error terms in the equations. Correlogram analysis may be used as an aid in deciding which correlations may be treated as sampling error, rather than true correlation of error terms. Given the estimates of the correlations of the errors, a Generalized Least Squares regression is run for the set of equations. 3 SLS estimates are used instead of GLS estimates when the data require IV regression to get consistent estimates and OLS regression to estimate the correlation of the error terms before solving for the simultaneous solution of the regression coefficients.

References

ABERBACH, J. D., and J. L. WALKER (1970) "Political trust and racial ideology." *American Political Science Review* 64 (December): 1199–1219.

ART, R. J. (1968) *The TFX Decision.* Boston: Little, Brown.

BAILEY, S. K., and E. MOSHER (1968) *ESEA: The Office of Education Administers a Law.* Syracuse, N.Y.: Syracuse University Press.

BARTLETT, M. S. (1935) "Some aspects of time-correlation problems in regard to tests of significance." *Journal of the Royal Statistical Society* 98: 536–543.

BERELSON, B. R., P. F. LAZARSFELD, and W. N. McPHEE (1954) *Voting.* Chicago: University of Chicago Press.

BERNSTEIN, M. H. (1955) *Regulating Business by Independent Commission.* Princeton, N.J.: Princeton University Press.

BLALOCK, H. (1970) "Estimating measurement error using multiple indicators and several points in time." *American Sociological Review* 35 (February): 101–111.

BLAU, P. M. (1970) "A formal theory of differentiation in organizations." *American Sociological Review* 35 (April): 201–218.

BLAU, P. M., and W. R. SCOTT (1962) *Formal Organizations.* San Francisco: Chandler.

BLAU, P. M., and R. A. SCHOENHERR (1971) *The Structure of Organizations.* New York: Basic Books.

BLAU, P. M., W. V. HEYDEBRAND, and R. E. STAUFFER (1966) "The structure of small bureaucracies," *Administrative Science Quarterly* 31: 179–191.

BOHRNSTEDT, G. (1969) "Observations in the measurement of change." *Sociological Methodology 1969.* 1: 113–136.

BONACICH, P. (1972) "Using the sign rule to make inferences from simple block theories." Paper presented at the annual meeting of the American Sociological Association.

BRAYBROOKE, D., and C. E. LINDBLOM (1963) *A Strategy of Decision.* New York: Free Press.

BURNS, J. M. (1956) *Roosevelt: The Lion and the Fox.* New York: Harcourt, Brace.

CAMPBELL, A., P. E. CONVERSE, W. E. MILLER, and D. E. STOKES (1960) *The American Voter.* New York: Wiley.

CAMPBELL, D. T., and J. C. STANLEY (1963) *Experimental and Quasi-Experimental Designs for Research.* Chicago: Rand McNally.

CHILDERS, G., B. MAYHEW, and L. GRAY (1971) "System size and structural differentiation in military organizations: testing a baseline model of the division of labor." *American Journal of Sociology* 76 (March): 813–830.

CLAUSEN, A. (1973) *How Congressmen Decide: A Policy Focus.* New York: St. Martin's.

COLEMAN, J. (1968) "The mathematical study of change," in H. M. Blalock and A. B. Blalock (eds.), *Methodology in Social Research.* New York: McGraw–Hill.

CONNERY, R. H. (ed.) (1968) "Urban Riots." *Proceedings of the American Academy of Political Science* 29.

CORSON, J. J. (1963) "Equipping men for growth in the public service." *Public Administration Review* 23 (September): 529–547.

DAHRENDORF, R. (1959) *Class and Class Conflict in Industrial Society.* Stanford, Calif.: Stanford University Press.

DAVIS, J. W. (1970) *The National Executive Branch.* New York: Free Press.

DAVIS, J. W., and R. B. RIPLEY (1967) "The bureau of the budget and executive branch agencies: notes on their interaction." *Journal of Politics* 29 (September): 749–769.

DAVIS, O. A., M. A. H. DEMPSTER, and A. WILDAVSKY (1966) "A Theory of the Budgetary Process." *American Political Science Review* 60 (September): 529–547.

DAVIS, O. A., M. A. H. DEMPSTER, and A. WILDAVSKY (1967) "To the editor." *American Political Science Review* 61 (March): 152–153.

DAWSON, R., and J. ROBINSON (1963) "Inter-party competition, economic variables, and welfare policies in the American states." *Journal of Politics* 25 (May): 256–289.

DOMHOFF, C. (1970) "How the power elite set national priorities," in K. Chen (ed.), *National Priorities.* San Francisco: San Francisco Press.

DONOVAN, J. C. (1967) *The Politics of Poverty.* New York: Pegasus.

DOWNS, A. (1957) *An Economic Theory of Democracy.* New York: Harper.

DOWNS, A. (1967) *Inside Bureaucracy.* Boston: Little, Brown.

DROR, Y. (1968) *Public Policy-Making Re-Examined.* San Francisco: Chandler.

DUNCAN, O. D. (1969) "Contingencies in constructing causal models: an illustration." *Sociological Methodology 1969.* 1: 74–112.

DUNCAN, O. D., R. P. CUZZORT, and D. DUNCAN (1961) *Statistical Geography.* New York: Free Press.

DYE, T. R. (1965) "Malapportionment and public policy in the American states." *Journal of Politics* 27 (August): 586–601.

DYE, T. R. (1966) *Politics, Economics, and the Public.* Chicago: Rand McNally.

EASTON, D. (1953) *The Political System.* New York: Knopf.

EASTON, D. (1965a) *A Framework for Political Analysis.* Englewood Cliffs, N.J.: Prentice–Hall.

EASTON, D. (1965b) *A Systems Analysis of Political Life.* New York: Wiley.

ETZIONI, A. (1970) *The Active Society.* New York: Free Press.

EULAU, H. (1957) "The ecological basis of party systems: the case of Ohio." *Midwest Journal of Political Science* 1 (August): 125–135.

FEINGOLD, E. (1966) *Medicare: Policy and Politics.* San Francisco: Chandler.

FENNO, R. F. (1959) *The President's Cabinet.* New York: Vintage.

FENNO, R. F. (1966) *The Power of the Purse.* Boston: Little, Brown.

FLAX, M. J. (1972) *A Study in Comparative Urban Indicators.* Washington, D.C.: Urban Institute.

FREEMAN, J. L. (1965) *The Political Process: Executive Bureau–Legislative Committee Relations,* rev. ed. New York: Random House.

FRIEDMAN, W. (1959) *Law in a Changing Society.* Berkeley, Calif.: University of California Press.

FRITSCHLER, A. L. (1969) *Smoking and Politics: Policy-Making and the Federal Bureaucracy.* New York: Appleton–Century–Crofts.

FROMAN, L. A. (1968) "The categorization of policy contents," in A. Ranney (ed.), *Political Science and Public Policy.* Chicago: Markham.

FRY, B. R., and R. F. WINTERS (1970) "Politics of redistribution." *American Political Science Review* 64 (June): 508–522.

GAWTHROP, L. (1969) *Bureaucratic Behavior in the Executive Branch: An Analysis of Organizational Change.* New York: Free Press.

GIST, J. A. (1974) "The effect of budget controllability on the theory of incrementalism." Paper presented at the annual meeting of the Midwest Political Science Association, Chicago, April 26.

GOLEMBIEWSKI, R. T. (1969) "Organization development in public agencies: perspectives on theory and practice." *Public Administration Review* 29 (May): 237–248.

GOULDEN, J. (1972) *The Superlawyers: The Small and Powerful World of the Great Washington Law Firms.* New York: Weybright and Falley.

HAAS, E., and L. COLLEN (1963) "Administrative practice in university departments." *Administrative Science Quarterly* 8 (June): 44–60.

HAMMOND, P. Y. (1963) *Super carriers and B–36 bombers,* ICP–37. Indianapolis: Bobbs–Merrill.

HANNAN, E. J. (1960) *Time Series Analysis.* London: Methuen.

HARRIS, C. (ed.) (1963) *Problems in Measuring Change.* Madison, Wisc.: University of Wisconsin Press.

HARRIS, R. (1966) *A Sacred Trust.* New York: New American Library.

HAUSER, R. M., and A. GOLDBERGER (1971) "The treatment of unobserved variables in path analysis," in H. Costner (ed.), *Sociological Methodology 1971.* San Francisco: Jossey Bass.

HEISE, D. R. (1969) "Problems in path analysis causal inference." *Sociological Methodology 1969.* 1: 38–73.

HEISE, D. R. (1970) "Causal inference from panel data." *Sociological Methodology 1970.* 2: 3–27.

HEISE, D. R. (1972) "Employing nominal variables, induced variables, and block variables in path analysis." *Sociological Methods and Research* 1 (November): 147–173.

HENDERSHOT, G., and T. JAMES (1972) "Size and growth as determinants of administrative-production ratios in organizations." *American Sociological Review* 37 (April): 149–153.

HIBBS, D. A. (1972) "Problems of statistical estimation and causal inference in dynamic, time-series regression models." Paper delivered at the annual meeting of the American Political Science Association, Washington, D.C.

HITCH, C., and R. McKEAN (1960) *The Economics of Defense in a Nuclear Age.* Cambridge, Mass.: Harvard University Press.

HOBBIE, R. A. (1975) "A methodological and empirical examination of William A. Niskanen's theory of supply by bureaus." Ph.D. dissertation. Columbus: The Ohio State University.

HOFFERBERT, R. I. (1966) "Relation between public policy and some structural and environmental variables in the American states." *American Political Science Review* 60 (March): 73–82.

HOLLANDER, E., and R. HUNT (eds.) (1971) *Current Perspectives in Social Psychology,* 3d ed. New York: Oxford University Press.

HOLMES, W. M. (1974) "Social conditions and policy change." Ph.D. dissertation. Columbus: The Ohio State University.

HORN, S. (1970) *Unused Power.* Washington, D.C.: Brookings.

HUMMON, N. (1971) "A mathematical theory of differentiation among organizations." *American Sociological Review* 36 (April): 297–303.

JENNRICH, R. I. (1970) "Asymptotic X^2 test for the equality of two correlation matrices." *Journal of American Statistical Association* 65: 904–912.

KAUFMAN, H. (1972) *The Limits of Organizational Change.* University, Ala.: University of Alabama Press.

KAUFMAN, H., and D. SEIDMAN (1970) "The morphology of organizations." *Administrative Science Quarterly* 15 (December): 439–451.

KANTER, A. (1972) "Congress and the defense budget: 1960–1970." *American Political Science Review* 66 (March): 129–143.

KESSEL, J. H. (1968) *The Goldwater Coalition.* Indianapolis: Bobbs–Merrill.

KESSEL, J. H. (1972) "The parameters of presidential politics." Paper presented at the annual meeting of the American Political Science Association, Washington, D.C.

KEY, V. O. (1940) "The lack of a budgetary theory." *American Political Science Review* 34 (December): 1137–1144.

KEY, V. O. (1949) *Southern Politics.* New York: Vintage.

KEY, V. O. (1961) *Public Opinion and American Democracy.* New York: Knopf.

KEY, V. O. (1966) *The Responsible Electorate.* Cambridge, Mass.: Harvard University Press.

KIESLER, C., B. COLLINS, and N. MILLER (1969) *Attitude Change.* New York: Wiley.

KULLBACK, S. (1970) "On testing correlation matrices." *Applied Statistics* 16: 80–85.

LAND, K. (1969) "Principles of path analysis." *Sociological Methodology 1969*. 1: 3–37.

LASSWELL, H. D. (1956) *The Decision Process: Seven Categories of Functional Analysis*. College Park, Md.: University of Maryland Press.

LELOUP, L. (1973) "Explaining agency appropriation change, success, and legislative support: A comparative study of agency budget determination." Ph.D. dissertation. Columbus: The Ohio State University.

LEMAY, M. (1973) "Expenditures and non-expenditure measures of state urban policy output." *American Politics Quarterly* 1 (October): 511–536.

LINDBLOM, C. E. (1959) "The science of muddling through." *Public Administration Review* 19 (Spring): 79–88.

LINDBLOM, C. E. (1965) *The Intelligence of Democracy*. New York: Free Press.

LOCKARD, D. (1959) *New England State Politics*. Princeton, N.J.: Princeton University Press.

LOWI, T. J. (1964) "American business, public policy, case studies, and political theory." *World Politics* 16 (July): 677–715.

LUNDBURG, F., and L. STEWART (1968) *The Rich and the Super-Rich*. New York: Bantam Books.

MALINVAUD, E. (1970) *Statistical Methods of Econometrics*, 2d ed. New York: American Elsevier.

MAYHEW, B., T. JAMES, and G. CHILDERS (1972a) "System size and structural differentiation in military organizations: testing a harmonic series model of the division of labor." *American Journal of Sociology* 77 (January): 750–765.

MAYHEW, B., R. LEVINGER, J. McPHERSON, and T. JAMES (1972b) "System size and structural differentiation in formal organizations: a baseline generator for two major theoretical propositions." *American Sociological Review* 37 (October): 629–633.

MILBRATH, L. (1969) "Political participation as a function of social position," in J. L. Price (ed.) *Social Facts: Introductory Readings*. London: Macmillan.

MILLER, W. E., and D. E. STOKES (1963) "Constituency influence in Congress." *American Political Science Review* 57 (March): 45–56.

MILLS, C. W. (1956) *The Power Elite*. New York: Oxford University Press.

MORELAND, W. B. (1973) "The limits of policy discretion: a non-incremental, time-series analysis of agency appropriations." Ph.D. dissertation. Columbus: The Ohio State University.

MOYNIHAN, D. P. (1969) *Maximum Feasible Misunderstanding*. New York: Free Press.

NATCHEZ, P. B., and I. C. BUPP (1973) "Policy and priority in the budgetary process." *American Political Science Review* 67 (September): 951–963.

NISKANEN, W. A. (1971) *Bureaucracy and Representative Government*. Chicago: Aldine–Atherton.

NOVICK, D. (ed.) (1965) *Program Budgeting*. Cambridge, Mass.: Harvard University Press.

PALUMBO, D. J. (1969) "Power and role specificity in organization theory." *Public Administration Review* 29 (May): 237–248.

POLSBY, N. (1965) *Congress and the President.* Englewood Cliffs, N.J.: Prentice–Hall.

REICH, C. A. (1962) *Bureaucracy and the Forests.* Santa Barbara, Calif.: Center for the Study of Democratic Institutions.

REIN, M. (1970) *Social Policy: Issues of Choice and Change.* New York: Random House.

RIPLEY, R. B. (1969) "Congress and clean air: the issue of enforcement, 1963," in F. N. Cleaveland (ed.), *Congress and Urban Problems.* Washington, D.C.: Brookings.

RIPLEY, R. B. (1972a) *The Politics of Economic and Human Resource Development.* Indianapolis: Bobbs–Merrill.

RIPLEY, R. B. (1972b) *Kennedy and Congress.* New York: General Learning Press.

RIPLEY, R. B., W. B. MORELAND, and R. N. SINNREICH (1973a) "Policy-making: a conceptual scheme." *American Politics Quarterly* 1 (January): 3–42.

RIPLEY, R. B., G. A. FRANKLIN, W. M. HOLMES, and W. B. MORELAND (1973b) "Structure, environment, and policy actions: exploring a model of policy-making." *Sage Professional Papers in American Politics* 1: 04–006.

RIPLEY, R. B., W. M. HOLMES, G. A. FRANKLIN, and W. B. MORELAND (1974) "Explaining changes in budgetary policy actions." *Administration and Society* 6 (May): 22–47.

RIVLIN, A. M. (1974) *Social Policy: Alternate Strategies for the Federal Government.* Brookings Institution general series reprint 288.

ROHERTY, J. M. (1970) "Policy implications and applications for international relations research for defense and security," in N. D. Palmer (ed.), *A Design for International Relations Research.* Monograph 10 of the American Academy of Political and Social Science, October.

ROSSITER, C. (1960) *Parties and Politics in America.* Ithaca, N.Y.: Cornell University Press.

ROURKE, F. E. (1969) *Bureaucracy, Politics and Public Policy.* Boston: Little, Brown.

SALISBURY, R. H. (1968) "The analysis of public policy: a search for theories and roles," in A. Ranney (ed.), *Political Science and Public Policy.* Chicago: Markham.

SALISBURY, R. H., and J. HEINZ (1970) "A theory of policy analysis and some preliminary applications," in I. Sharkansky (1970), *Policy Analysis in Political Science.* Chicago: Markham.

SAMUEL, Y., and B. F. MANNHEIM (1970) "A multidimensional approach to a typology of bureaucracy." *Administrative Science Quarterly* 15 (June): 216–228.

SAYRE, W. S., and H. A. KAUFMAN (1965) *Governing New York City.* New York: Norton.

SCAMMON, R. C., and B. J. WATTENBERG (1970) *The Real Majority.* New York: Coward–McCann, & Geoghegan.

SCHLESINGER, A. M., JR. (1957) *The Crisis of the Old Order.* Boston: Houghton Mifflin.

SCHLESINGER, J. A. (1955) "A two-dimensional scheme for classifying the states according to degree of inter-party competition." *American Political Science Review* 49 (December): 1120–1128.

SCHULTZE, C. L. (1968) *The Politics and Economics of Public Spending.* Washington, D.C.: Brookings.

SCHULTZE, C. L. (1971) "Testimony of Charles L. Schultze," pp. 2–5 in U.S. Congress Joint Economic Committee, Subcommittee on Priorities and Economy in Government. Part 1. *The Economics of National Priorities.* June 1, 2, and 4. 92d Cong., 1st sess. Washington, D.C.: Government Printing Office.

SCOTT, R. (1964) "Theory of organizations," in E. Faris (ed.), *Handbook of Modern Sociology.* New York: Basic Books.

SHARKANSKY, I. (1965) "Four agencies and an appropriations subcommittee: a comparative study of budget strategies." *Midwest Journal of Political Science* 9 (August): 254–281.

SHARKANSKY, I. (1967) "Government expenditures and public services in the American states." *American Political Science Review* 61 (December): 1066–1077.

SHARKANSKY, I. (1968) *Spending in the American States.* Chicago: Rand McNally.

SHARKANSKY, I. (1969) *The Politics of Taxing and Spending.* Indianapolis: Bobbs–Merrill.

SHARKANSKY, I. (1970) "Government expenditures and public services in the American states," in Sharkansky (ed.), *Policy Analysis in Political Science.* Chicago: Markham.

SHARKANSKY, I. (1972) *Public Administration,* 2d ed. Chicago: Markham.

SHULL, S. A. (1974) A comparative examination of agency policy response to structural, environmental, and budgetary stimuli." Ph.D. dissertation. Columbus: The Ohio State University.

SIMON, H. A. (1953) "Birth of an organization: Economic Cooperation Administration." *Public Administration Review* 13 (Autumn): 227–236.

SIMON, H. A. (1957) *Administrative Behavior.* New York: Free Press.

SIMON, R. (1968) *The Sociology of Law.* San Francisco: Chandler.

SMITH, B. L. R. (1967) "To the editor." *American Political Science Review* 61 (March): 150–152.

SPEIGEL, H. B. C. (1968) *Citizen Participation in Urban Development.* Washington, D.C.: NTL Institute for Applied Behavioral Research.

STOKES, D. E. (1966) "Spatial models of party competition," in A. Campbell (ed.), *Elections and the Political Order.* New York: Wiley.

STOKES, D. E. (1971) "Compound paths in political analysis," in J. F. Herndon and J. L. Bernd (eds.), *Mathematical Applications in Political Science V.* Charlottesville, Va.: University of Virginia.

STROMBERG, J. L. (1970) *The Internal Mechanisms of the Defense Budget Process: Fiscal 1953–1968.* Santa Monica, Calif.: Rand.

SUNDQUIST, J. L. (1968) Politics and Policy. Washington, D.C.: Brookings.

TINTNER, G. (1968) "Time-series: general." pp. 49–57 in *International Encyclopedia of the Social Sciences,* vol. 16. New York: Macmillan.

TRUMAN, D. B. (1969) "Functional interdependence: elective leaders, the White House, and the congressional party," in A. Wildavsky (ed.), *The Presidency*. Boston: Little, Brown.

U.S. National Science Foundation (1971) *An Analysis of Federal R&D Funding by Budget Function*. Surveys of Science Resources Series. Washington, D.C.

VAN METER, D. S., and H. B. ASHER (1973) "Causal analysis: its promise for policy studies." *Policy Studies Journal* 2 (Winter): 103–109.

WAHLKE, J. C. (1967) "Public policy and representative government: the role of the represented." Paper presented at the 7th Congress of the International Political Science Association.

WEBER, M. (1946) *Essays in Sociology*. Edited by H. H. Gerth and C. W. Mills. New York: Oxford University Press.

WEIDENBAUM, M. L., and D. LARKINS (1972) *The Federal Budget for 1973: A Review and Analysis*. Washington, D.C.: American Enterprise Institute.

WILDAVSKY, A. (1964) *The Politics of the Budgetary Process*. Boston: Little, Brown.

WILLIAMS, W. (1971) *Social Policy Research and Analysis*. New York: American Elsevier.

WONNACOTT, R. J., and T. H. WONNACOTT (1970) *Econometrics*. New York: Wiley.

WRIGHT, S. (1960) "Path coefficients and path regression: alternative or complementary concepts." *Biometrics* 16 (June): 189–201.

Index

Index